BLACK AMERICA SERIES

AKRON

BLACK AMERICA SERIES

AKRON

Abel A. Bartley

ARCADIA
PUBLISHING

ISBN 0-7385-3281-9

Published by Arcadia Publishing
Charleston, SC

Printed in the United States of America

Library of Congress Catalog Card Number: 2004103402

For all general information contact Arcadia Publishing at:
Telephone 843-853-2070
Fax 843-853-0044
E-mail sales@arcadiapublishing.com
For customer service and orders:
Toll-Free 1-888-313-2665

Visit us on the Internet at www.arcadiapublishing.com

Contents

ACKNOWLEDGMENTS

I would like to thank all of those who have had a hand in creating this work. This has truly been a labor of love. First, I need to say a special thanks to Stephen Paschen, who was so patient with me as I looked through the many pictures housed in the University of Akron Archives. I would like to also thank the members of the steering committee of the Shirla McClain Gallery of Akron Black History for their unselfish help in identifying pictures. The Shirla McClain Gallery is a wonderful resource for anyone interested in researching Akron's African-American community. I would also like to thank Edwin Parms and Opehlia Averitt for their help. I would also be remiss if I did not thank my wife, daughter, and parents for their patience and support during this project. Finally, I need to thank God for the many ways He helps me every day.

Introduction

Contemporary Akron, Ohio, is a city of more than 217,000 residents located south of Cleveland. Founded on December 6, 1825, by General Simon Perkins and Paul Williams, Akron originally had few African Americans. However, they were instrumental in its growth and history. Ohio's status as a free state, with interest in abolitionist activities, made it an attractive place for runaways and free Blacks. However, Ohio's attitude towards African Americans was at best an ambivalent one. The state legislature passed a series of Black codes, which limited the status and influence of Blacks during the early 1800s. These laws stripped African Americans of the franchise and forced Blacks to register with the clerk of courts. During the Civil War attitudes about freedom and equality somewhat changed, and Ohio began to remove some of the restrictions. After the Civil War African Americans began to enter Akron in much larger numbers, and they increasingly became more and more important to Akron's growth.

With the growth of the rubber industry Akron's population experienced phenomenal growth during the second and third decades of the twentieth century. Akron's population increased from 69,000 to well over 300,000. Part of this rapid growth was an influx of African Americans who flooded into the city to find employment in the expanding rubber industry. African Americans faced discrimination, which was common to others in similar cities. Therefore, this segregation forced them to form their own institutions, which fostered their growth and development. African Americans formed churches, schools, businesses, civic and social organizations, and other institutions, which were instrumental to their success.

Akron was also the incubator for a number of talented African-American musicians, artists, poets, and entrepreneurs. Much of Akron's story has never been told. Nevertheless, it is significant that African-American Akronites' accomplishments be recognized. Of equal importance are the many African Americans who live in the city going about their daily activities, quietly doing all the things that make a community lively and important to those who live there. This book celebrates both the known and unknown African Americans that make up the Akron African-American story.

One

Black Leaders

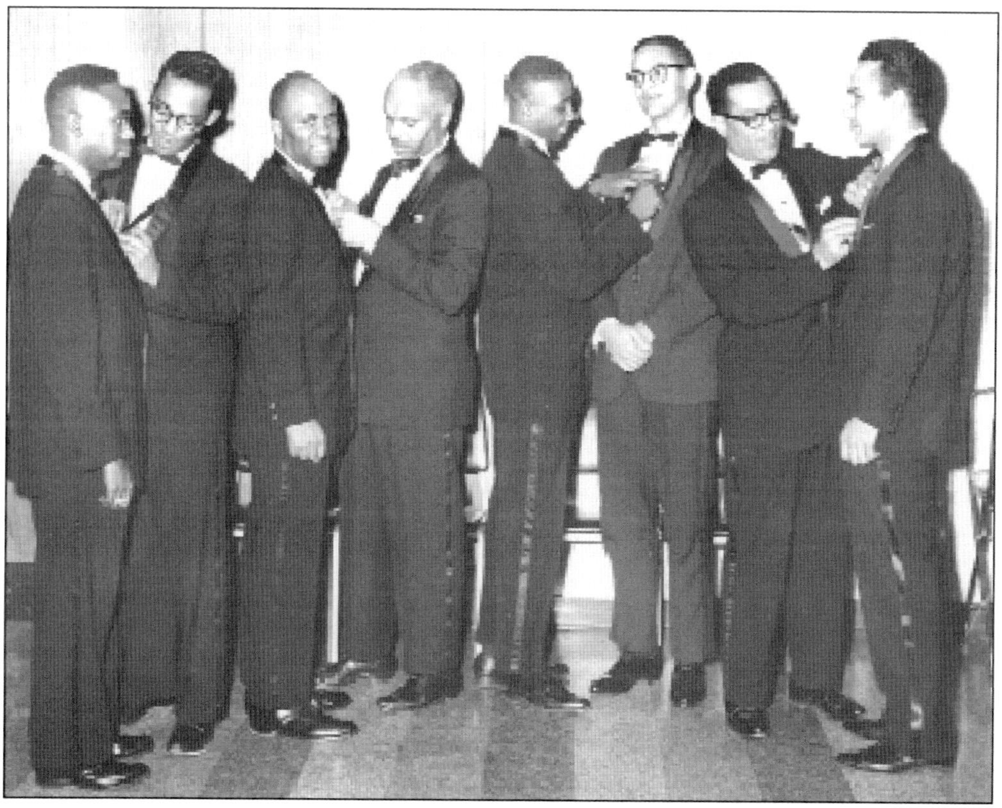

Men of the Alpha Phi Alpha fraternity check to make sure that everything is all right before they hold an affair. In the picture are, from let to right, Leon Butts, Buddy Tate, William Miller, Nate Martin (one of the first African-American police officers—John Suddeth was the first Black officer), Richard Neal, Booker Brown, George Nichols, and Archie Berry.

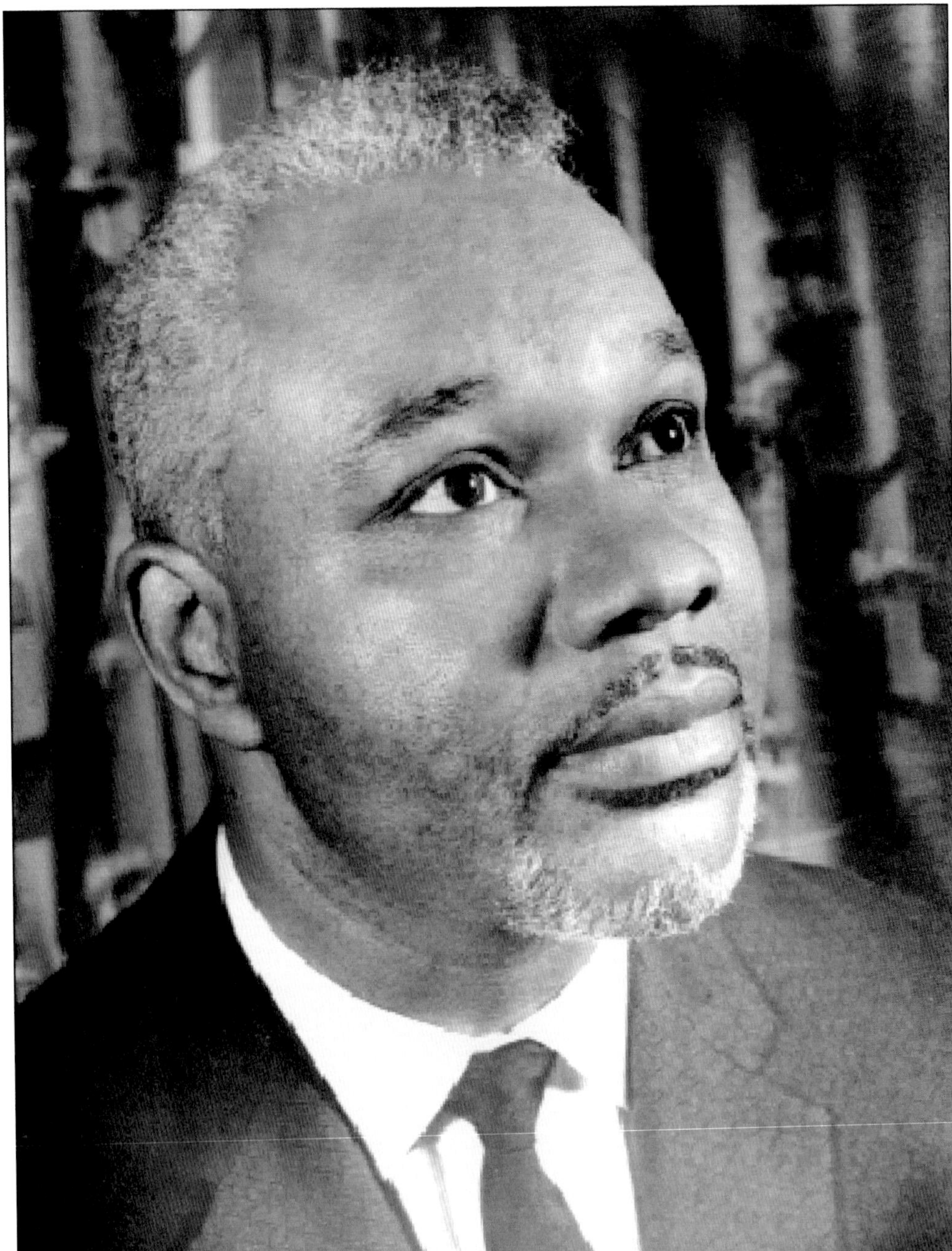

George Gay was an athlete who became a traffic officer in Akron. Gay, who went on to become a minister in New Jersey, was one of the best-known African-American officers. Many people in Akron remember him for his flamboyant style of directing traffic in Akron.

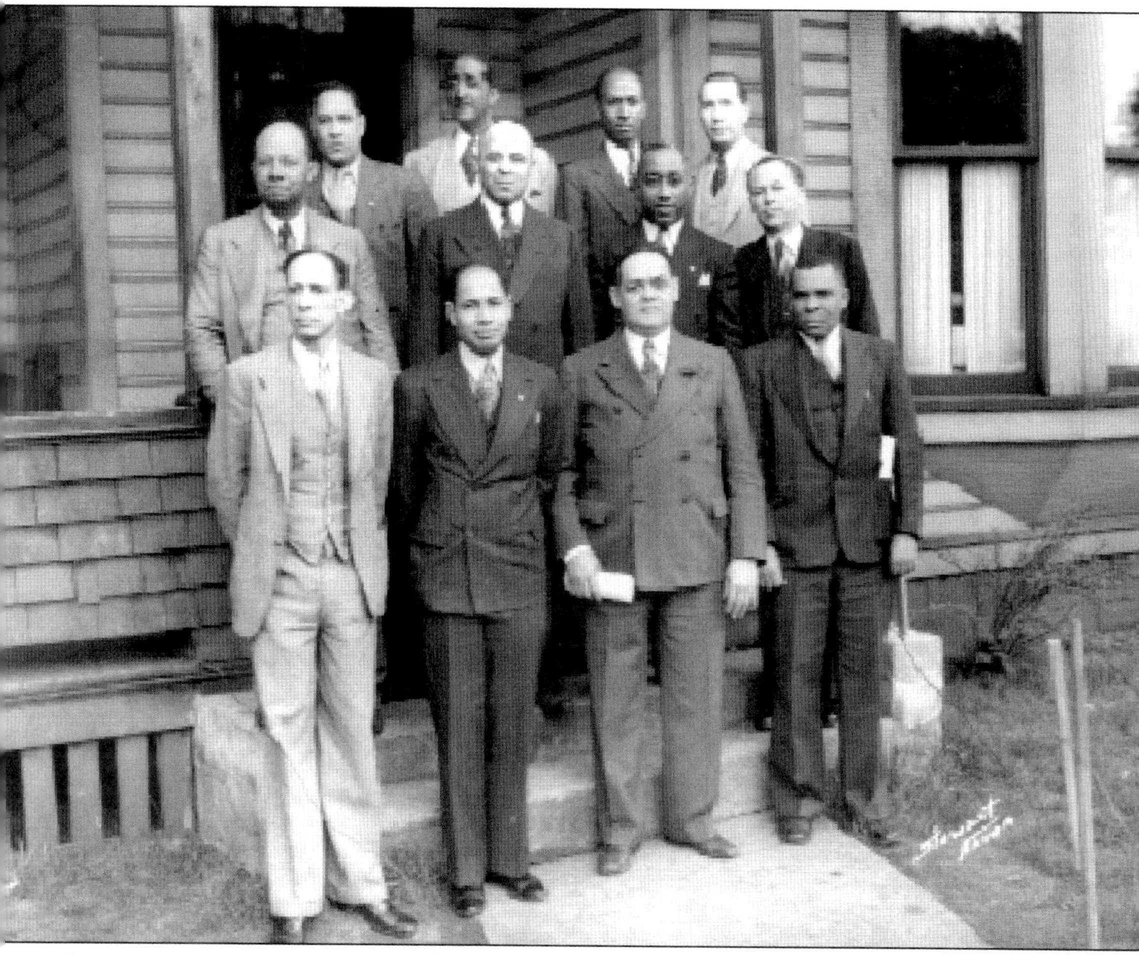

Akron was fortunate to have a good cadre of African-American leaders to guide and help the African-American community. In this photograph are three of the most powerful African-American lawyers in Akron: on the left in the second row, Samuel T. Kelley, on the left in the front row, Artee Fleming III, second from the left in the front row, Raymond Brown, and on the extreme right in the front row, Emmer Lancaster. Raymond Brown was executive director of the Akron Community Service Center.

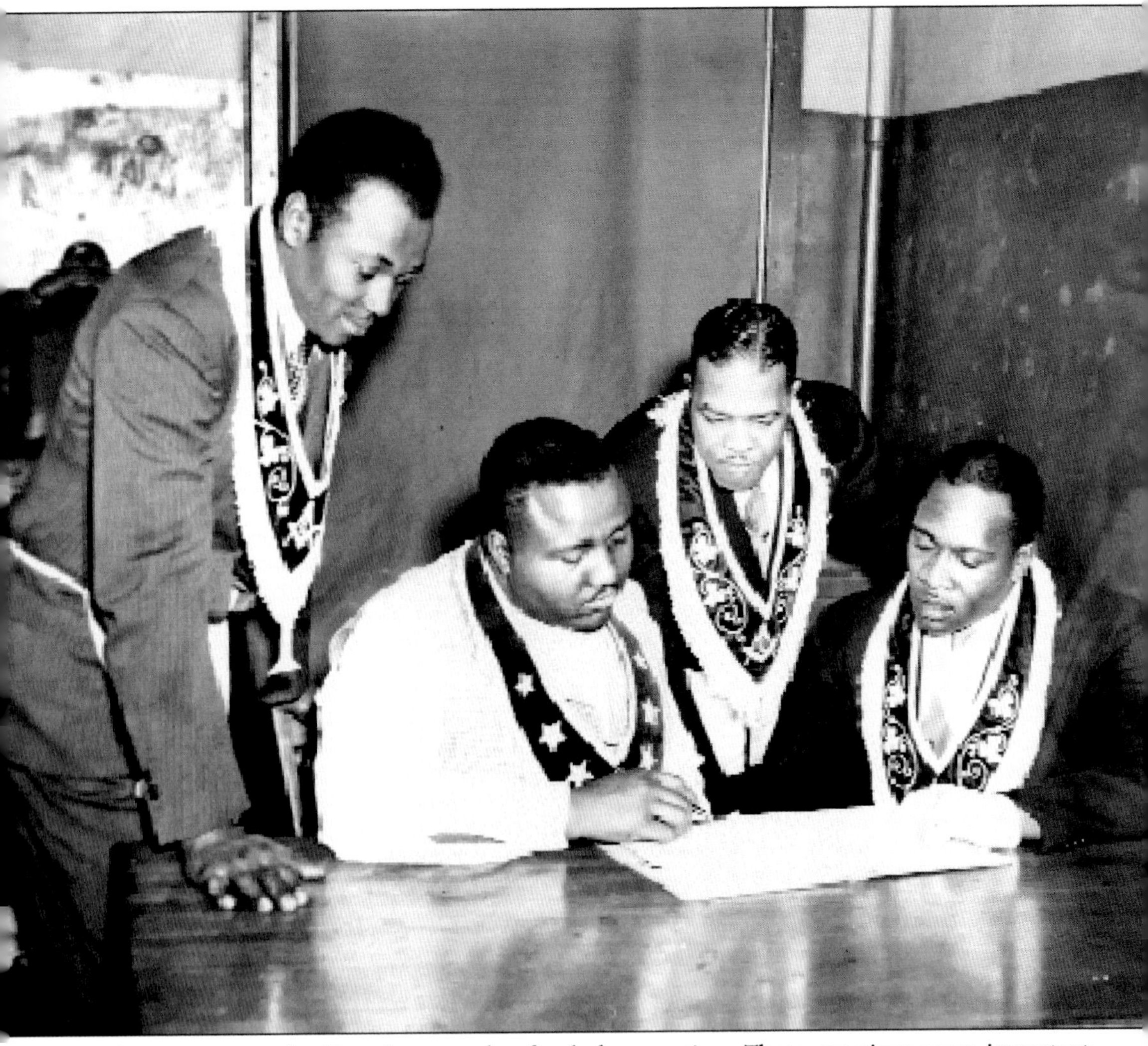

These men are checking the records of a lodge meeting. These meetings were important gatherings for African Americans.

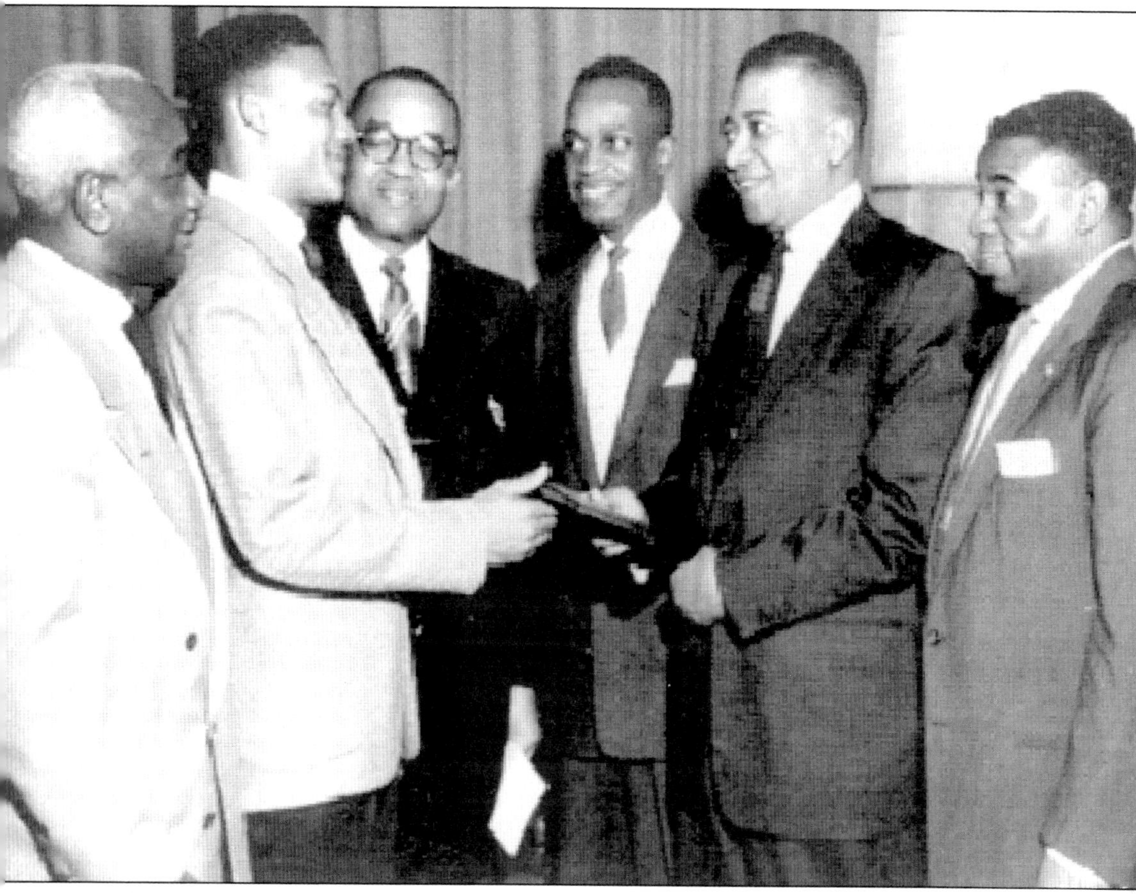

Several prominent African Americans participate in an award ceremony: from left to right, Wilbur Bratcher, an unidentified person, Herbert Bratcher, an unidentified person, and Dr. Wilford Bozeman. On the far right is Dr. Melvin Farris.The award recognized a worthy student who excelled in the Akron Public School system. Akron's African-American community was known for giving back to those less fortunate.

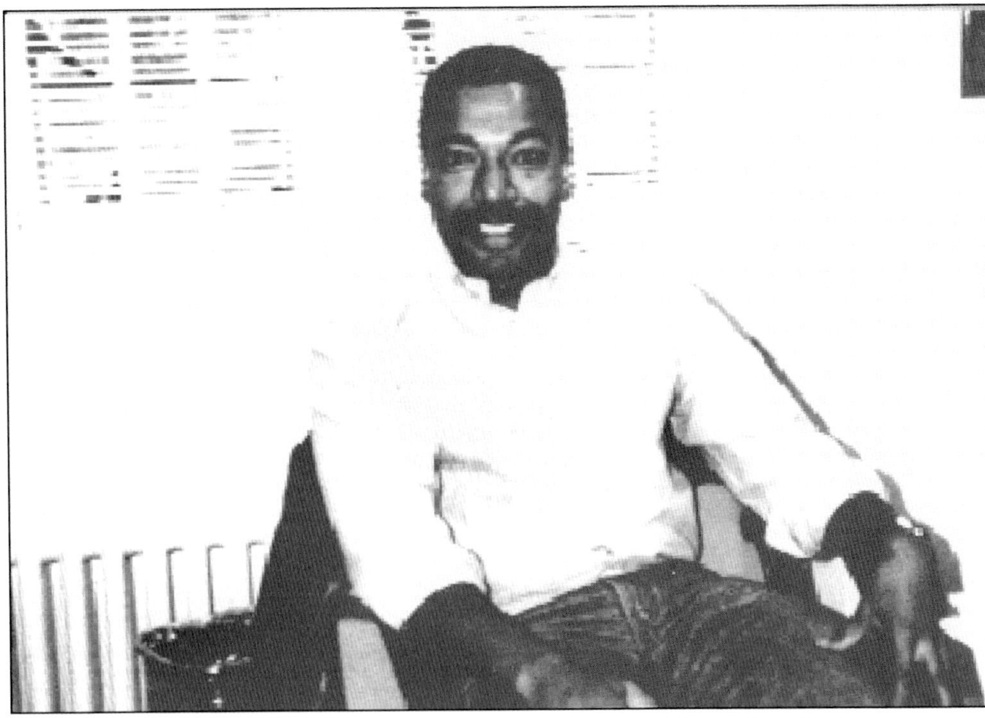

One of the great equalizers for African Americans in Akron was the public school system. It was the incubator of many talented people. Dr. Edward Hill, a graduate of Akron Public Schools, went on to become a department chairperson at Duke University.

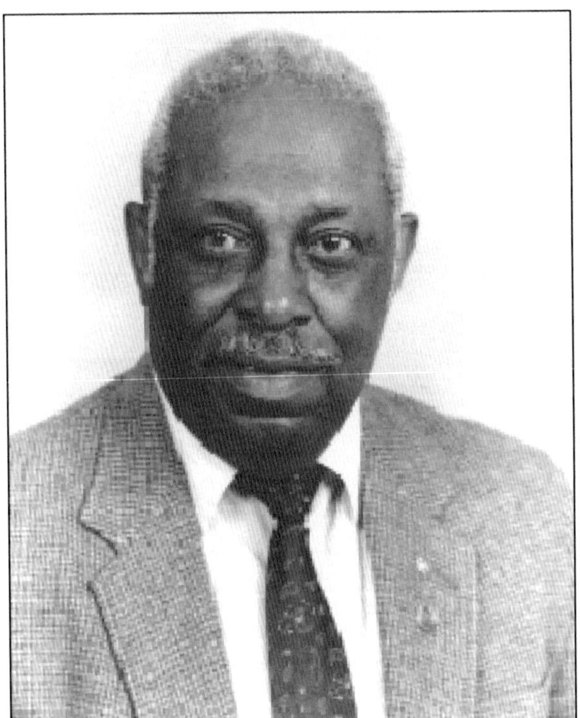

Spurgeon Moore was a very influential teacher and musician in Akron. Moore was a retired Lt. Col. who served in the 555 Paratroopers during the Second World War. This was the first Black paratrooper unit in the U.S. He was a leading figure in the struggle for civil rights in Akron. His mother Bertha Moore was also a very influential activist.

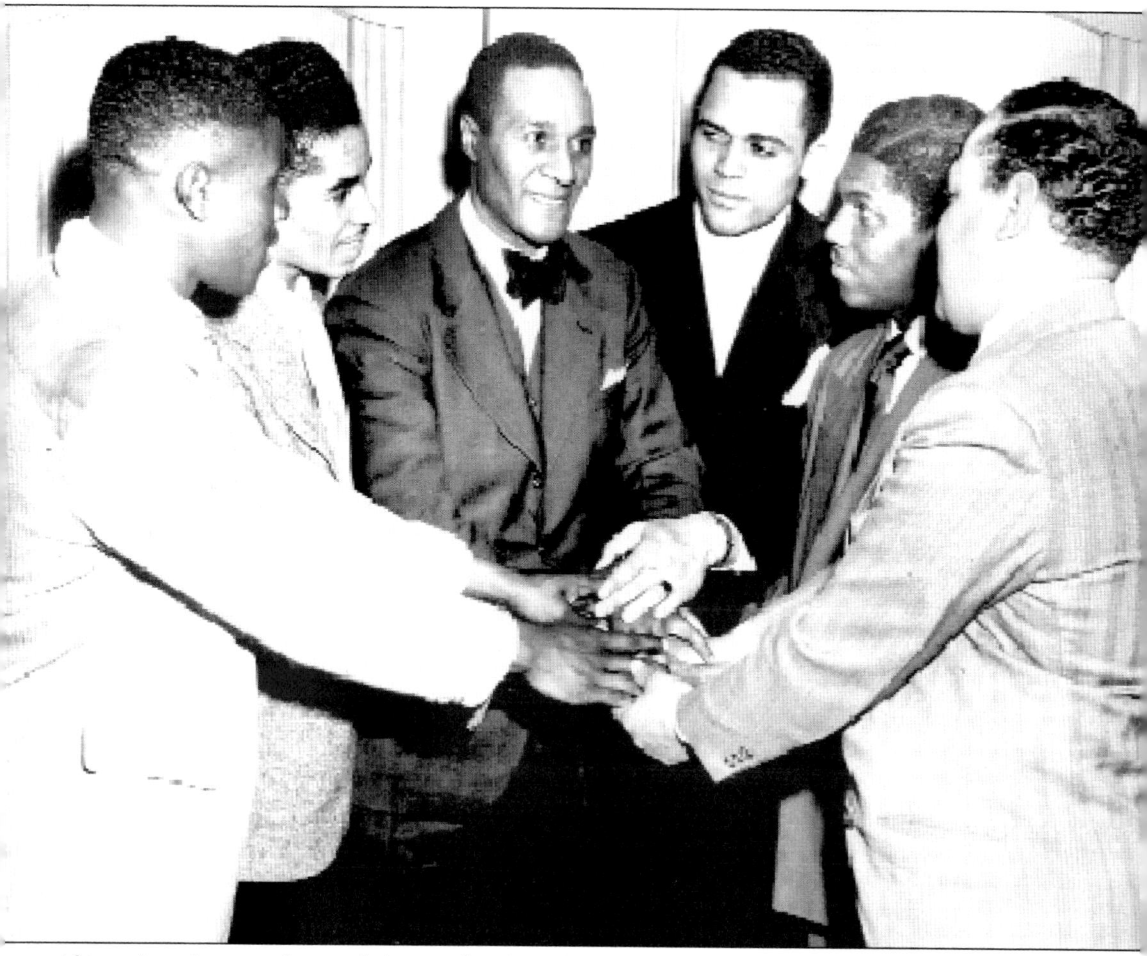

African Americans understood the need to have fundraisers to raise money for some important events. In this photograph six unidentified men celebrate the reaching of a goal. Akron's African-American community had a remarkable ability to raise funds for the things the community needed. They were a truly independent community, able to do many things for themselves.

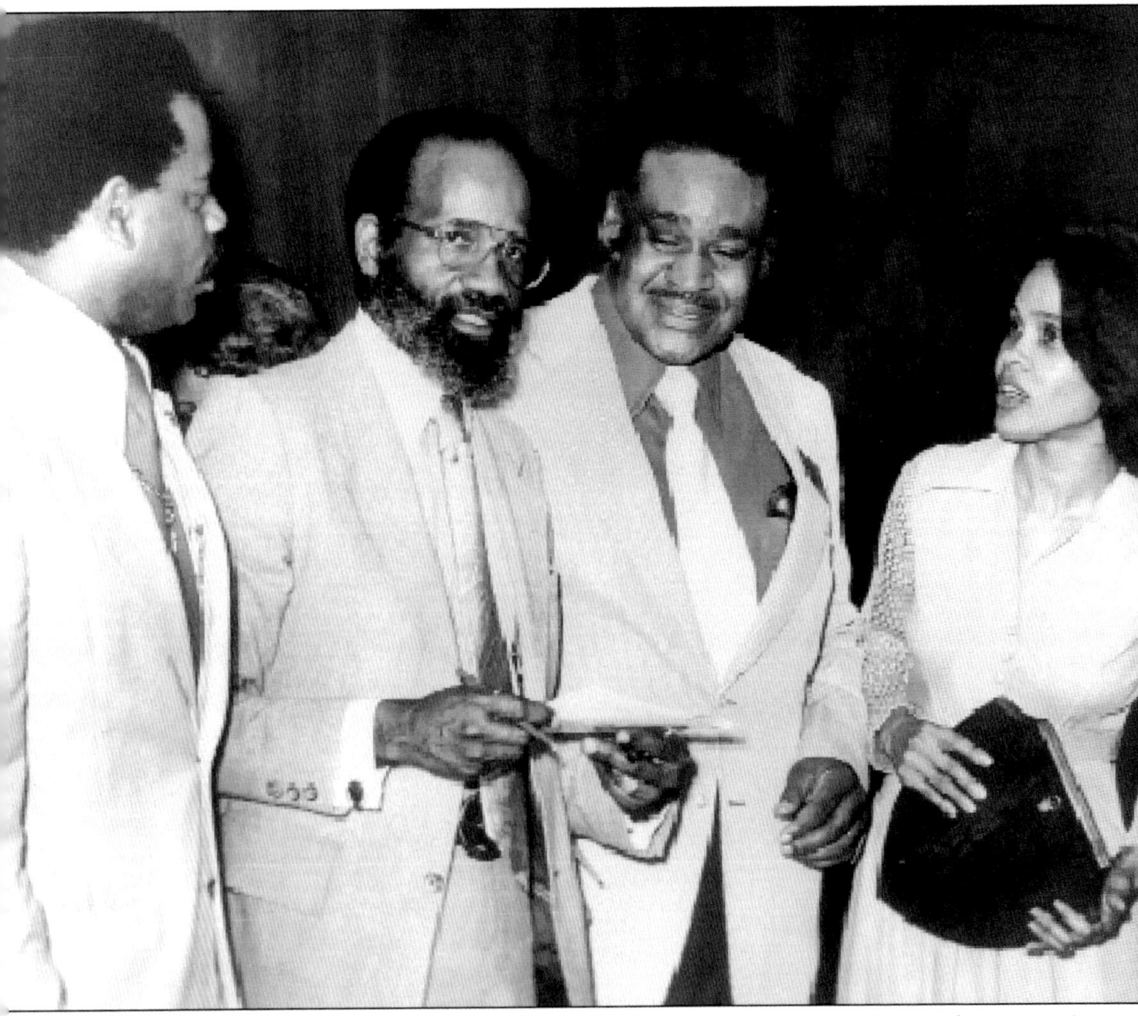

William Threatt, Leon Author, Vernon Odom (executive director of the Akron Urban League), and Shirla McClain discuss an important matter during a reception. The Urban League is a very important organization working within the African-American community. Akron's Urban League was especially active, serving a very important role, as a unifier of people within the community. Many important African-American social and civic events are held in the building owned and operated by the Urban League.

Dr. Melvin Farris was one of Akron's leading African-American physicians. He began his practice in 1946 after graduating from Ohio State University. He was president of the Frontier's Club, a member of the Urban League Board of Trustees, and a life member of the NAACP. It is very important that African-American youths have visible, Black role models.

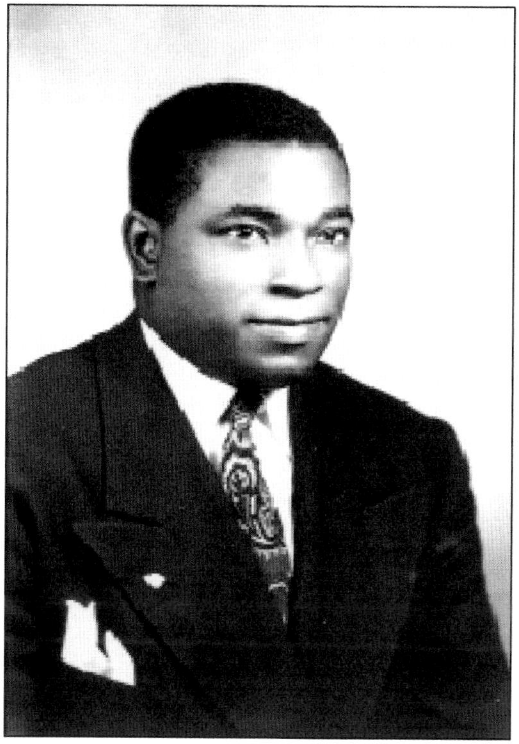

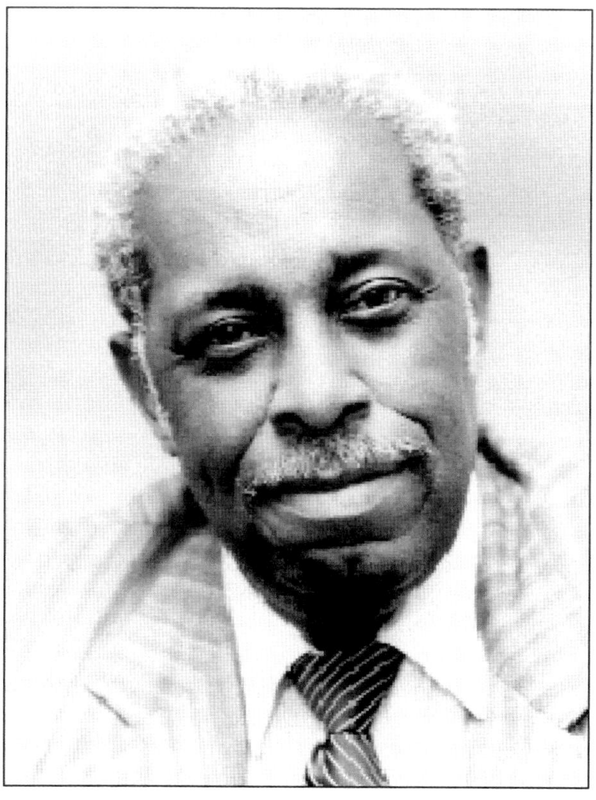

Spurgeon Moore at an older age continued to be a very important figure in Akron. He was very active in the veterans' affairs of Akron. Akron was very proud of the service of its African-American men and women. The VFW lodges proudly commemorated the accomplishments of Black soldiers.

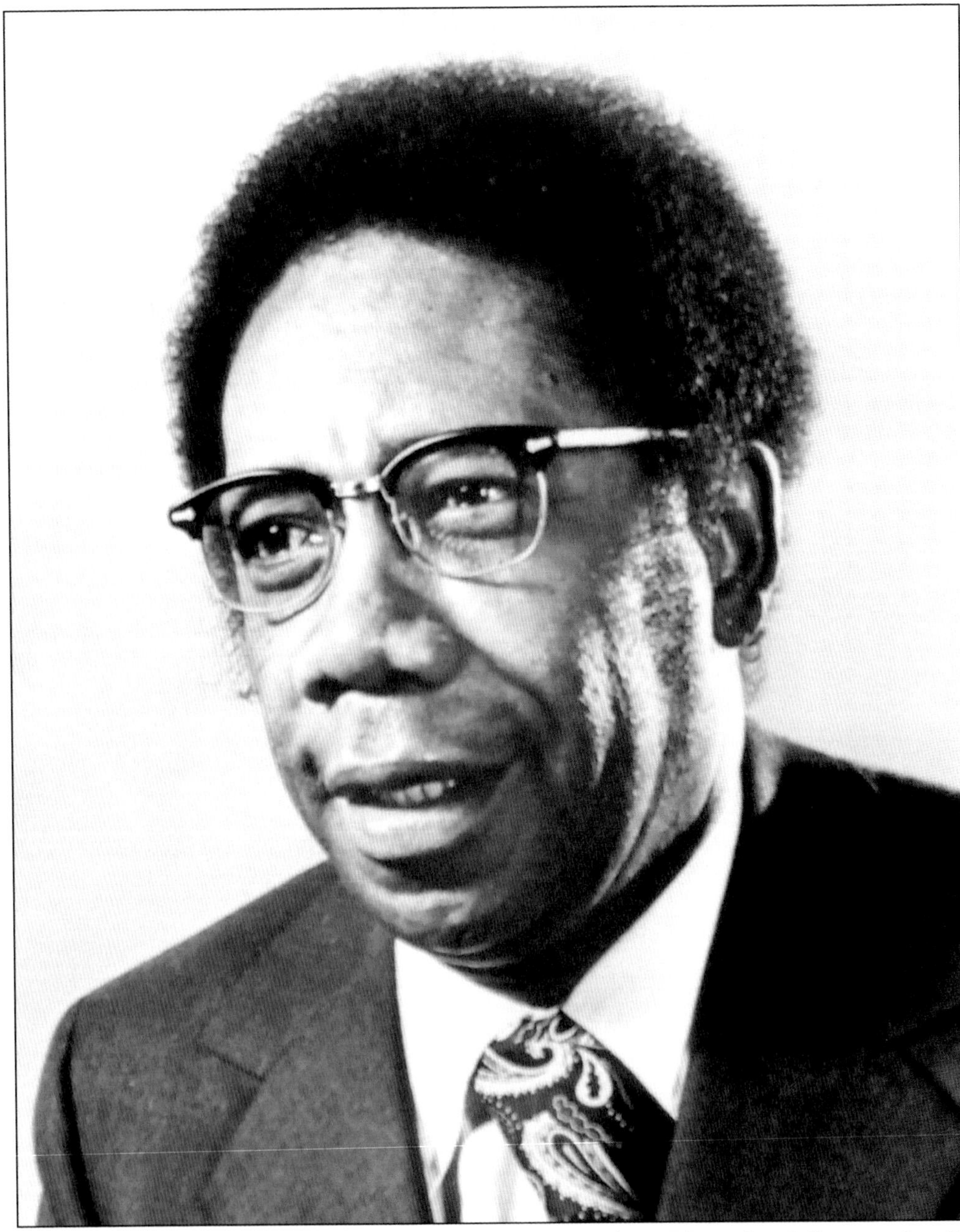

Reverend Dr. Eugene E. Morgan Jr. was pastor of Wesley Temple AME Zion church for more than 35 years. Wesley Temple is the oldest African-American church in Akron. Many of the most prominent African-American Akronites have been members of this church. Like all communities churches were an important part of the institutional complexity of Akron's African-American community.

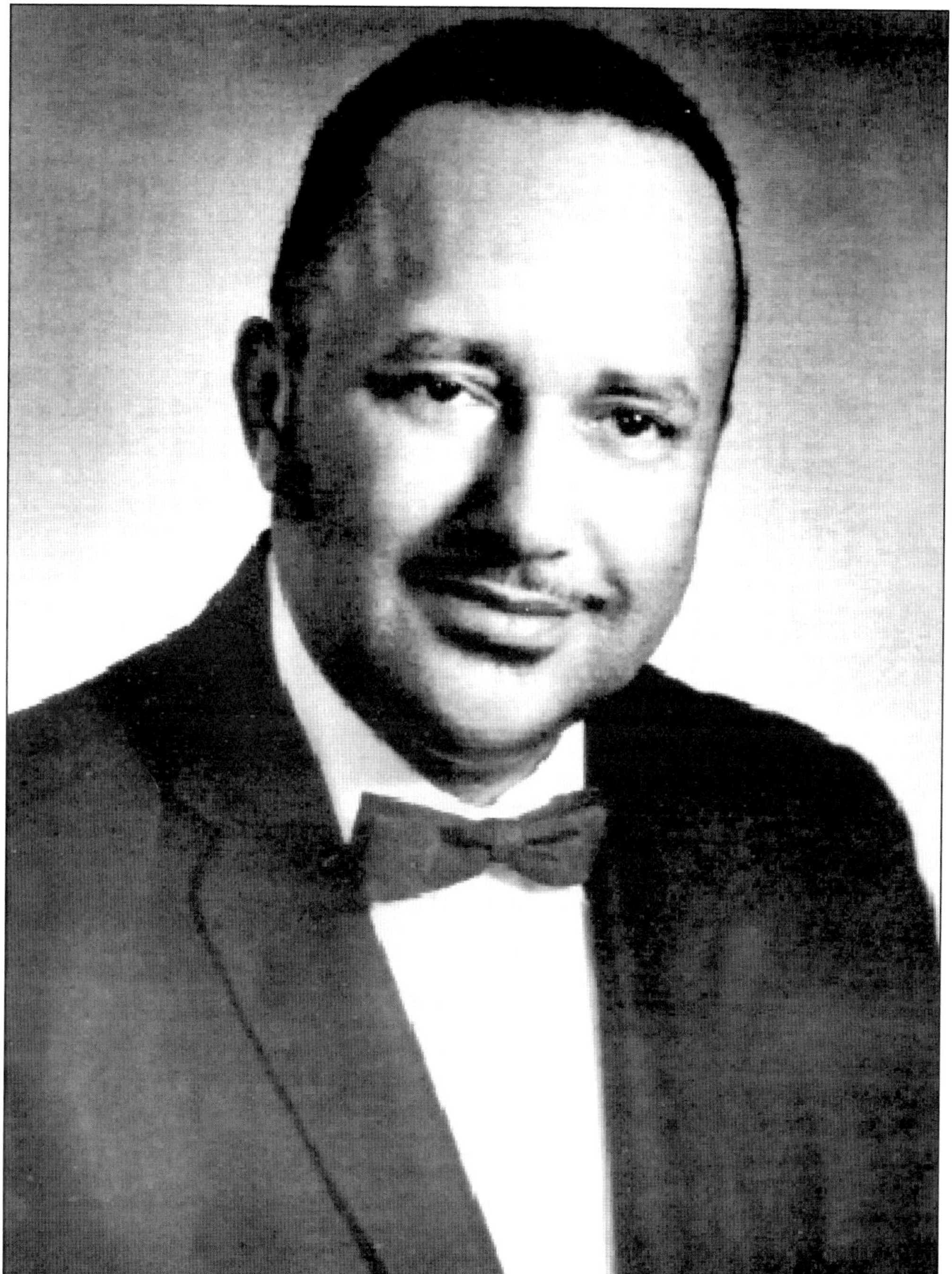

Akron was fortunate to have several good African-American physicians. Dr. E. Gates Morgan came to Akron in 1956. He was married to the famed jazz singer Delores Parker. He graduated from Virginia State College and Meharry Medical School and was the first African-American general surgeon in Akron. Dr. Morgan provided a vital link to the white community in Akron. His skill as a physician and his education made him a natural leader in the community. He was also the first African-American president of the Summit County Medical Society.

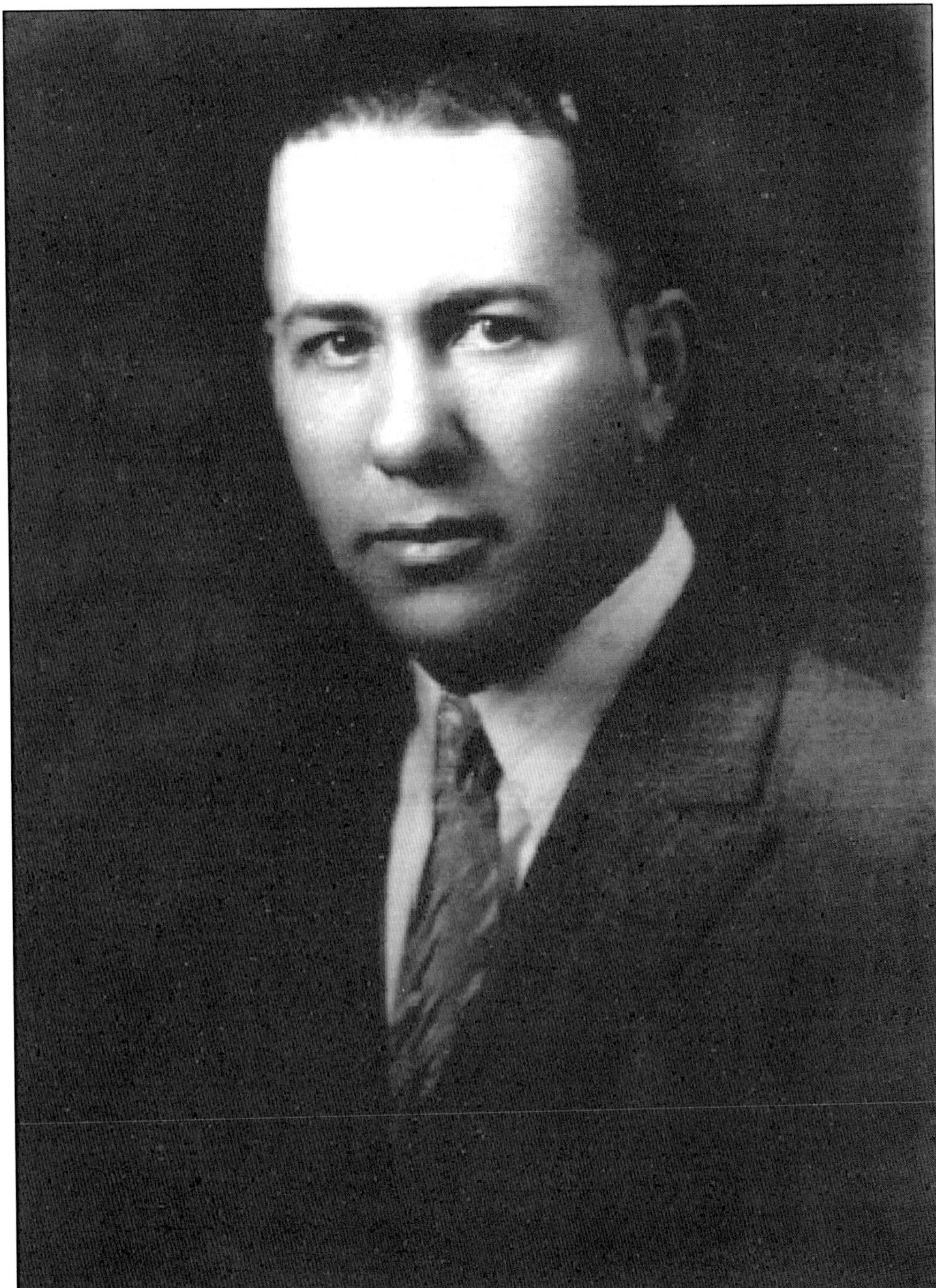

Akron's African Americans were very dedicated to building a community. Therefore they were part of the many national movements. Dr. John W. Dunbar was vice president of Akron's Negro Business League and was one of the first African-American dentists in Akron. He was a founding member of the Akron branch of the NAACP and the Association for the Colored Community, which evolved into the Urban League.

Dr. Abraham Murphy Perry was named after the famous African-American Kentucky Derby jockey Isaac Murphy. He was trained as a doctor at Meharry Medical College and came to Akron in 1934 after five years in nearby Barberton, Ohio. He was also a pianist for the well-known Fisk Jubilee Singers. Akron was the focal point for a number of talented migrants from the south.

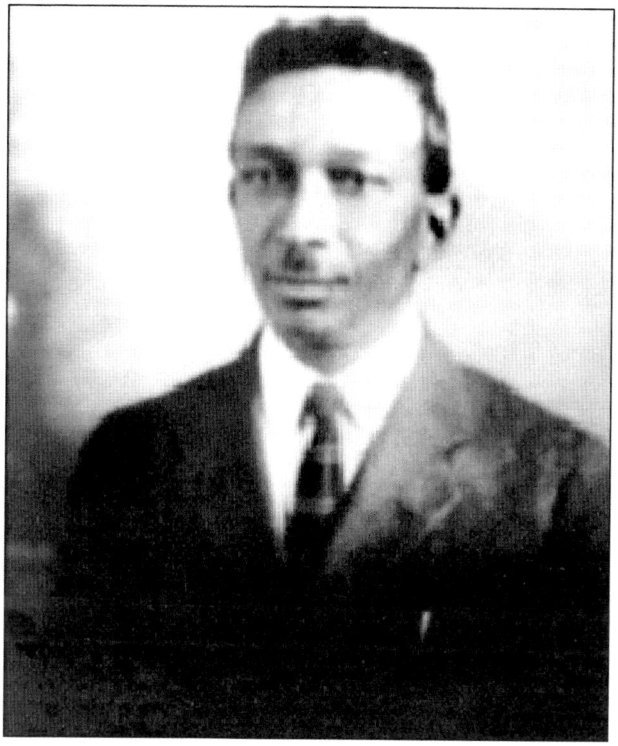

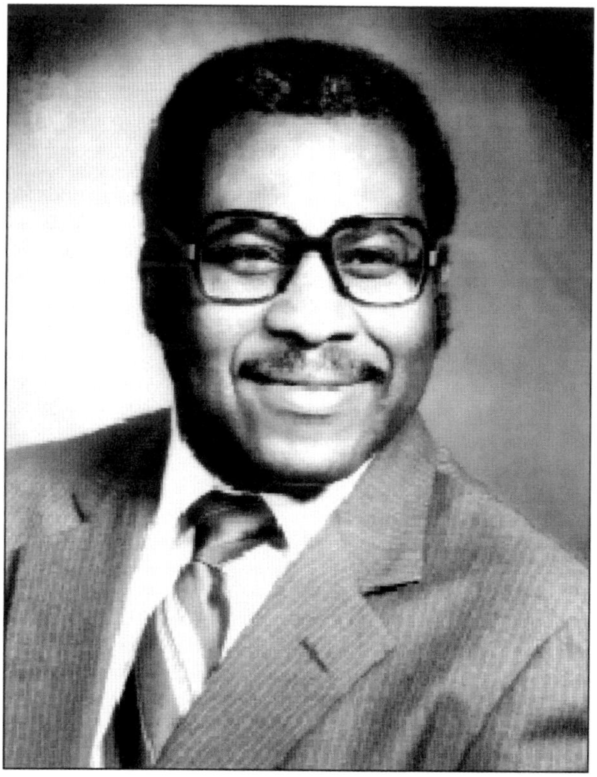

One of the most important institutions in the African-American community is the Black church. Pastor Ron Fowler of the Arlington Street Church of God, one of the most powerful and prestigious Black churches in the city, is well known to Black Akronites. The historical Arlington Street Church of God has been at the forefront of developing and training leaders in Akron. Pastor Fowler is one of the most recognized and important community leaders, fighting for better treatment and for opportunities for African Americans in Akron.

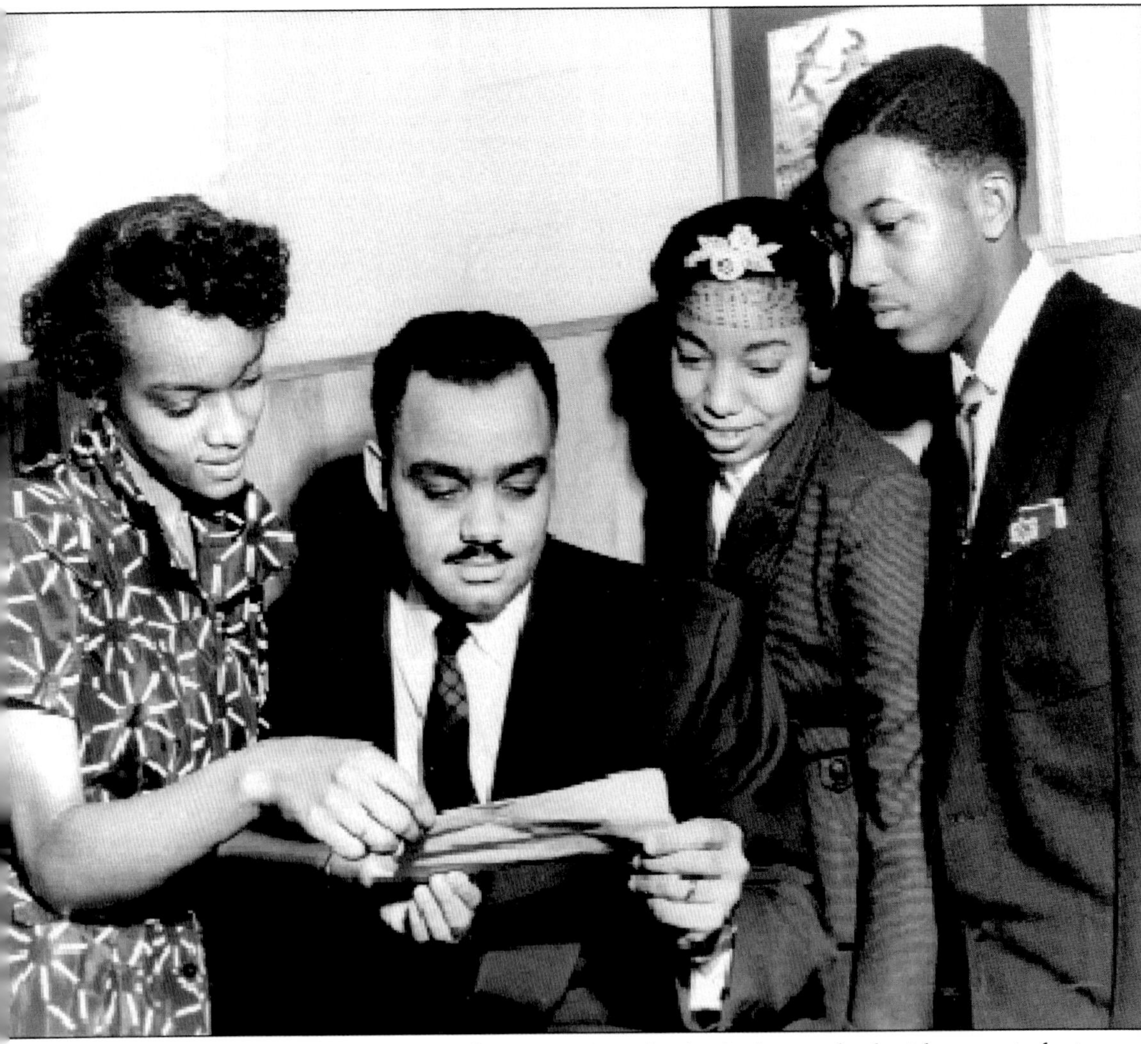

Dr. Eldridge Sharpe, an influential African-American dentist, looks at a check with some students from the Akron Public Schools. Dr. Sharpe was considered a prominent dentist in Akron.

Two

Education

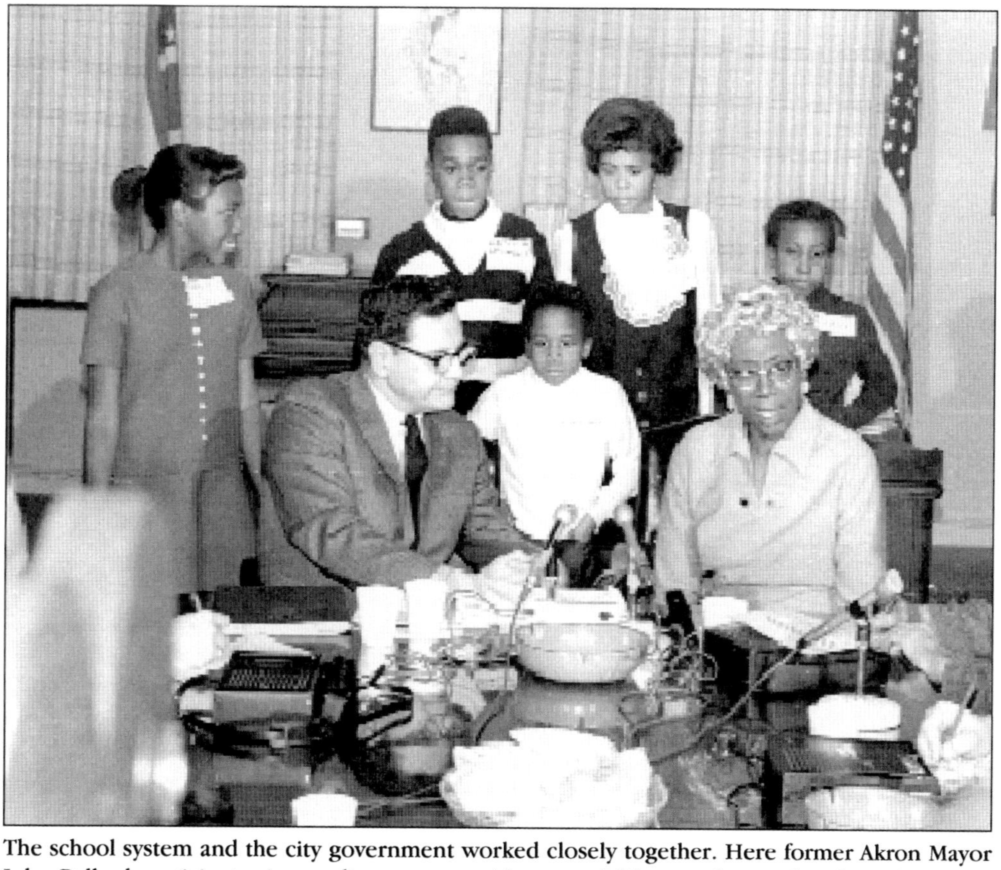

The school system and the city government worked closely together. Here former Akron Mayor John Ballard participates in a radio program with some children and a teacher from the Akron Public Schools' system. The Akron Public Schools' system was an important institution for educating and motivating African-American children.

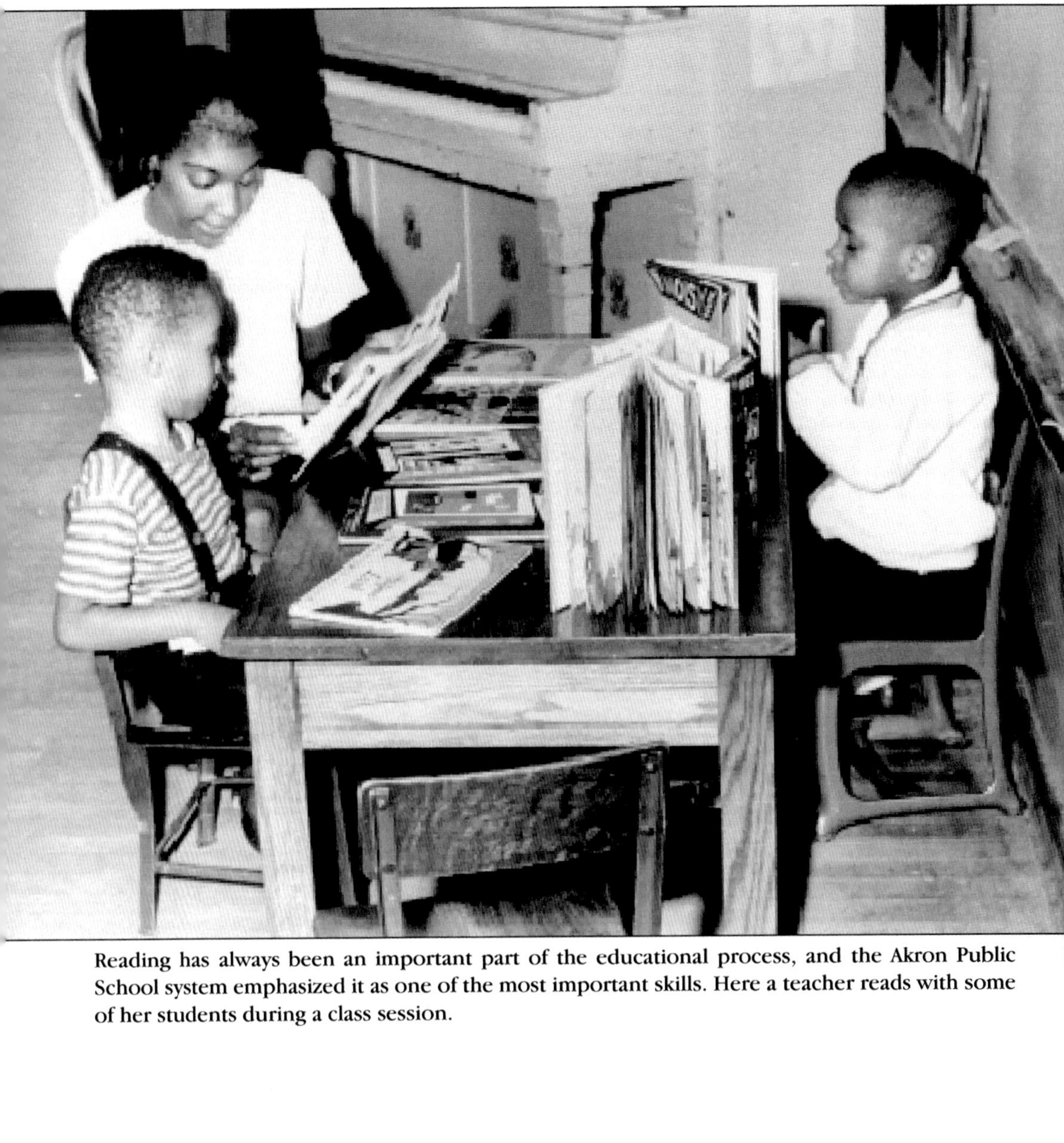

Reading has always been an important part of the educational process, and the Akron Public School system emphasized it as one of the most important skills. Here a teacher reads with some of her students during a class session.

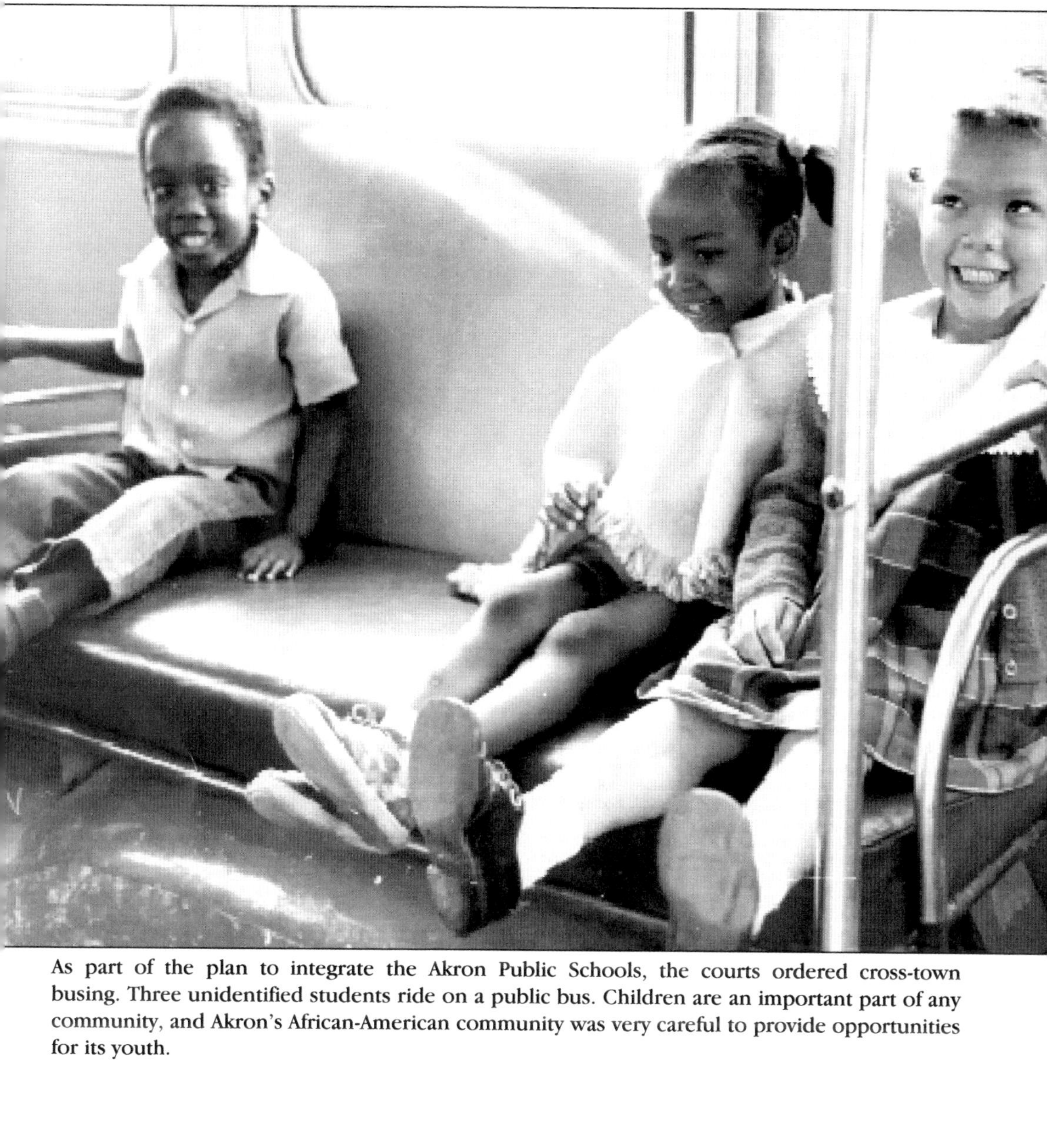

As part of the plan to integrate the Akron Public Schools, the courts ordered cross-town busing. Three unidentified students ride on a public bus. Children are an important part of any community, and Akron's African-American community was very careful to provide opportunities for its youth.

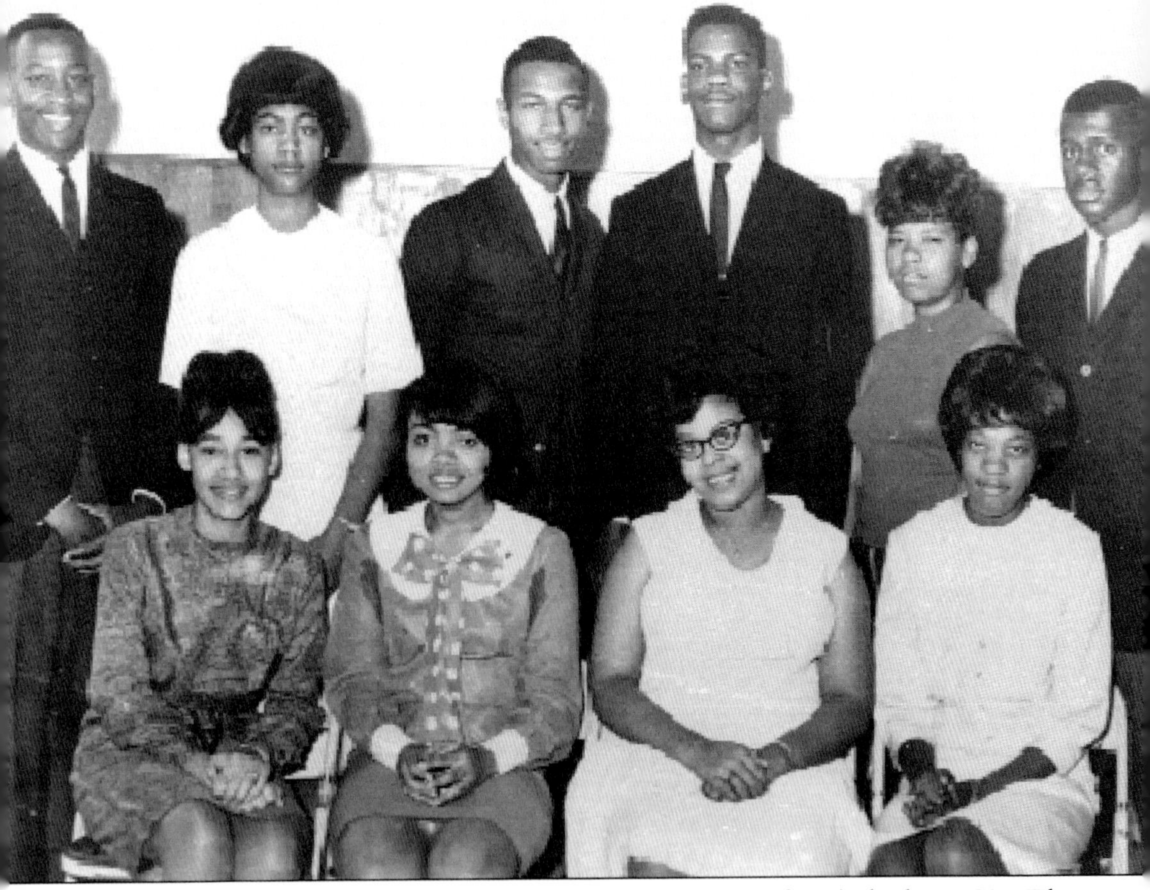

Students pose for a picture after a school function: second from left in the back row, Rita Wilson and next to her, David Burch—two proud graduates of the public school system. The other students are unidentified.

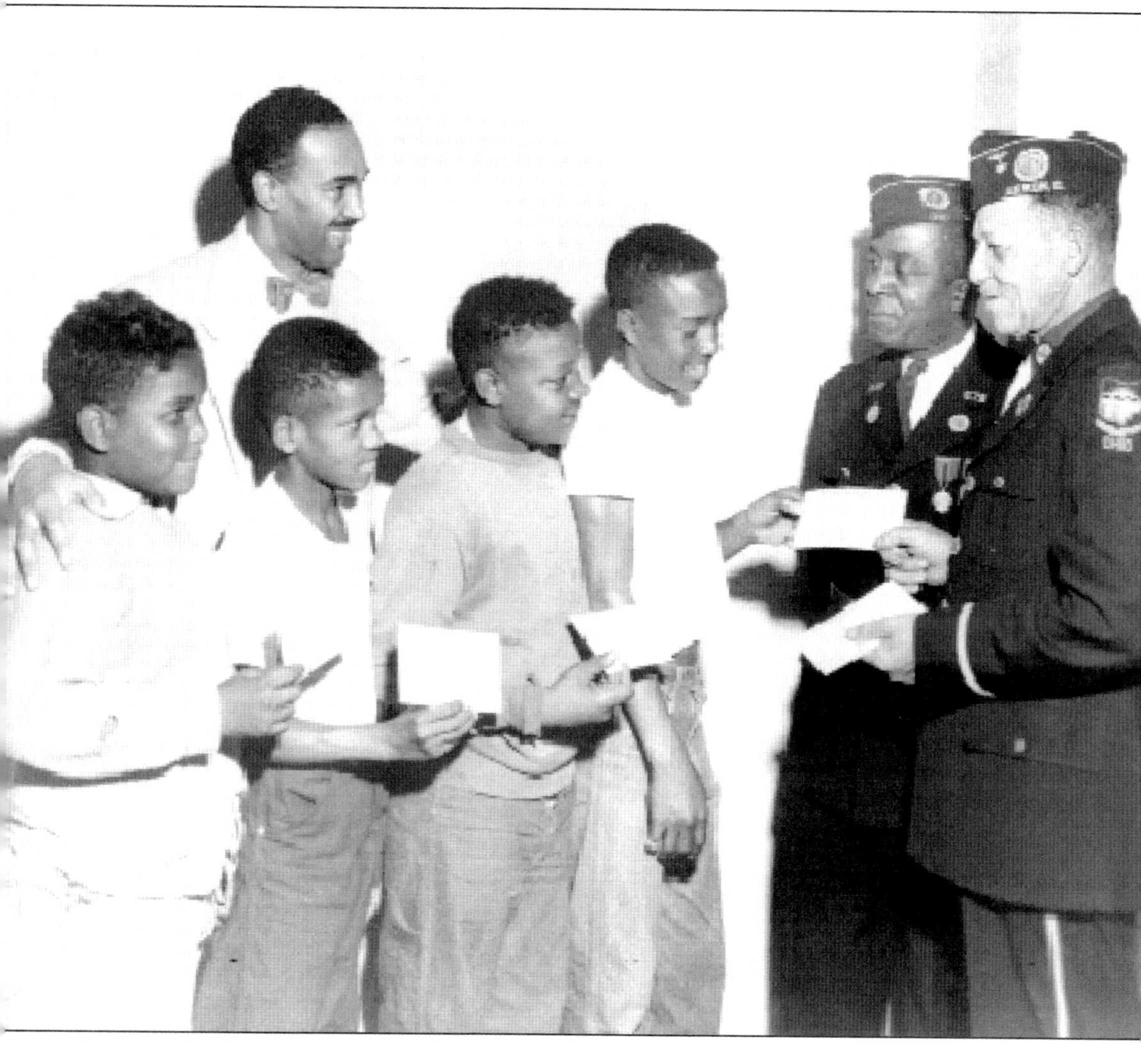

Attorney Rufus Thompson presents four unidentified students for awards from two unidentified Akron-branch American Legion members. The older generation of Akron feels a strong need to give back to those who come after them. The American Legion uses these opportunities to teach students about the sacrifices of past generations.

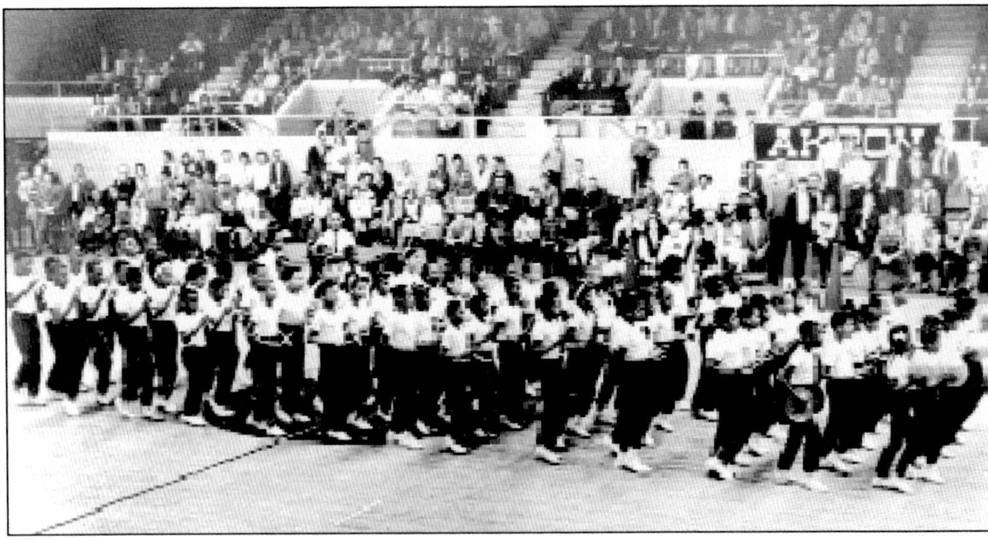

Akron has a number of influential organizations that play a special role in the community. One of the most successful programs for young people in Akron is the marching band. Here the Bryan School marching band gives a stirring performance.

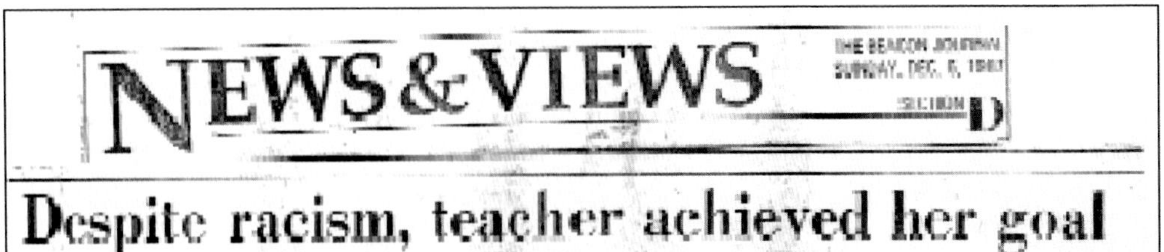

NEWS & VIEWS

THE BEACON JOURNAL SUNDAY, DEC. 6, 1987 SECTION D

Despite racism, teacher achieved her goal

BioGraph: Edith Delaney Mitchell

Edith Delaney Mitchell was the first African-American graduate of the University of Akron's teacher education program. She spent her career educating students in Ohio and especially Akron. Mitchell has been active in a number of organizations, including the Alpha Kappa Alpha sorority. She was one of the first female employees of the B.F. Goodrich company, which built tanks for the military.

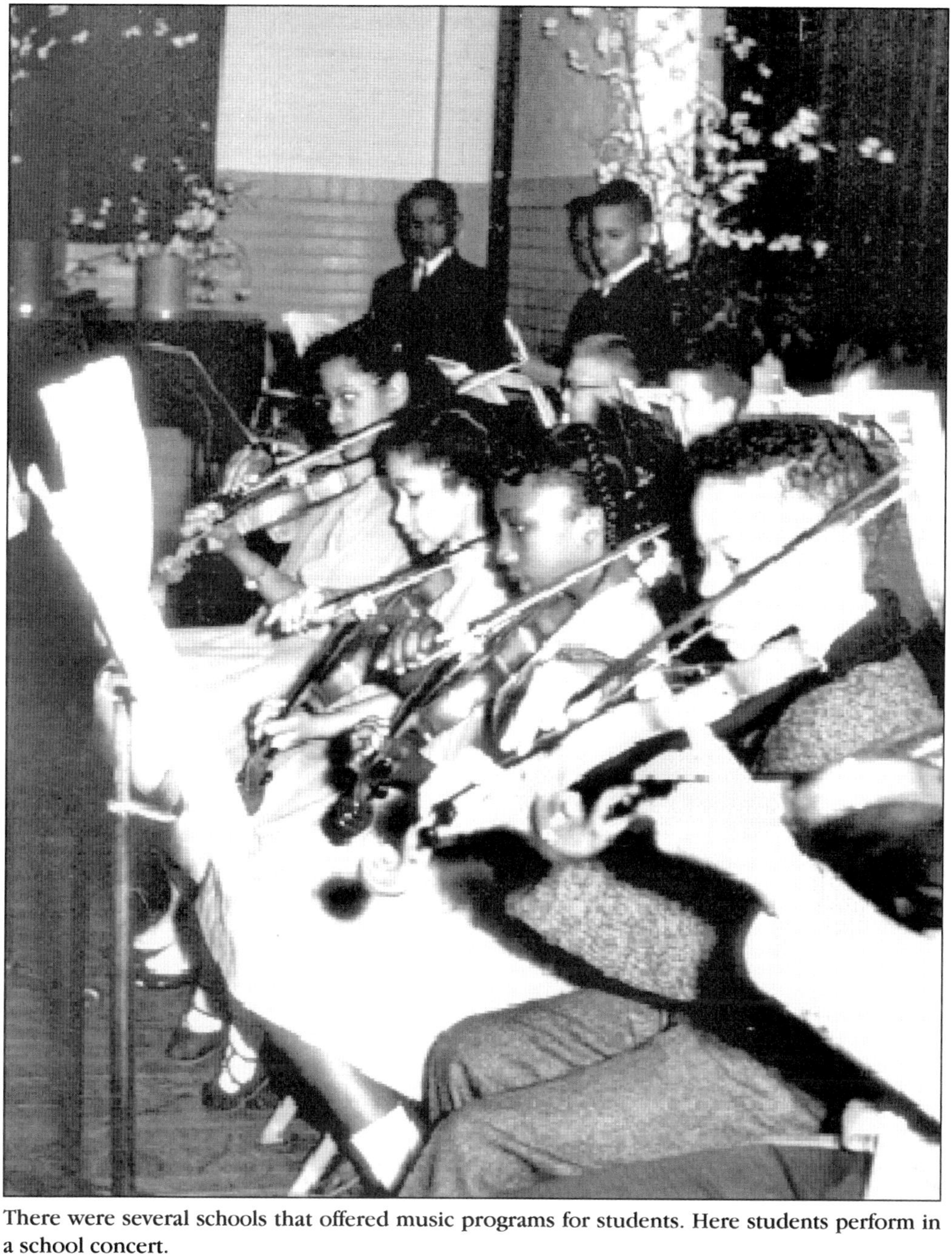

There were several schools that offered music programs for students. Here students perform in a school concert.

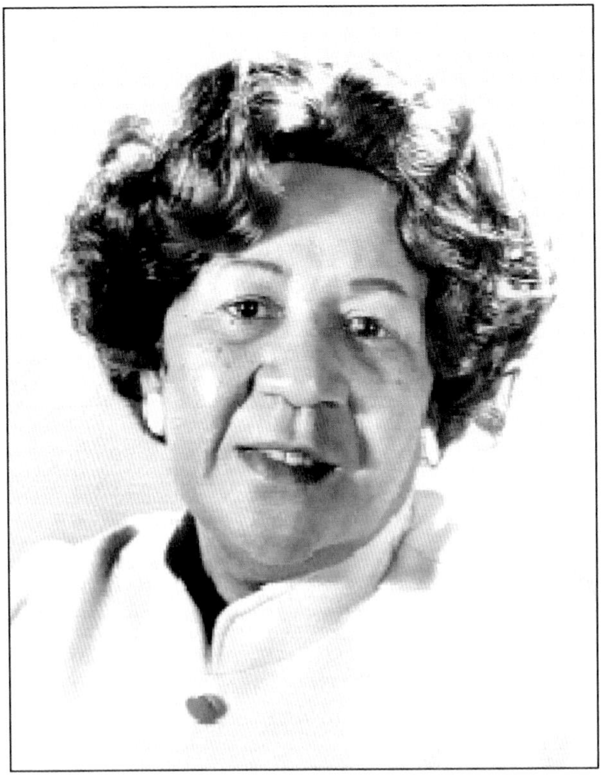

African-American women have played a pivotal role in the success of the Akron Public School system. Dr. Abbie Willacy served as a principal at one of the local schools.

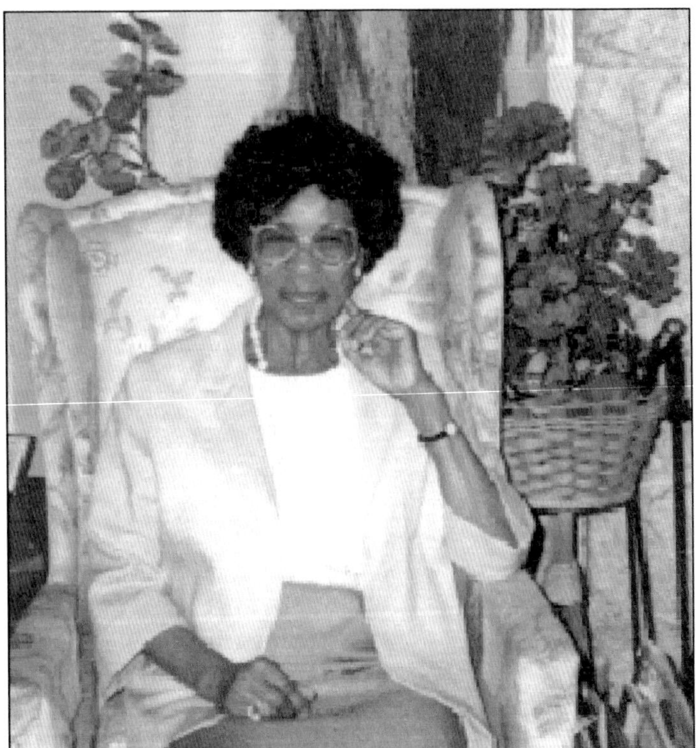

Mary Eagle served as an important member of the Mt. Zion Church. The center of the African-American community was the Black church. Women were very active in sponsoring church related activities.

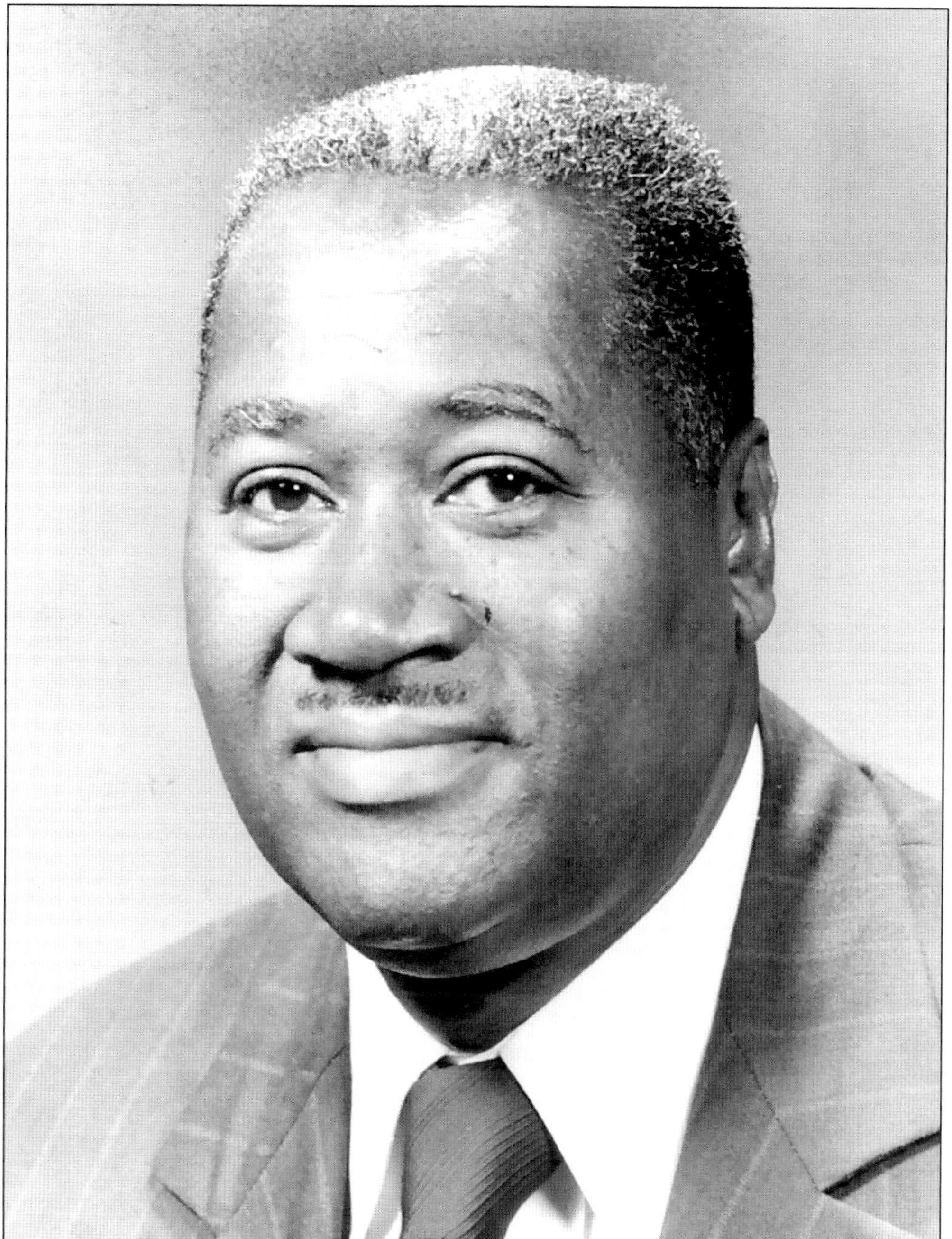

The Akron Public Schools' system offered African Americans the opportunity to demonstrate their skills. It was in the public school system that African Americans first received distinction for their administrative skills. James Ervin served as a public school administrator in the Akron Public Schools.

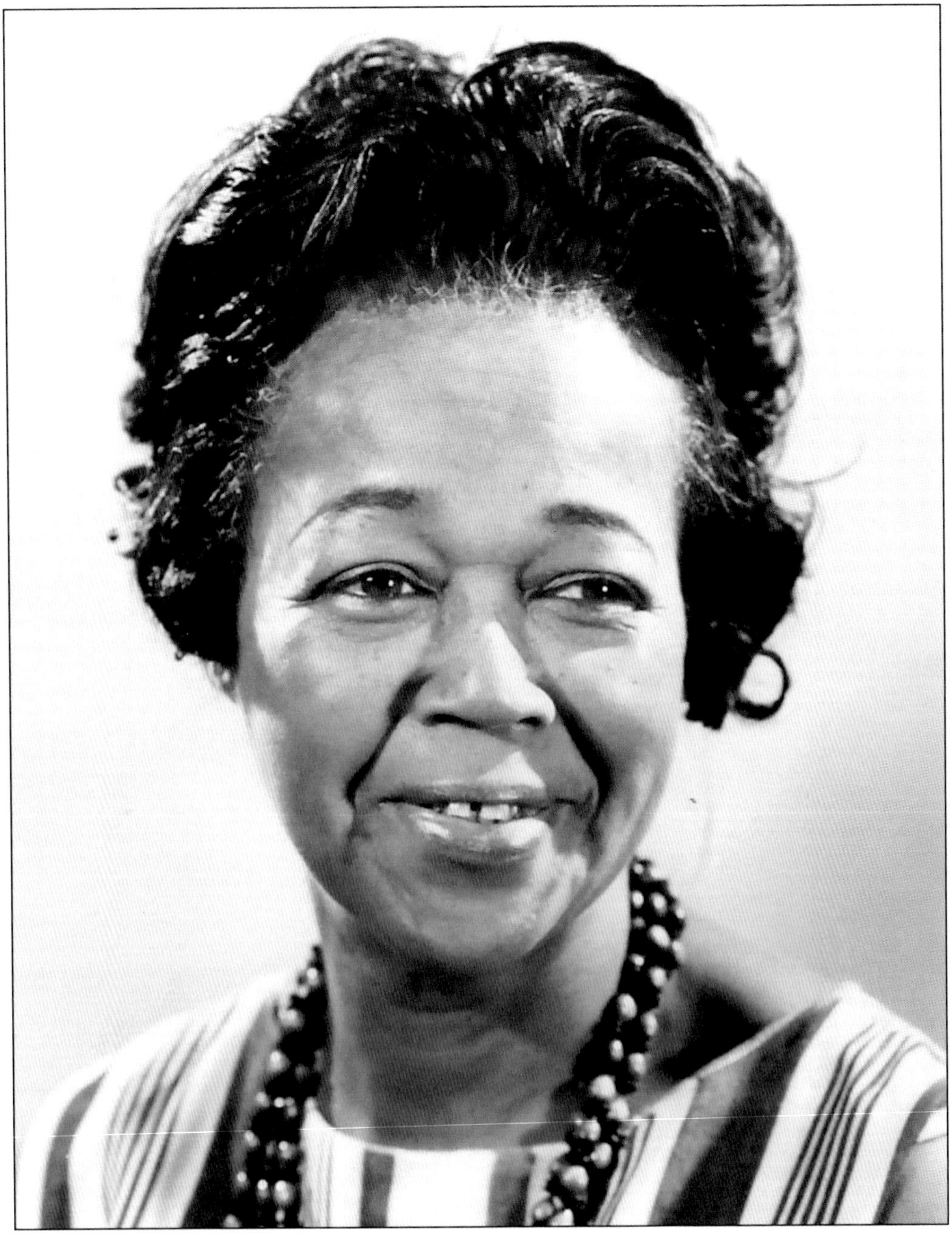

Women played an integral role in running the public schools, and Ester Spruill was a successful administrator and teacher in the school system. Public school education offered opportunities for both men and women.

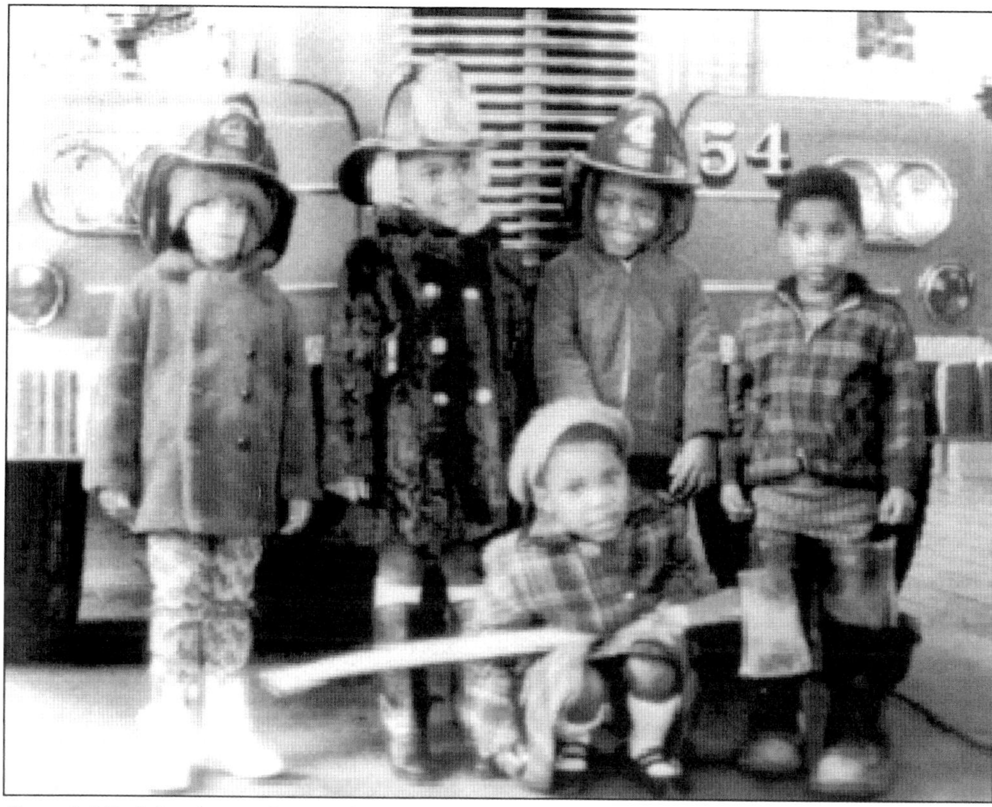

Akron Public Schools were known for was the many field trips they took the children on to introduce students to different experiences. Here you see children enjoying a fieldtrip to a fire station.

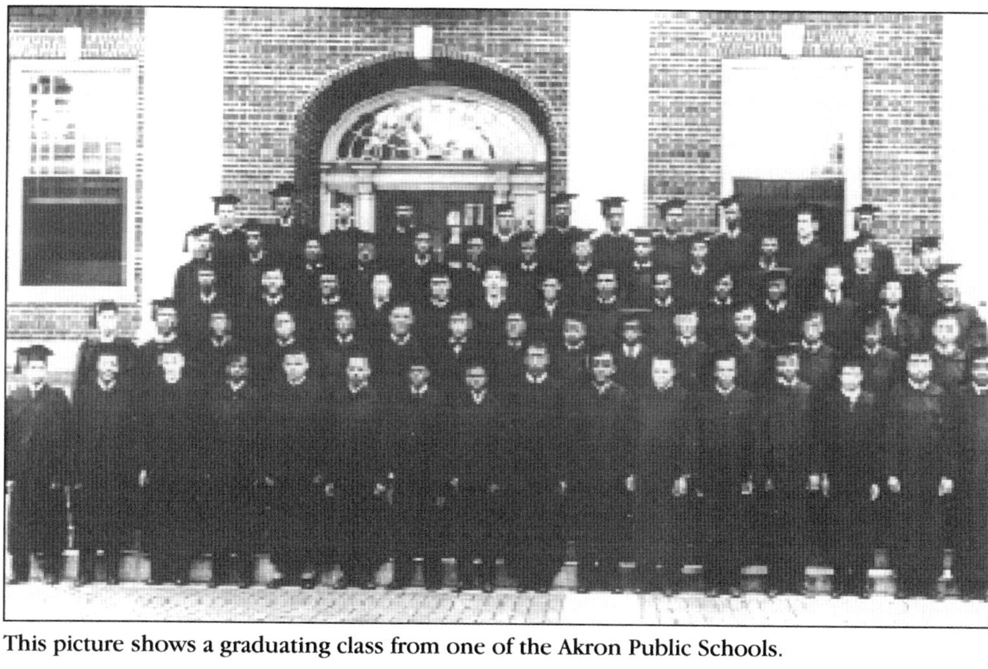
This picture shows a graduating class from one of the Akron Public Schools.

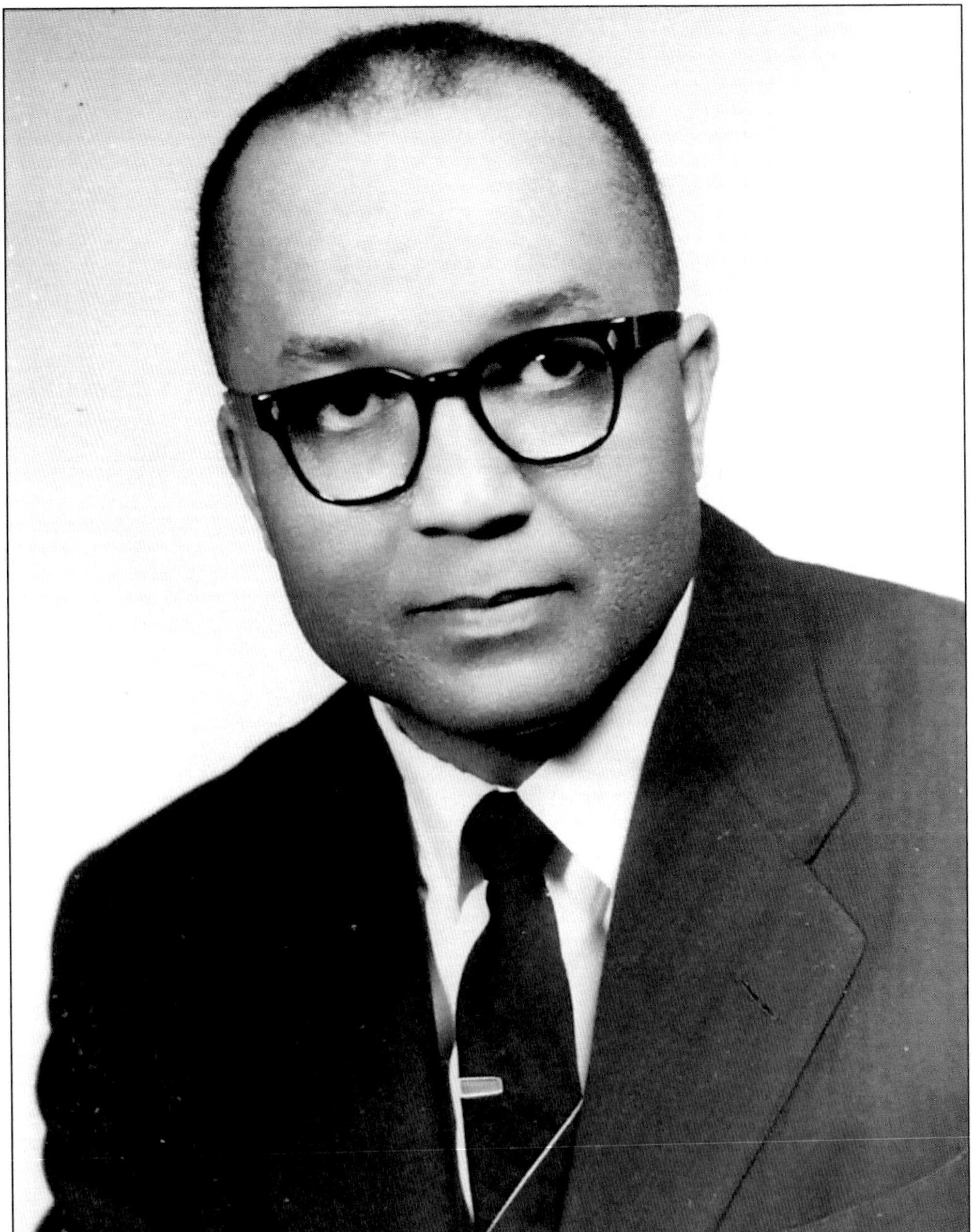

Herbert Brackens was one of the first African-American teachers to work for the Akron Public Schools' system. He began his teaching career in Akron in 1946.

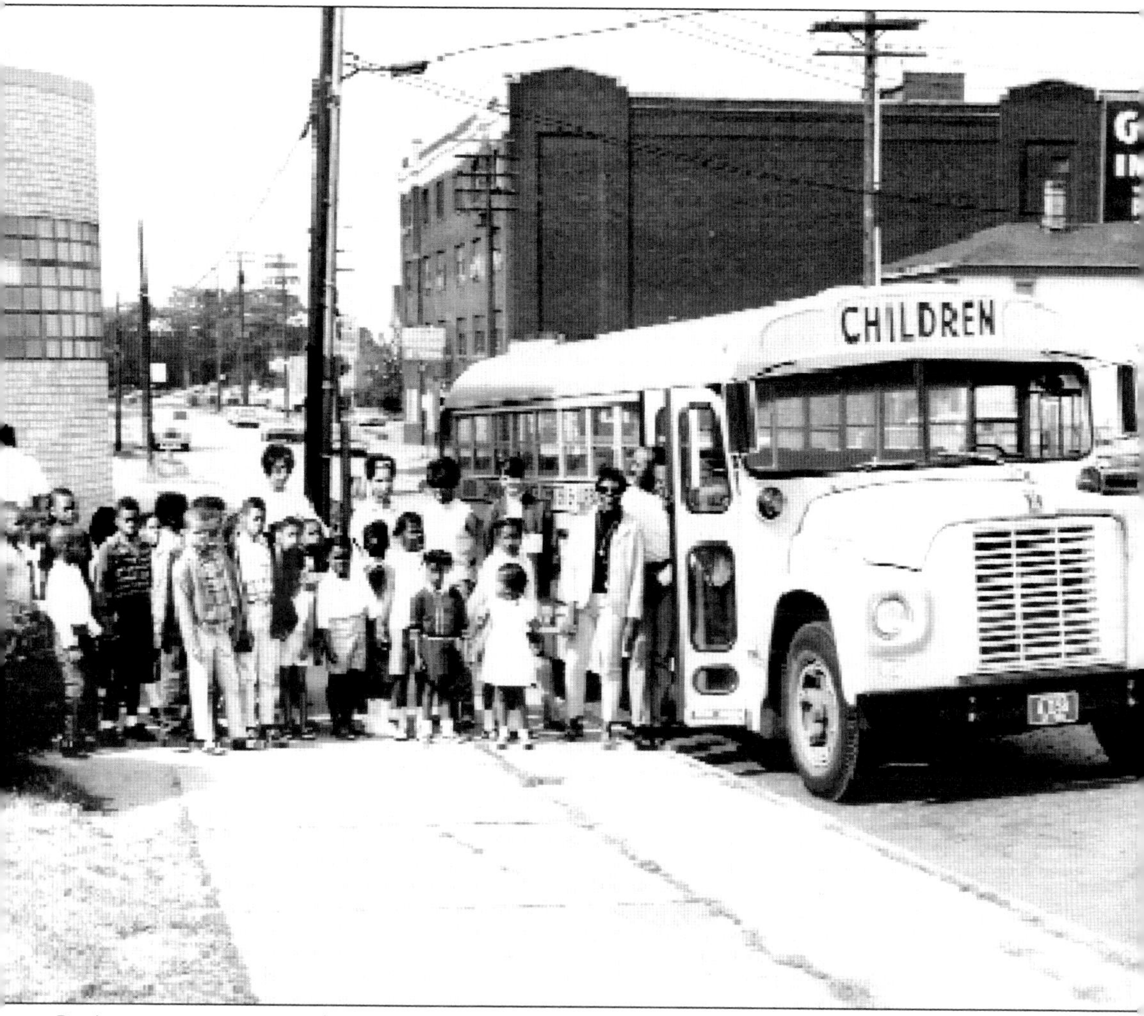

Busing was a controversial issue all over the United States, separating races and peoples. Busing was also controversial in the Akron area. However, it was an important factor in Akron's attempt to equalize education. Here students wait to board a bus at the Urban League *circa* 1970.

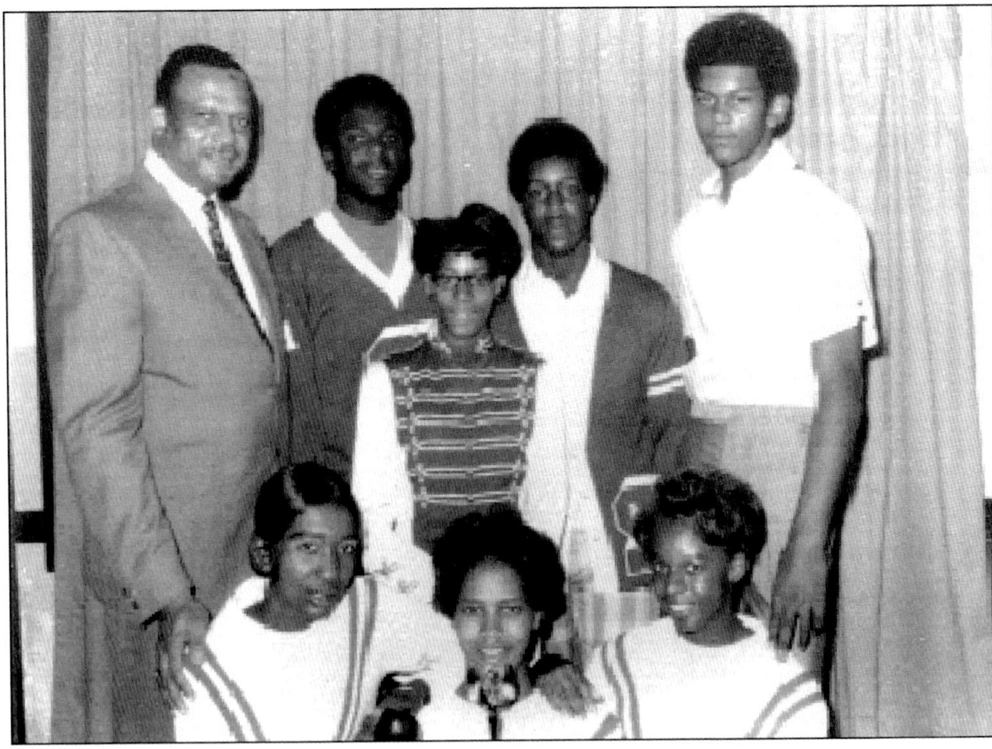

One of the first and most prominent school officials was school administrator Martin Chapman. He poses with some students who have won awards in school competitions.

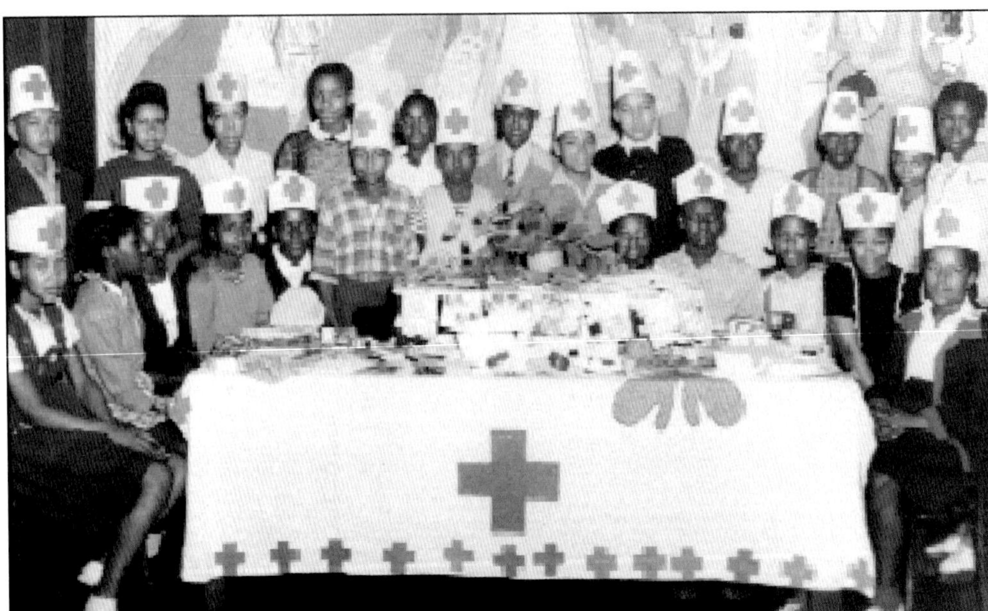

Students are taught the rudiments of life saving by the Red Cross. Here students participate in a Red Cross presentation.

One of the best-known poets in the country is Rita Dove. Dove is a native of Akron, Ohio, where she was a standout student. Here we see Dove as a young girl.

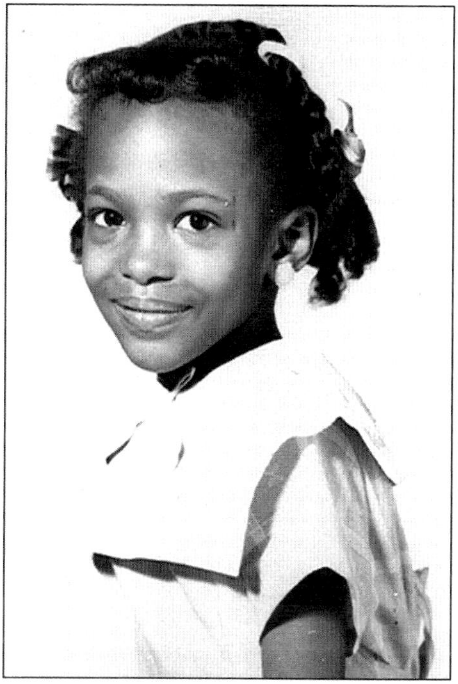

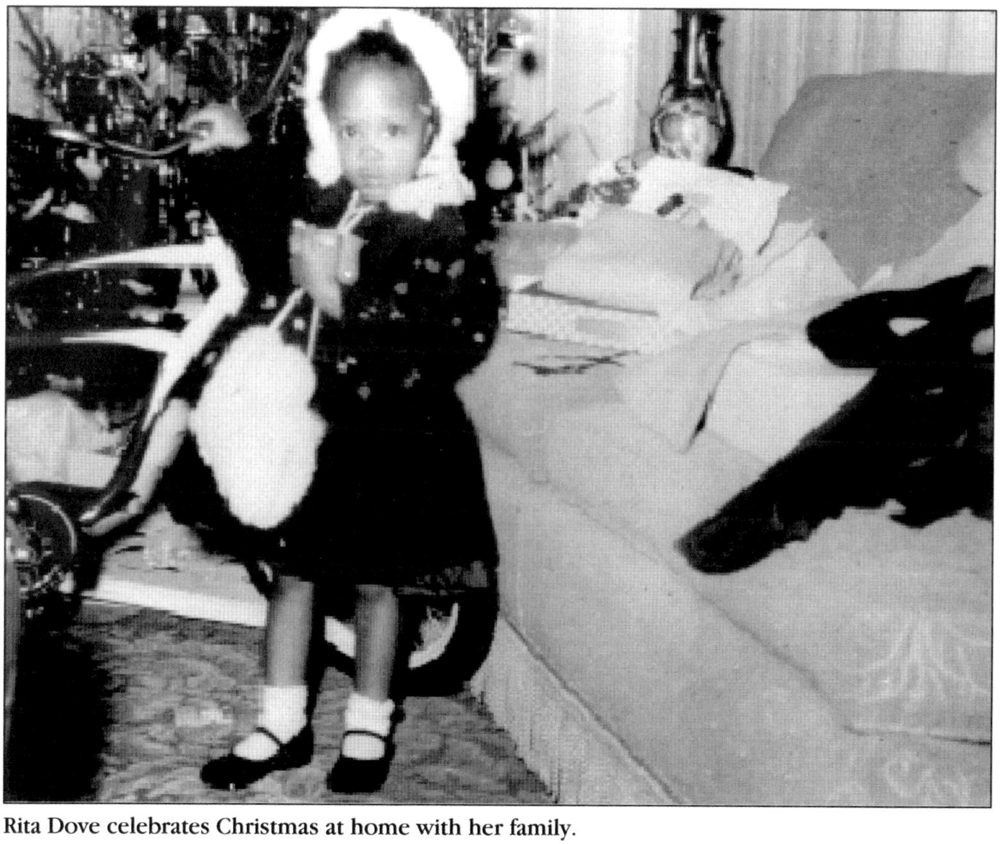

Rita Dove celebrates Christmas at home with her family.

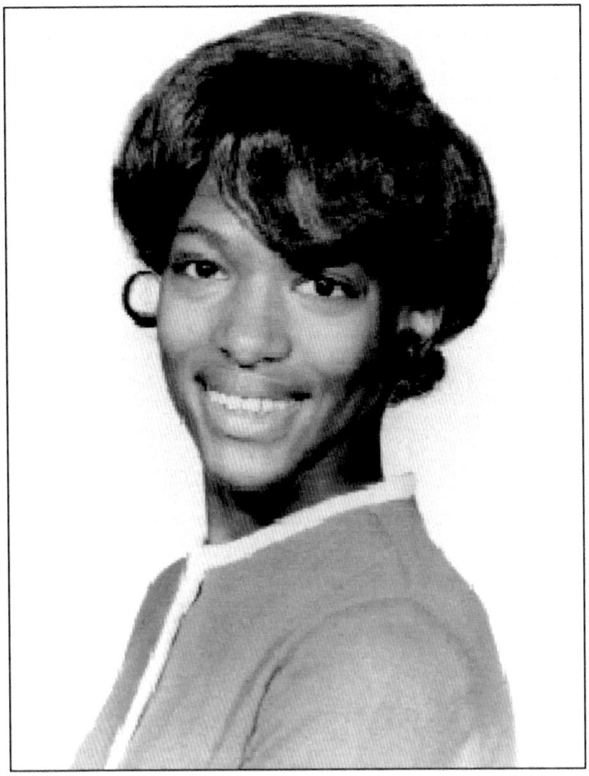

Here is a picture of Rita Dove as a student. Dove demonstrated her intellectual brilliance at an early age.

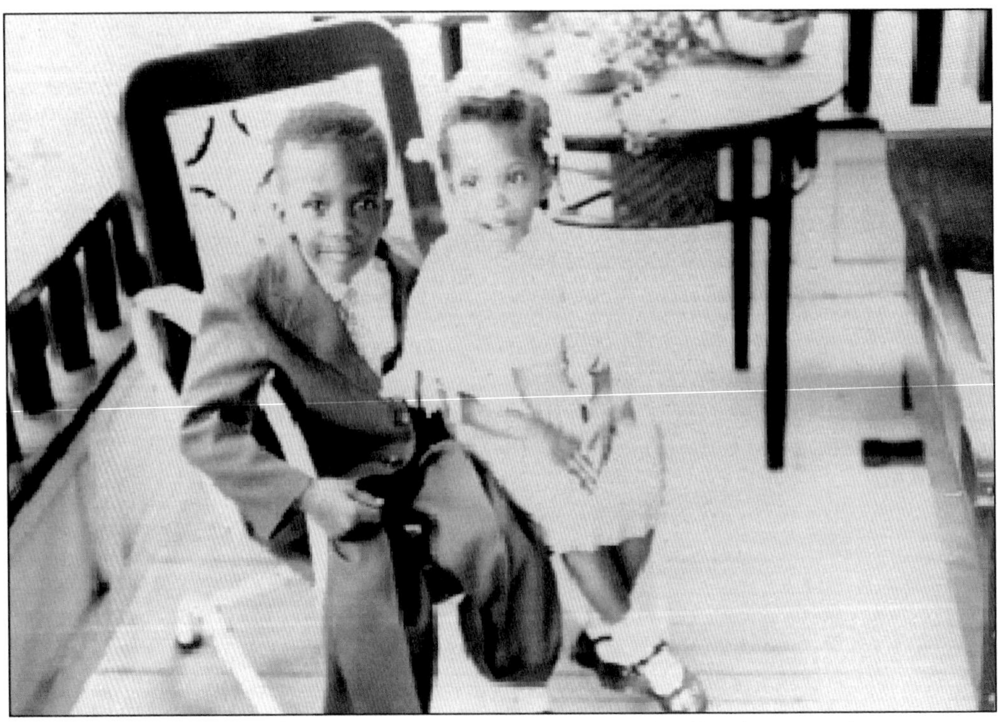

Rita Dove is shown here with an unidentified child on the porch of her home in Akron.

This is a baby picture of Rita Dove as she plays in the yard of her family's home.

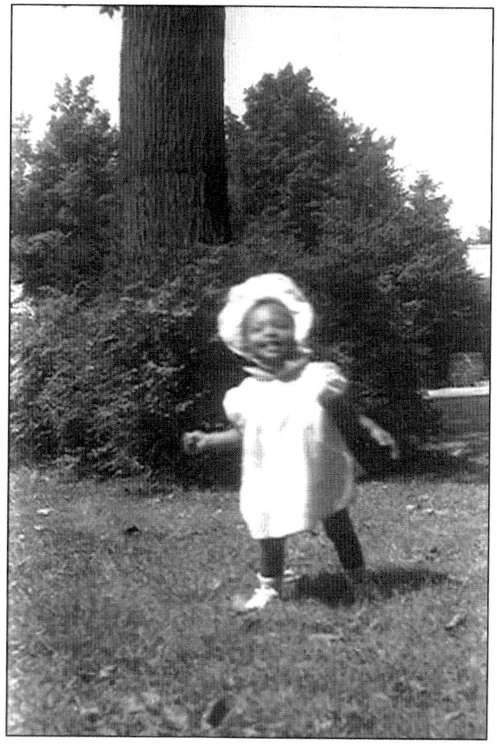

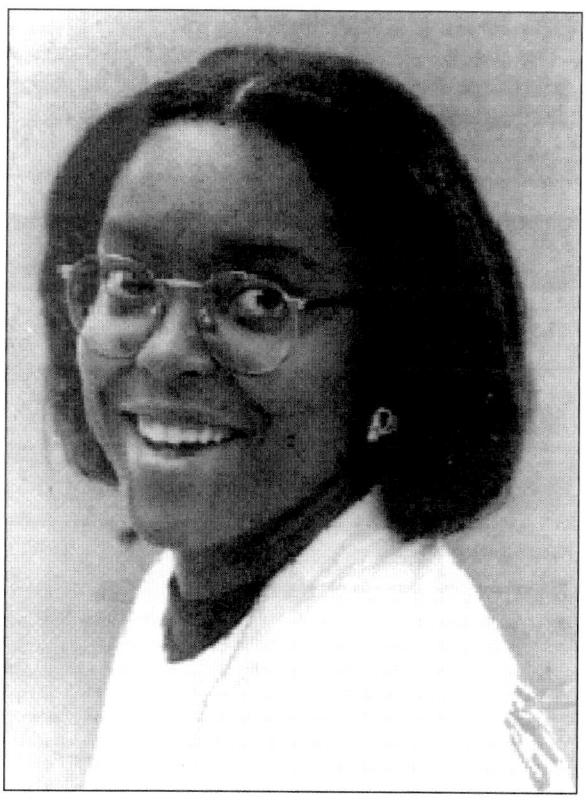

Rochell Parent was a standout athlete and student at Firestone High School.

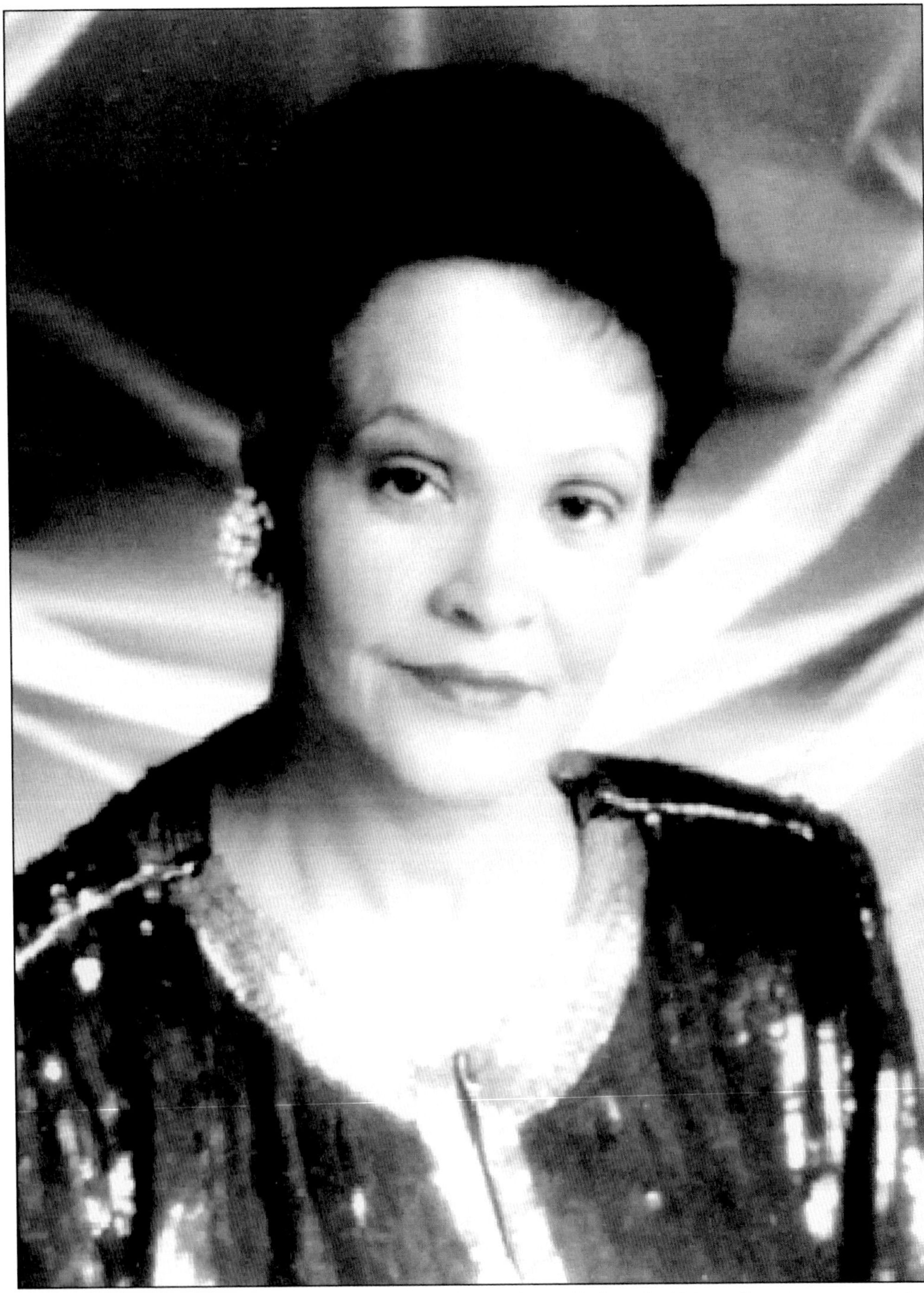

Dr. Shirla McClain is one of the best-known chroniclers of Akron's African-American past. After graduating from the University of Akron, she worked for the Akron Public Schools and did research on African Americans in Akron.

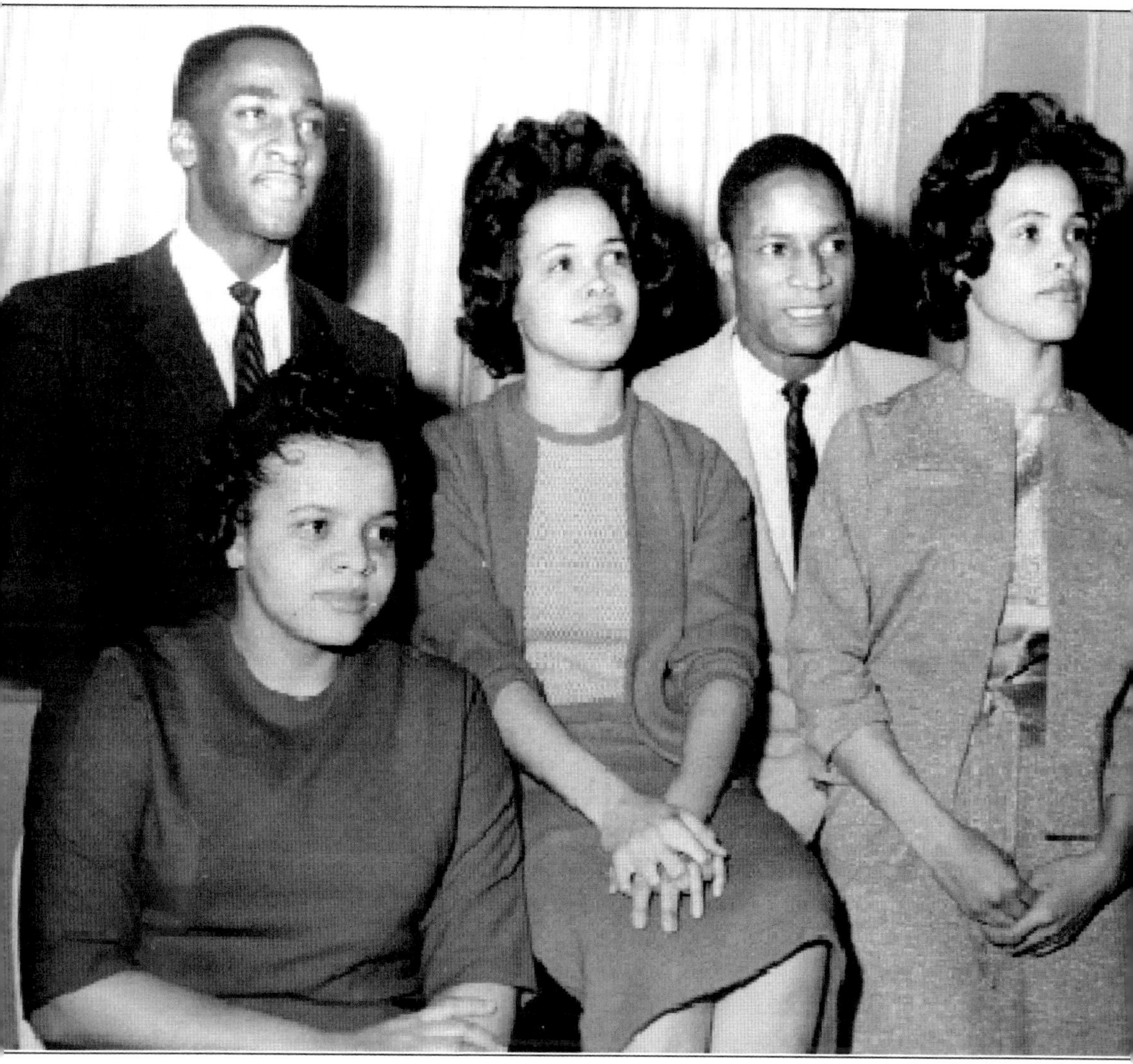

This group watches a performance. Included in the group are, from left to right, Allan Jackson, Bernice Fitzpatrick, Sheila McClain, Ambrose Brazelton, and Shirla McClain.

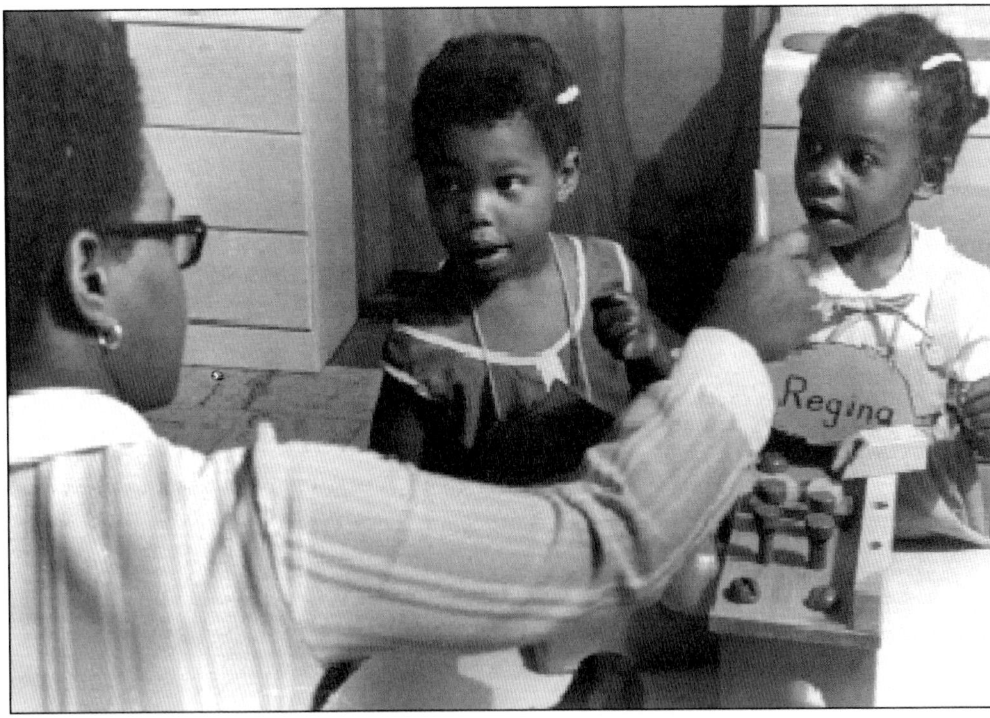

These two students listen intently as their teacher instructs them in a lesson.

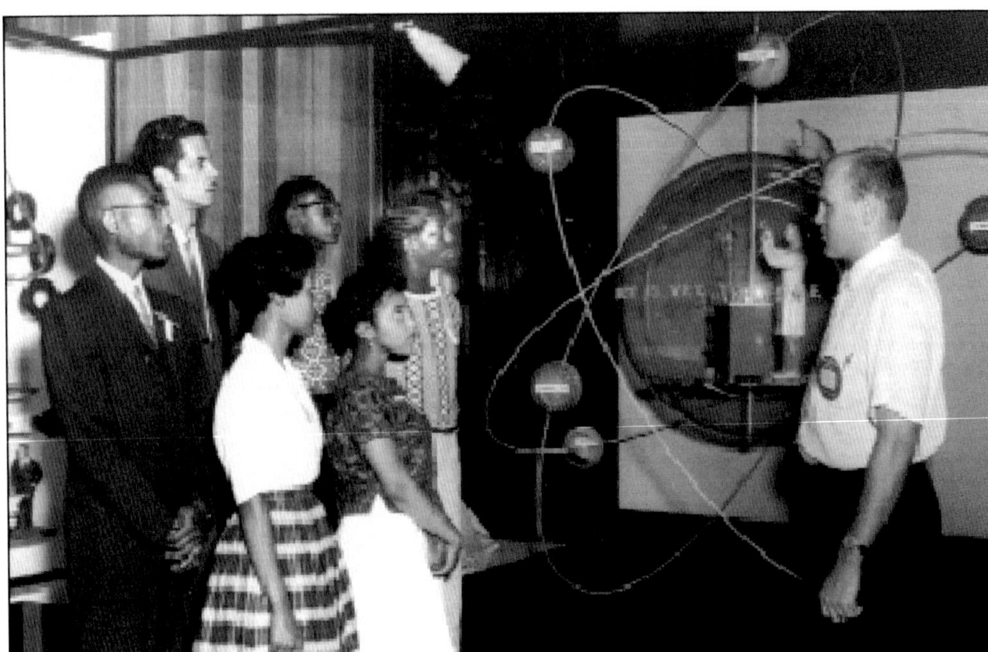

Akron was the rubber capital of the world. The many rubber companies had research labs that did groundbreaking studies of polymers. Students take a tour of the Rubber World museum and display.

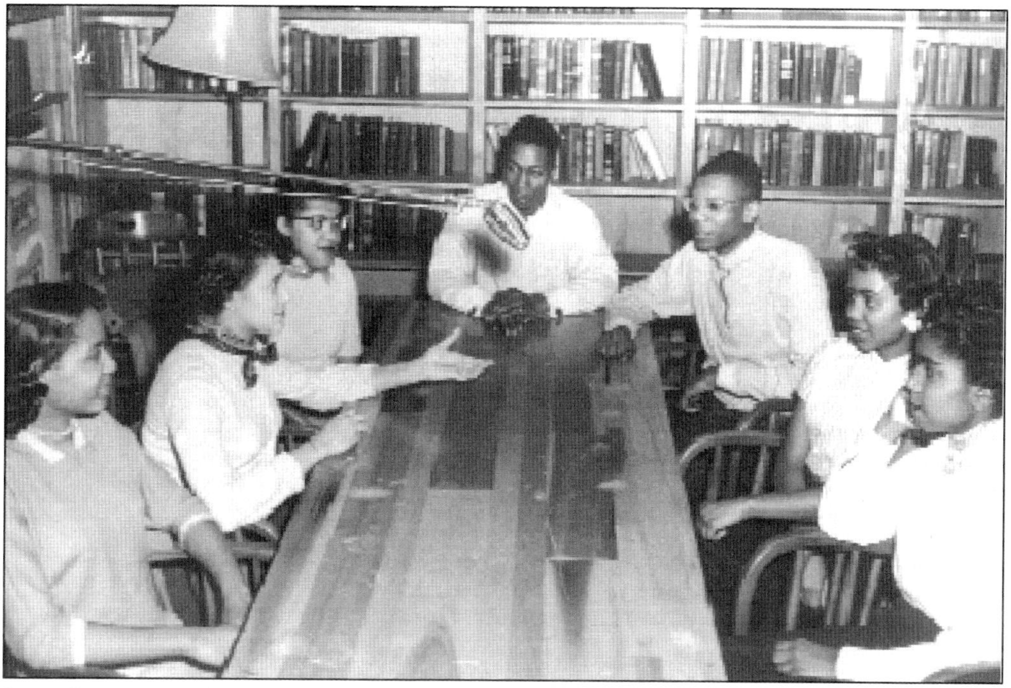

Several young people meet in the Urban League library. Shown in the picture are, second from left, Alberta Banton, center, Richard Thompson, next to him, Leonard Jetton, and on the far right, Jean Threatt.

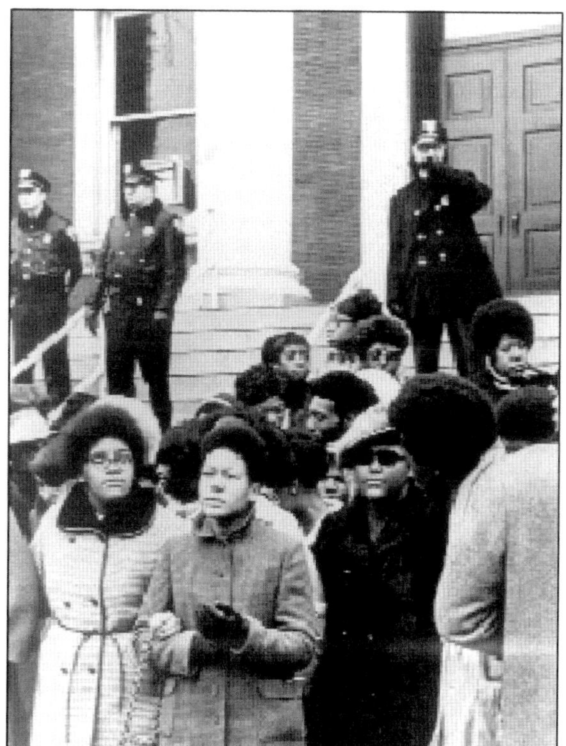

Students at the University of Akron were very active in pressing the university to open up new opportunities for minority students. Here student protest at Buchtel Hall, the schools' administration building.

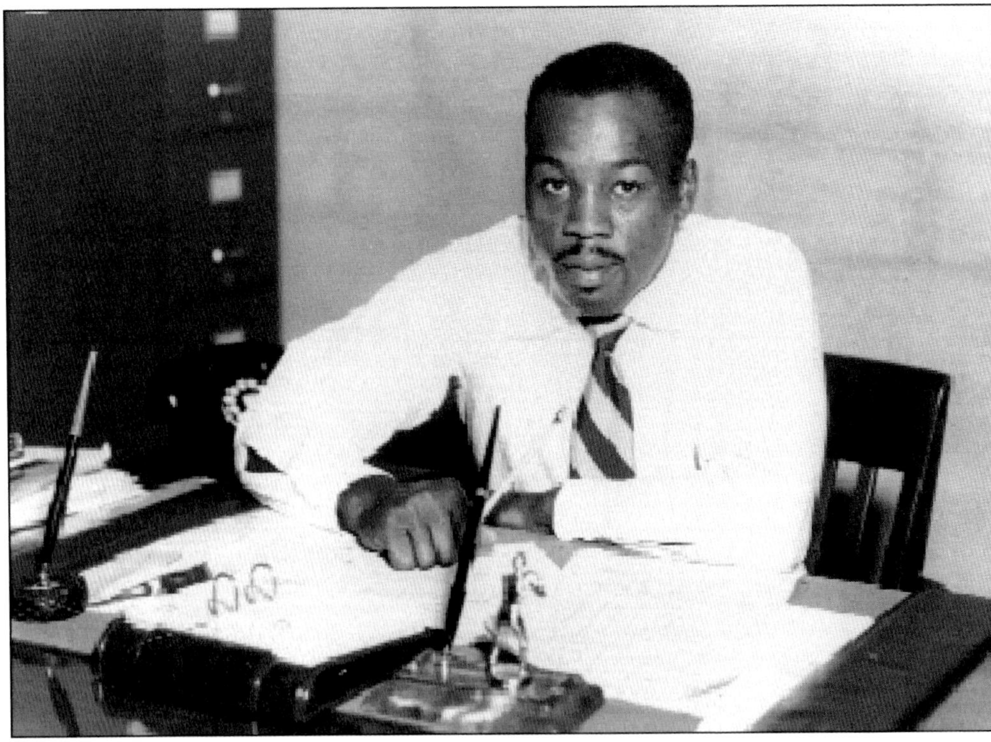

Gene Scruggs, a public school official, sits at his desk and works on a problem.

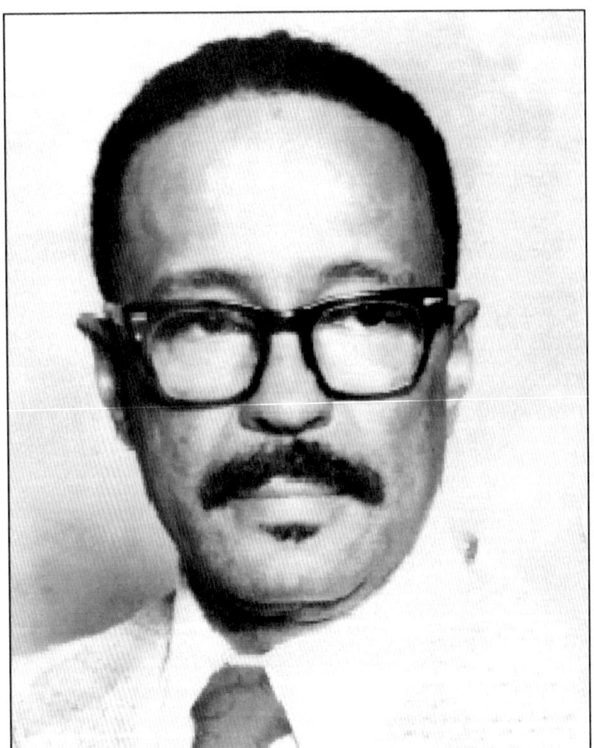

There were many African Americans who found employment in the Akron Public School system. This unidentified man was a teacher who worked for the system.

Three

WORK

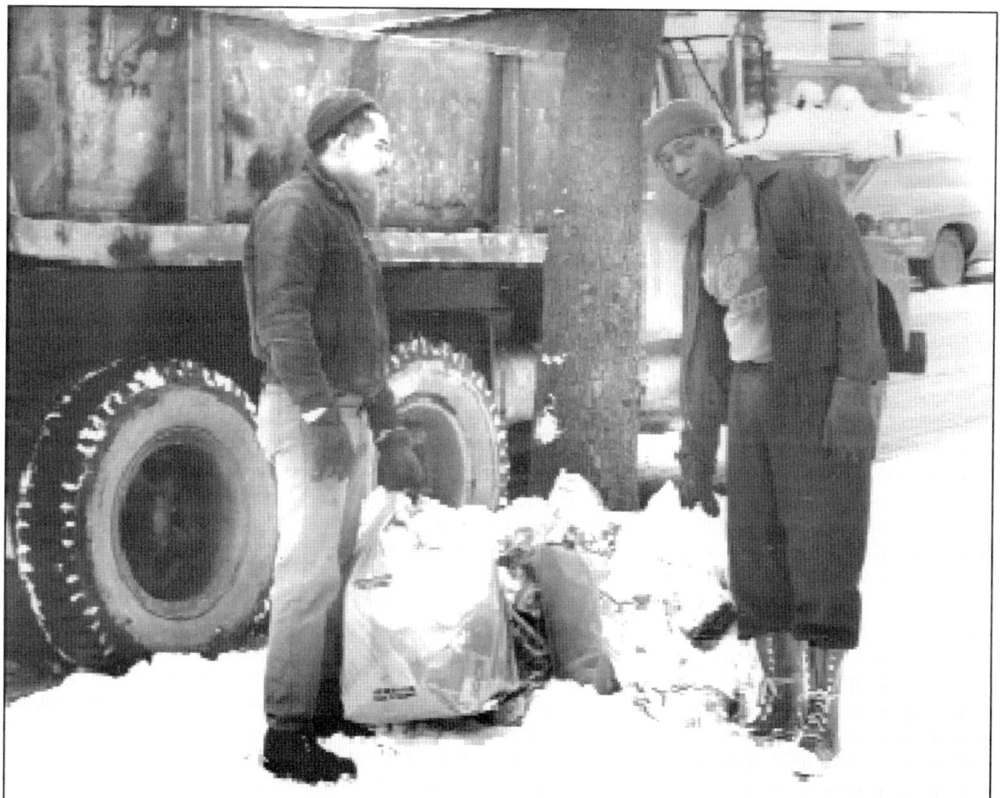

African Americans held a number of jobs in Akron. Some were well paying, well-respected jobs, and others were somewhat routine, every-day jobs needed to keep a society functioning. This picture shows two unidentified African-American sanitation workers in Akron.

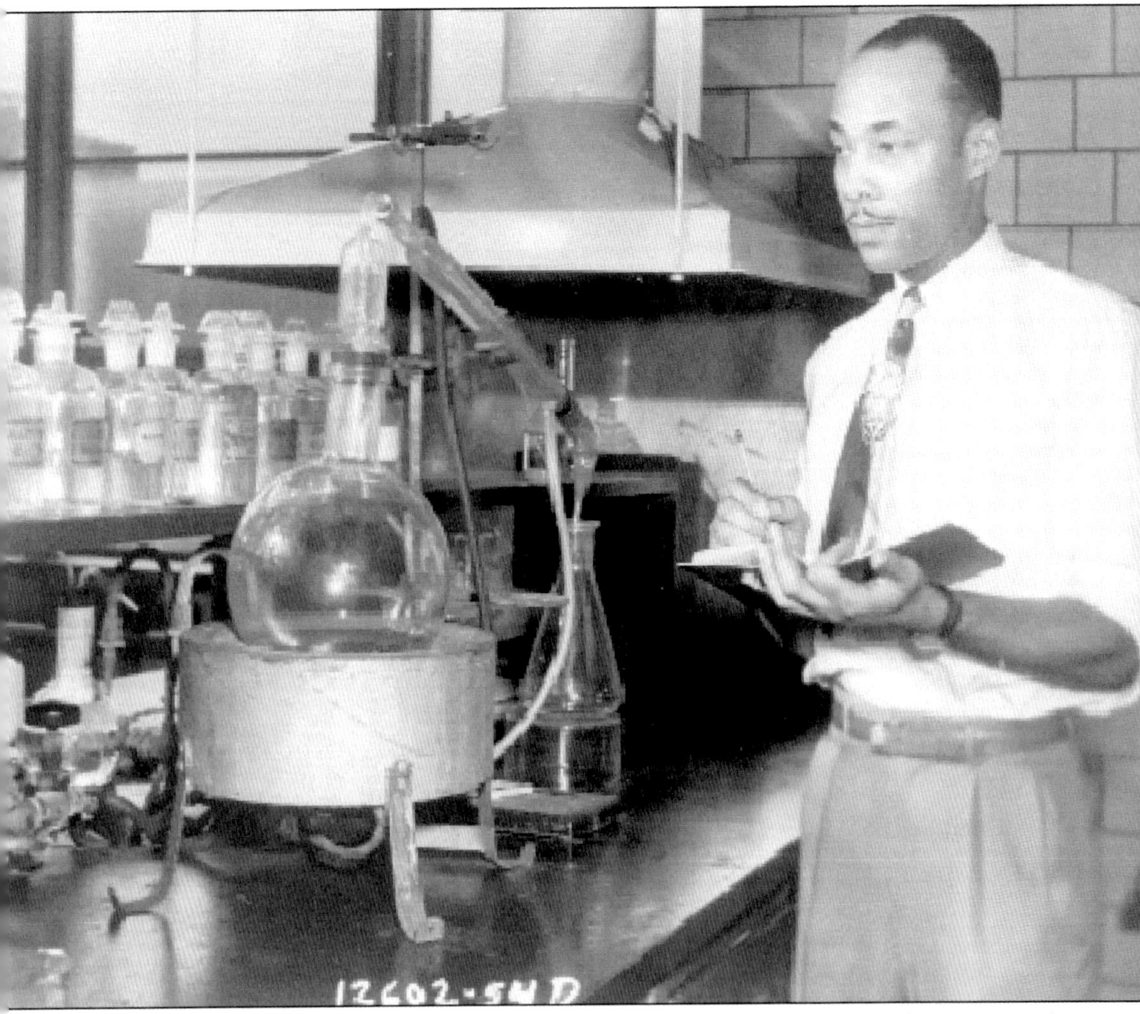

Talented African Americans were often hampered in their attempts to demonstrate their intellectual prowess. One of the few people who received an opportunity to demonstrate their intellectual ability was Ray Dove, who worked in a lab for Firestone. He was one of the limited number of African Americans who found employment in a rubber company lab.

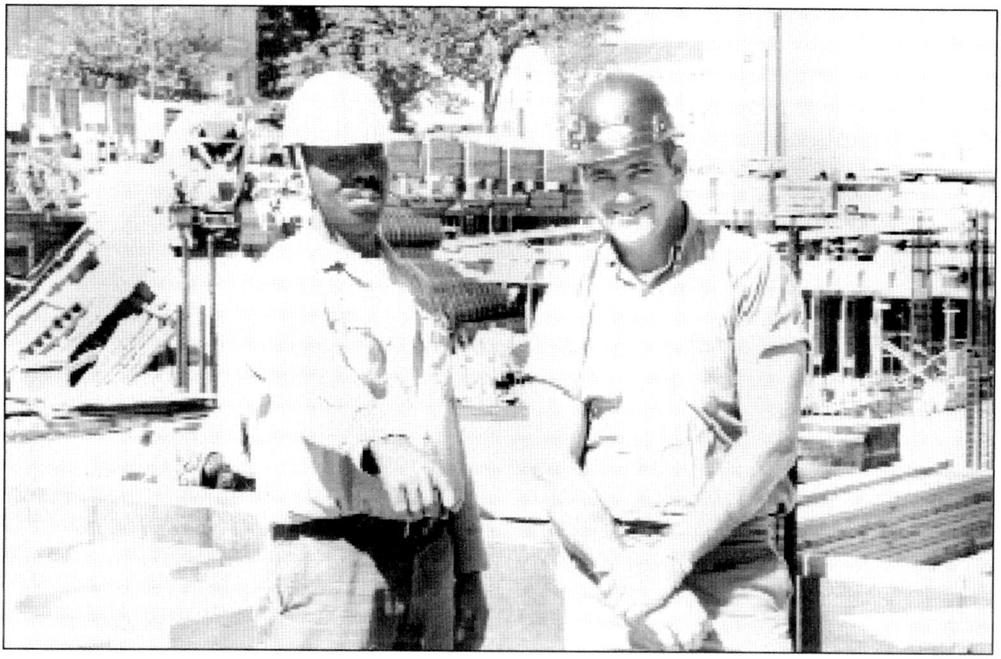

Andy Bullos (left) and Ted Miracle pose at a worksite.

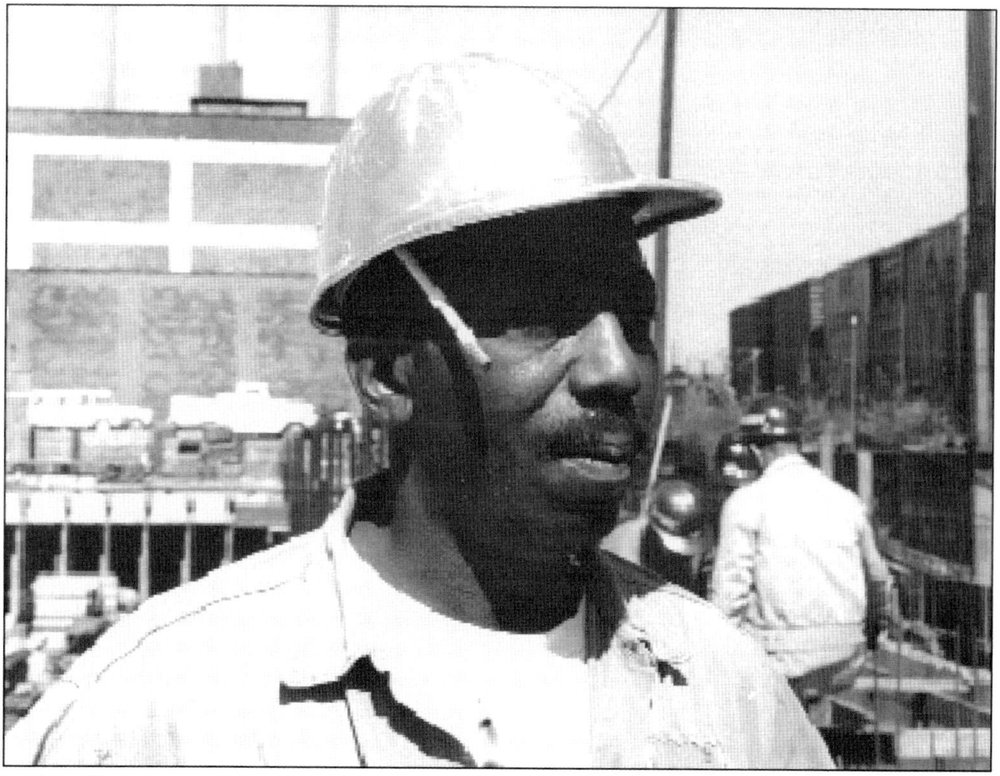

Andy Bullos was one of the few African Americans who rose to the level of foreman on a jobsite during the 1970s.

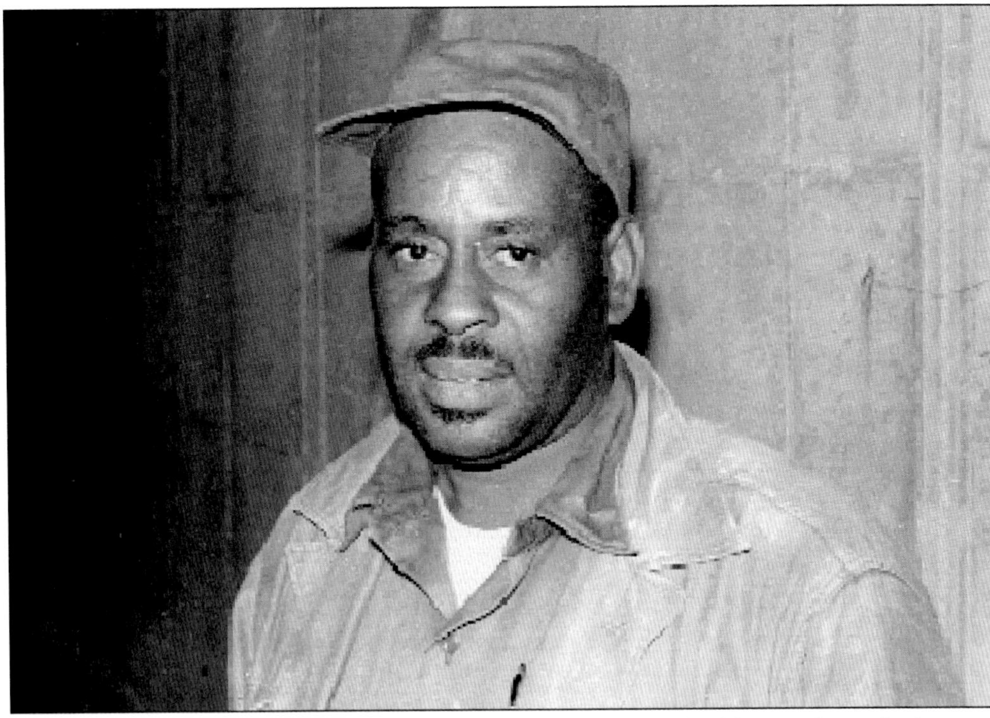

African Americans had a number of skills that were utilized in the building trades. Bob Cage was a plumber who worked on several construction sites.

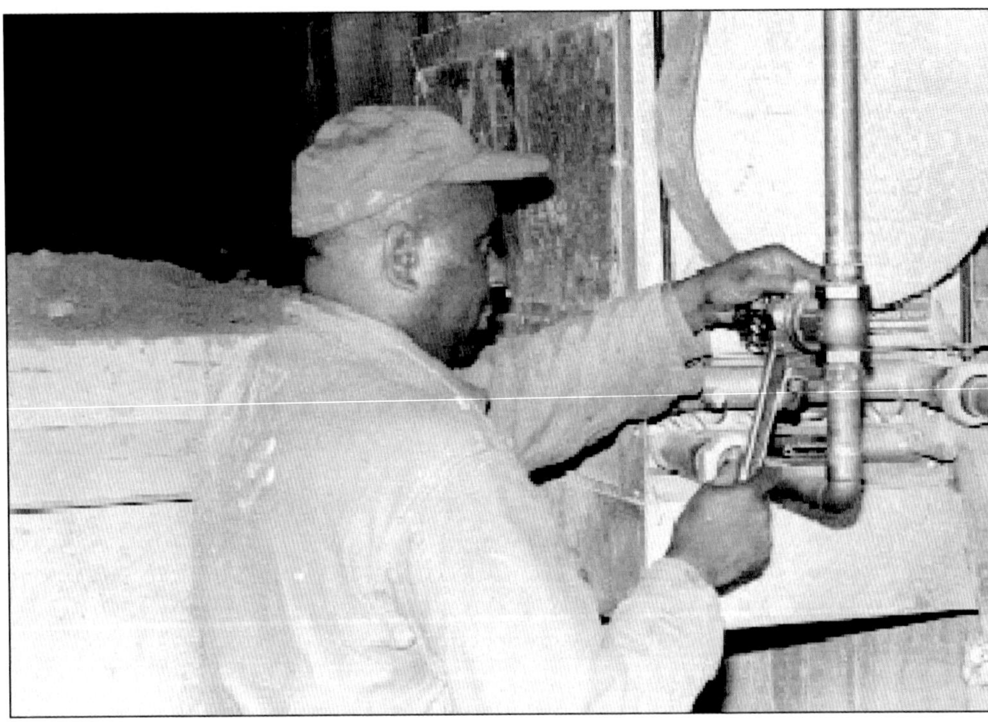

Here Cage works on a boiler in a building in Akron.

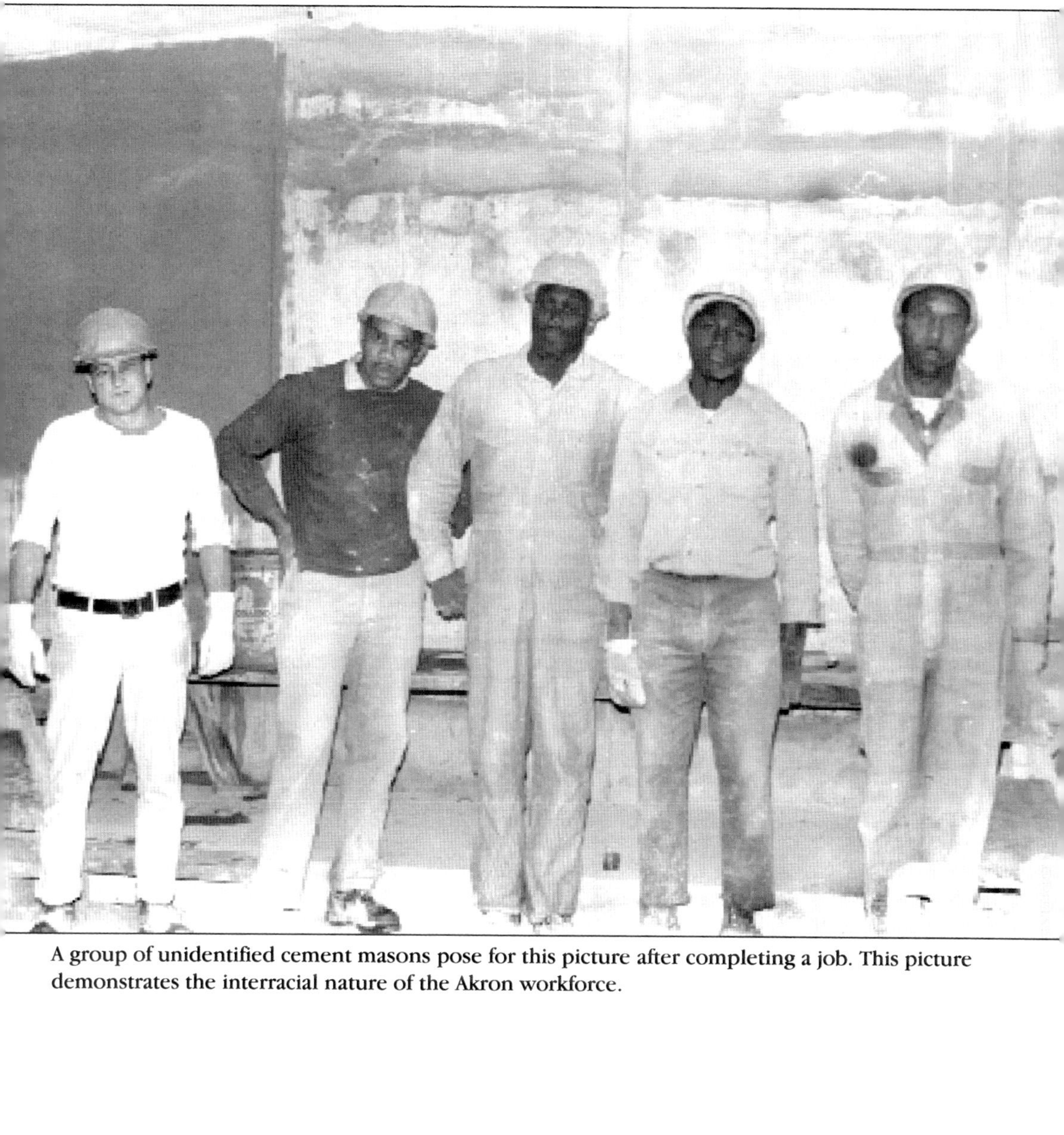

A group of unidentified cement masons pose for this picture after completing a job. This picture demonstrates the interracial nature of the Akron workforce.

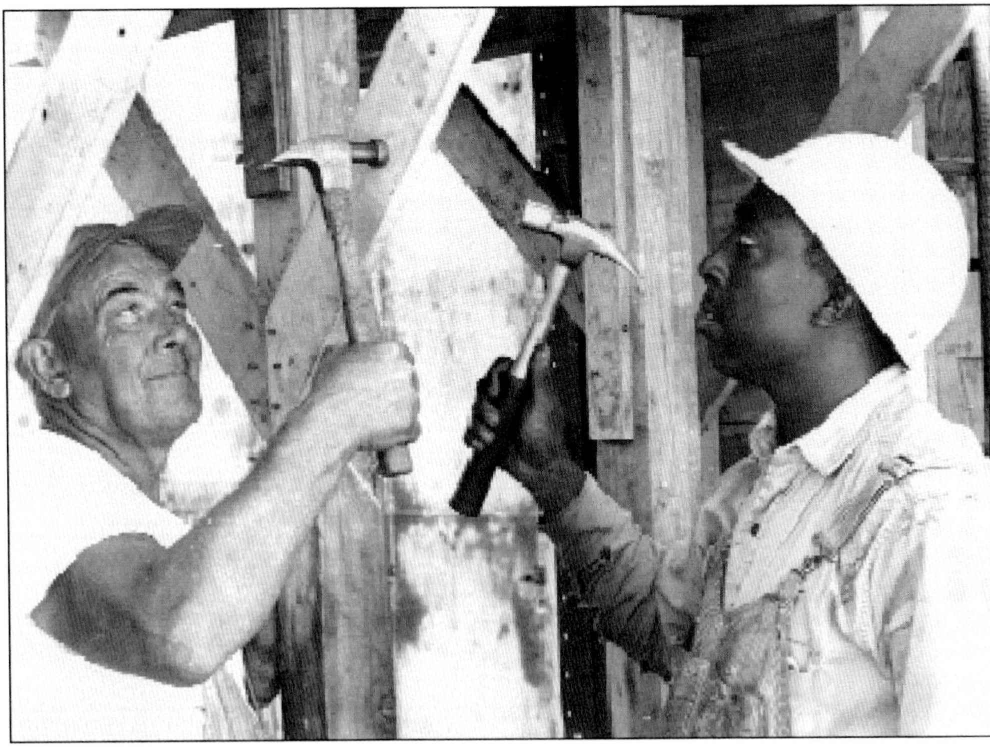

Clarence Hill, on right, and Mr. Price work cooperatively, hammering a board at a work site.

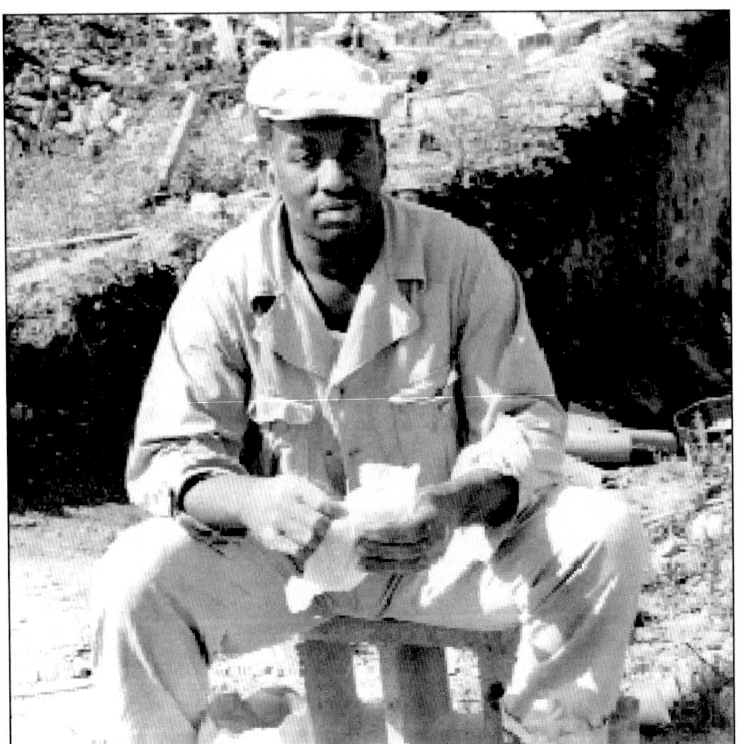

An unidentified worker takes a lunch break at a worksite.

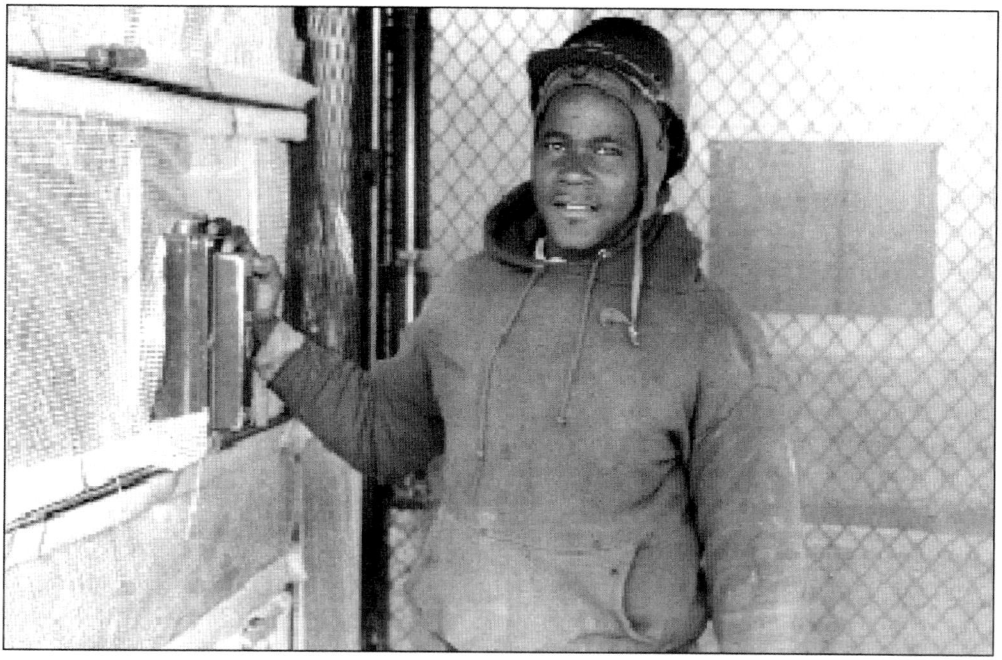

Ernest Grapson takes an elevator up to the floor where he will be working.

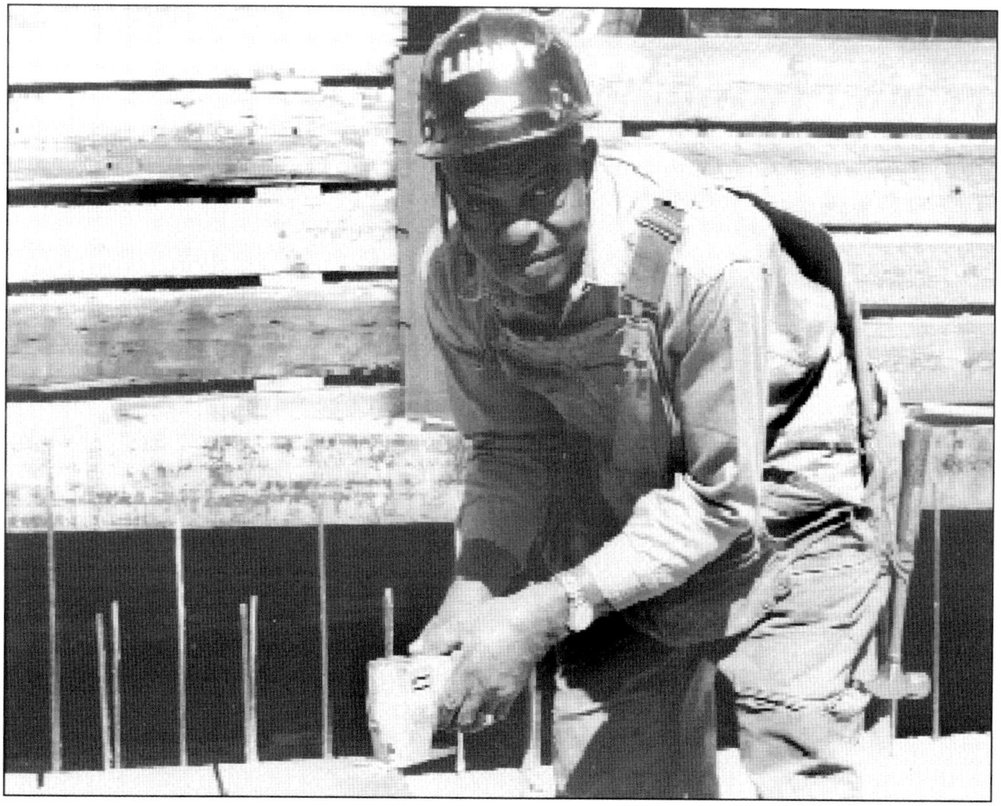

Fred Henry, a carpenter, uses an electric saw to cut a board.

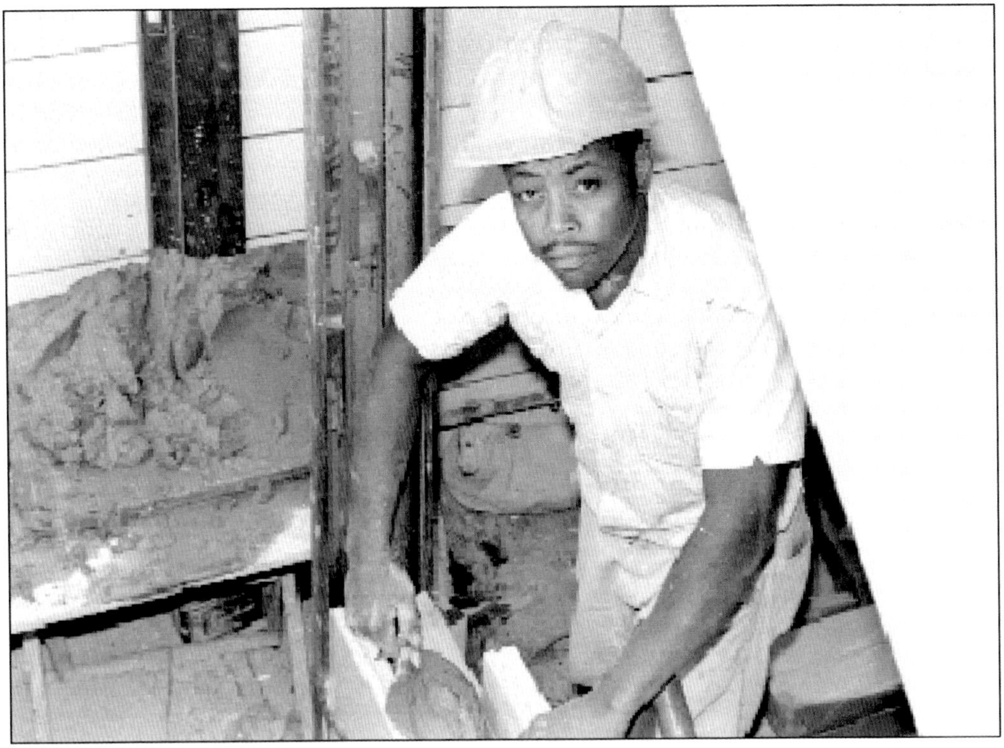

Garner Robinson worked as a brick mason on several important building projects in the Akron area.

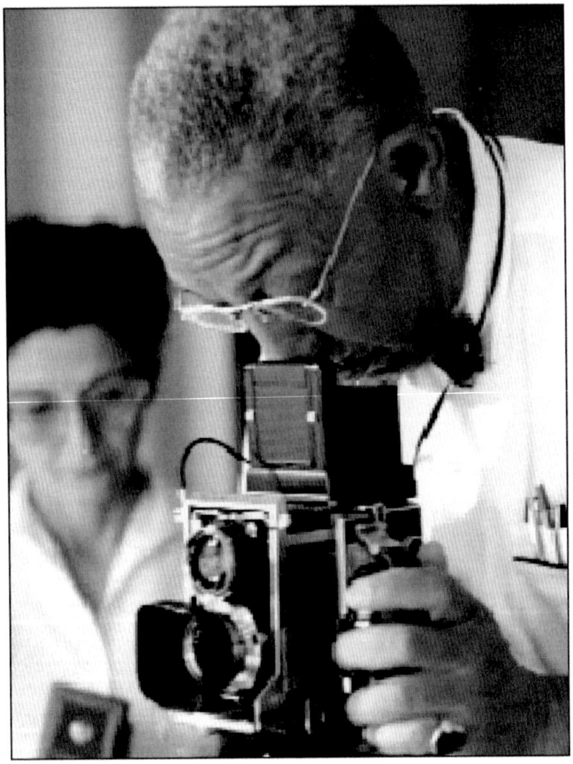

Horace Stewart was one of the best-known African-American photographers in the Akron area.

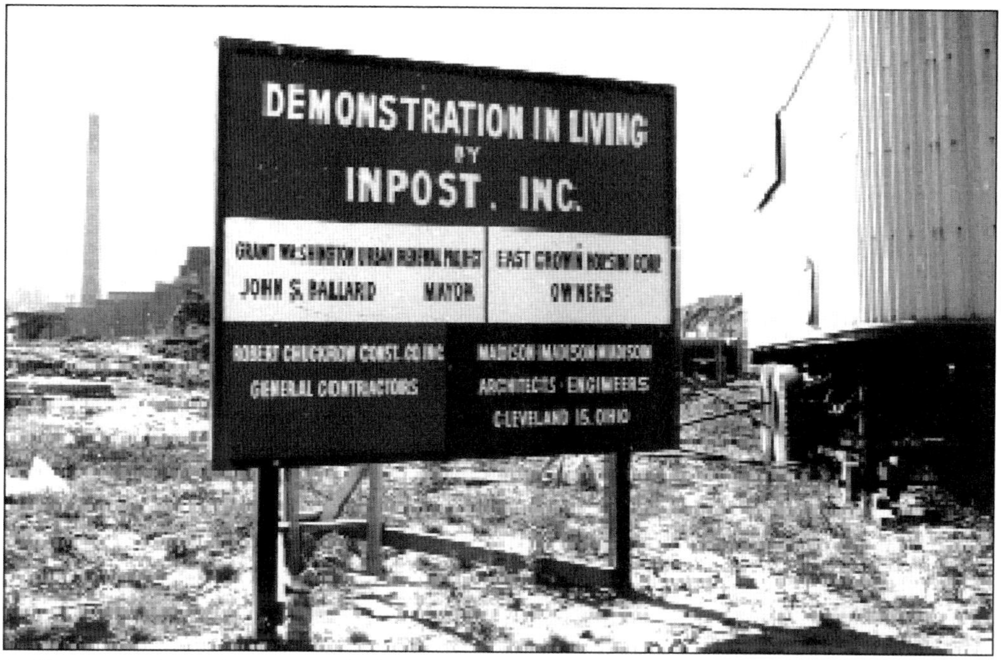

As Akron experienced economic decline, many African Americans found employment working in the urban renewal projects prevalent in the city.

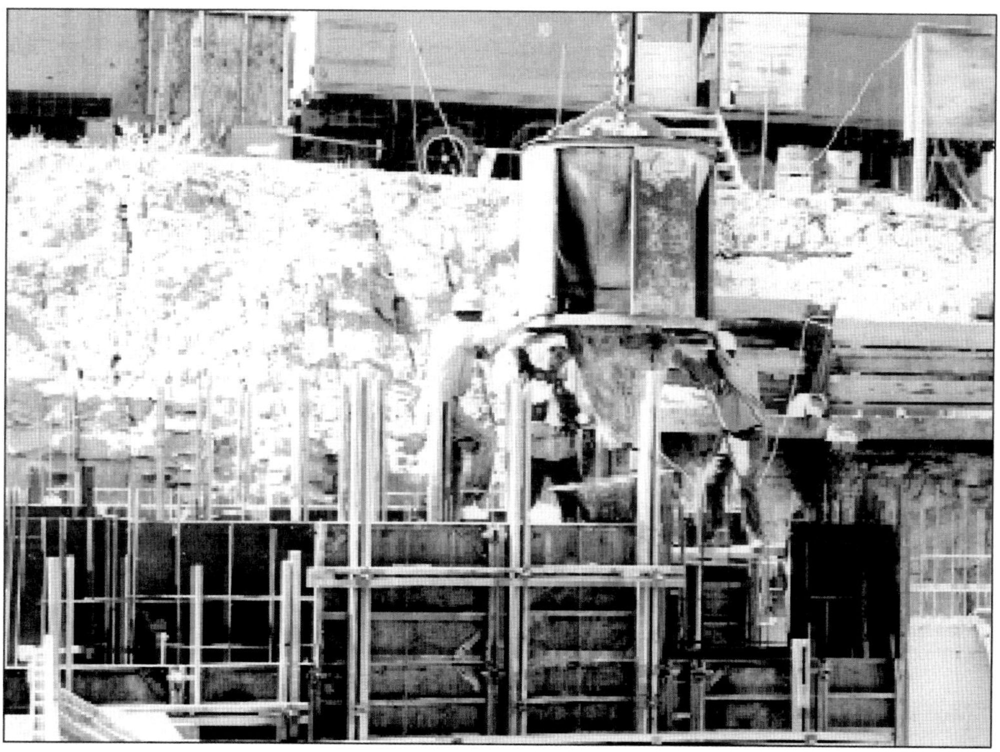

Construction on the University of Akron campus was one form of employment that was available. Here workers construct the Health Building on the university campus.

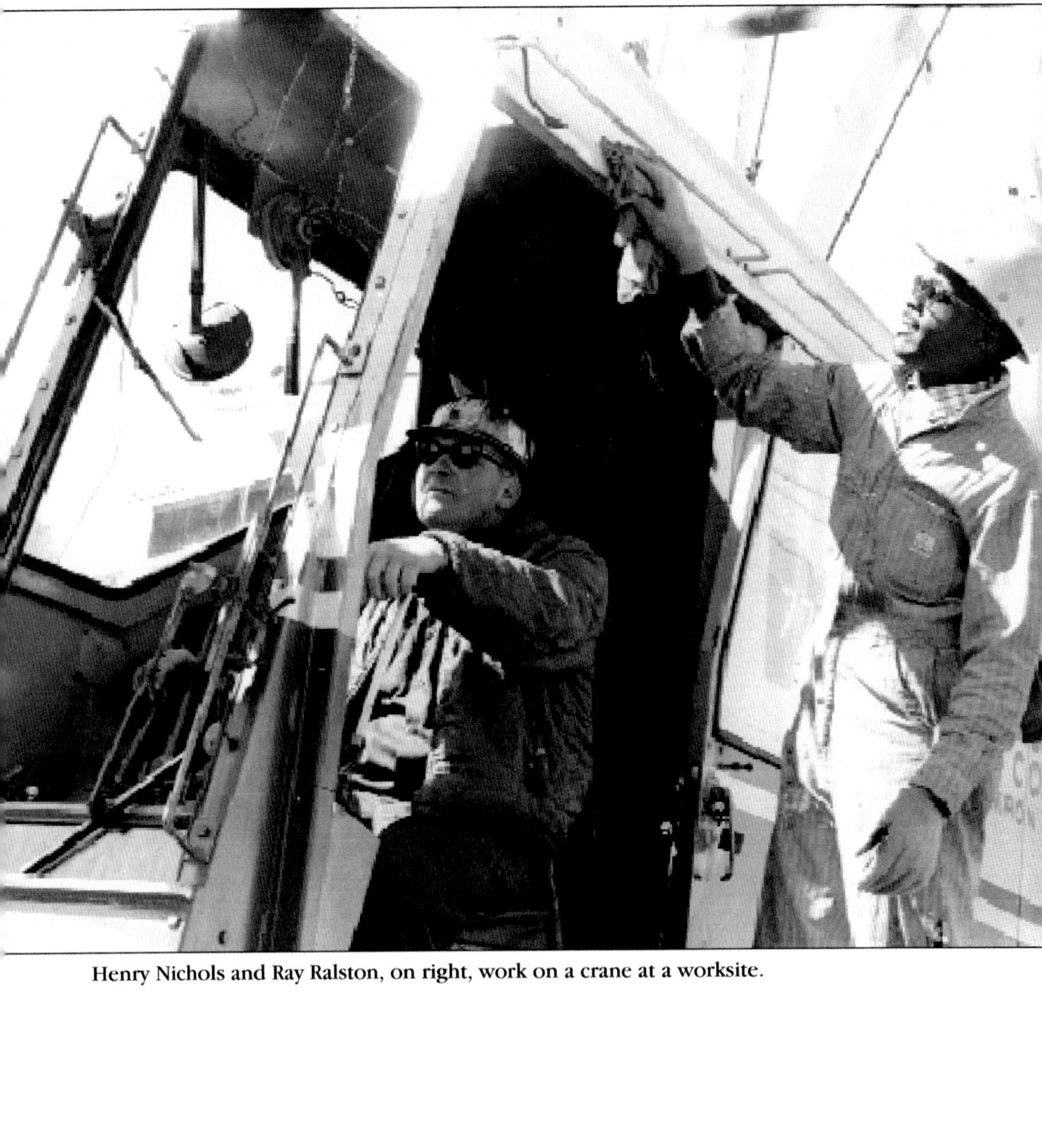

Henry Nichols and Ray Ralston, on right, work on a crane at a worksite.

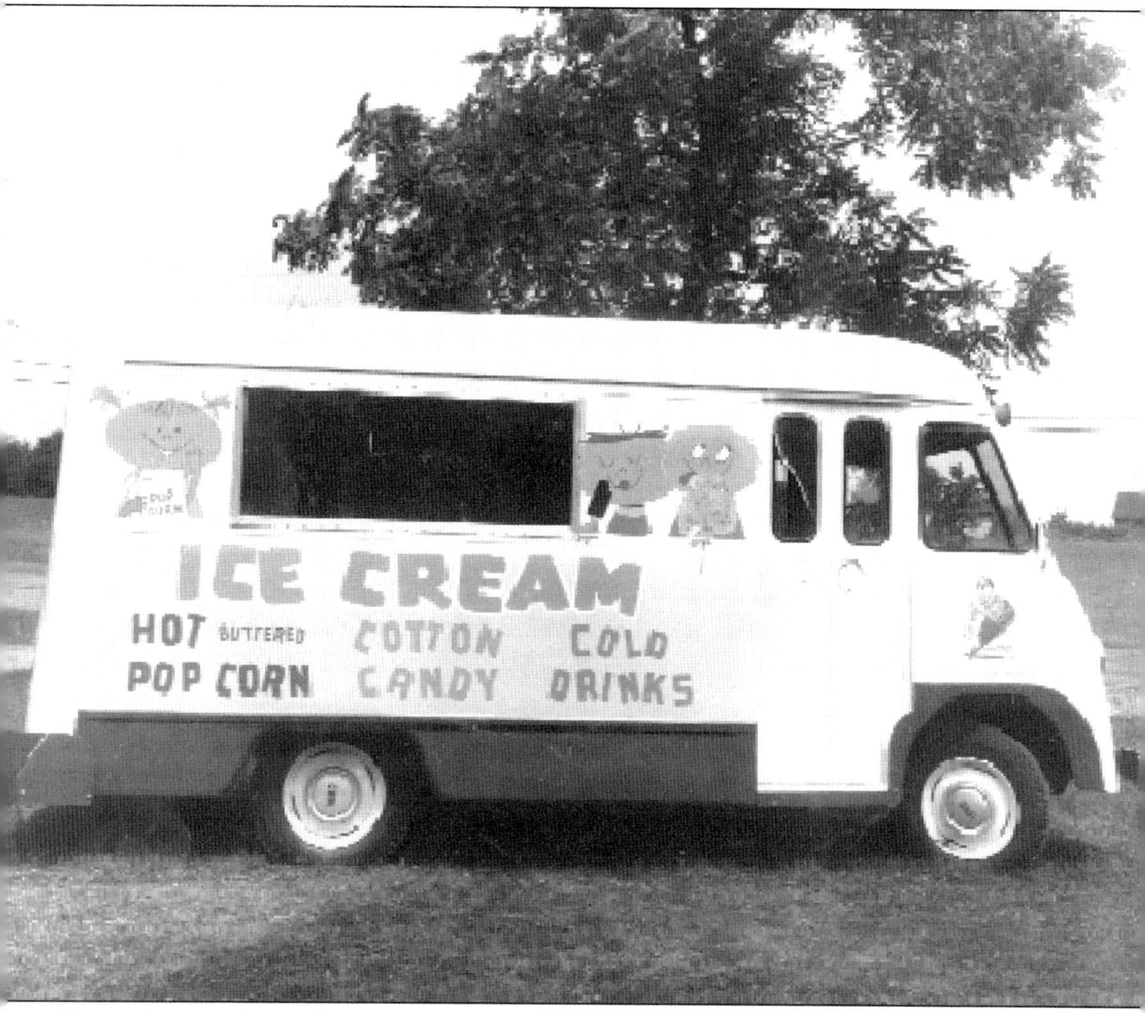

Akron photographer and activist Opie Evans owned a number of establishments. Here is a picture of one of his enterprises. This is an ice cream truck, which frequented the African-American neighborhoods.

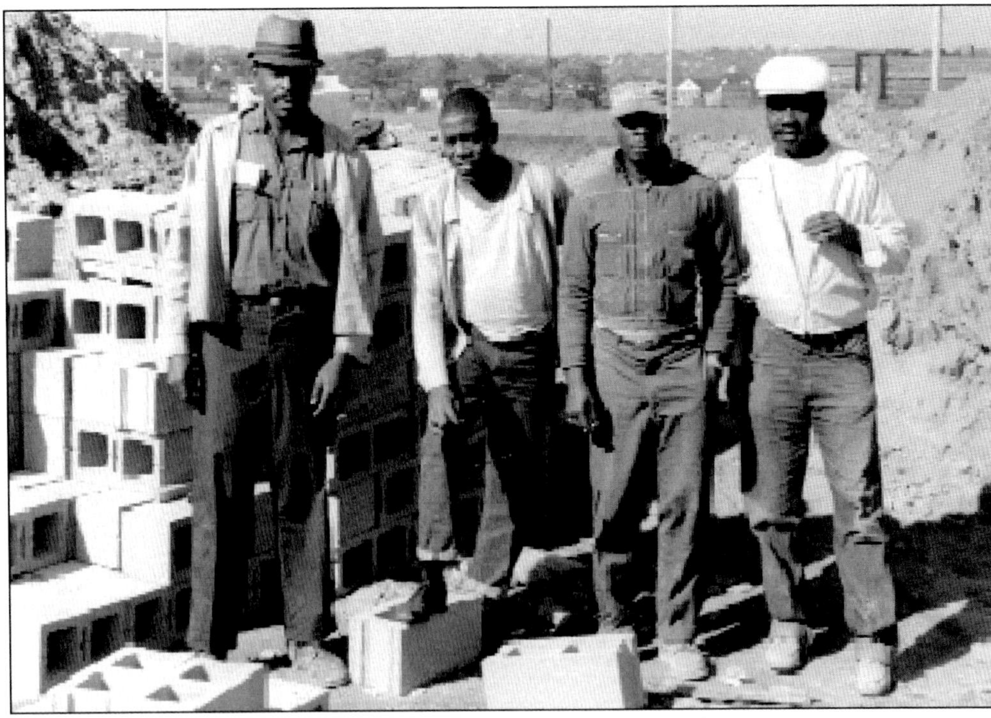

Several unidentified African-American laborers pose after work on the In Post Project.

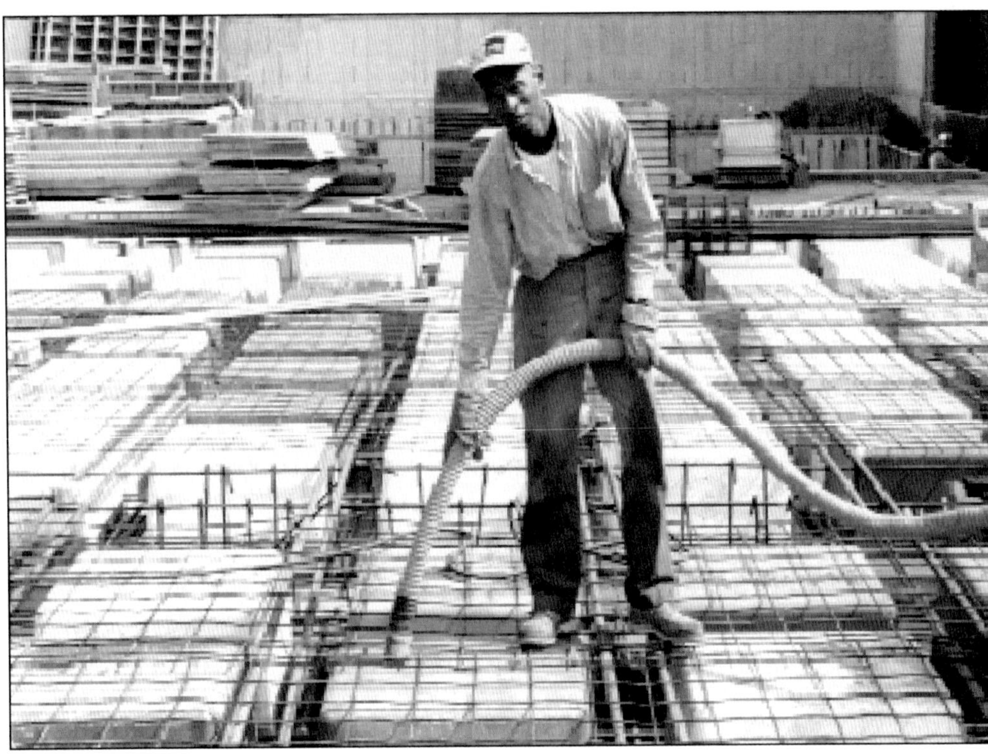

James Carter pours cement during work on a construction project.

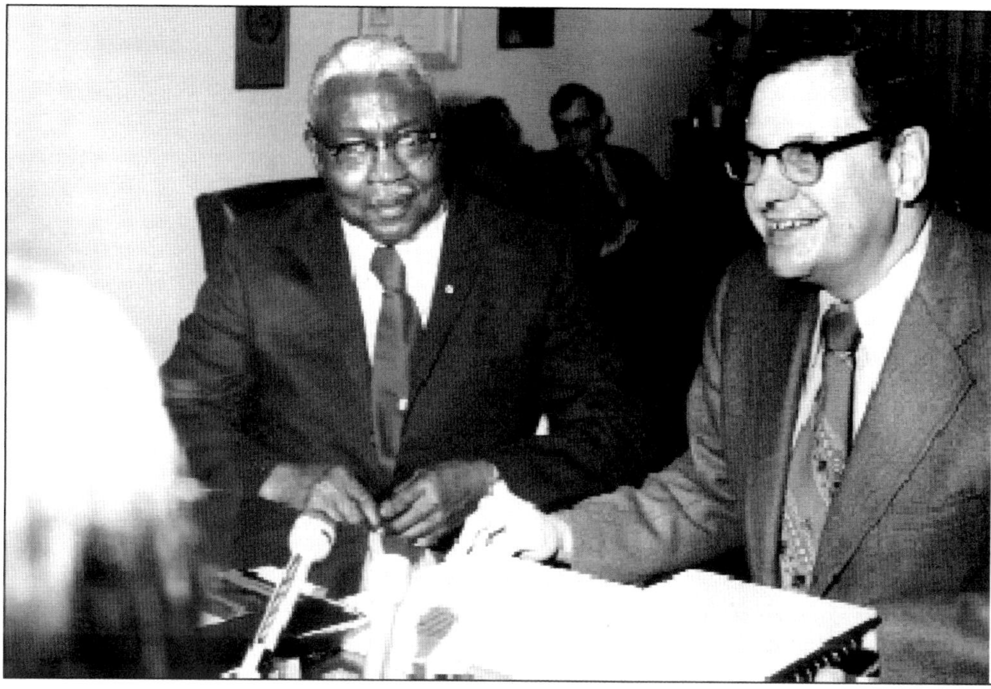

Mayor John Ballard laughs during a light moment with African-American entrepreneur and photographer Opie Evans.

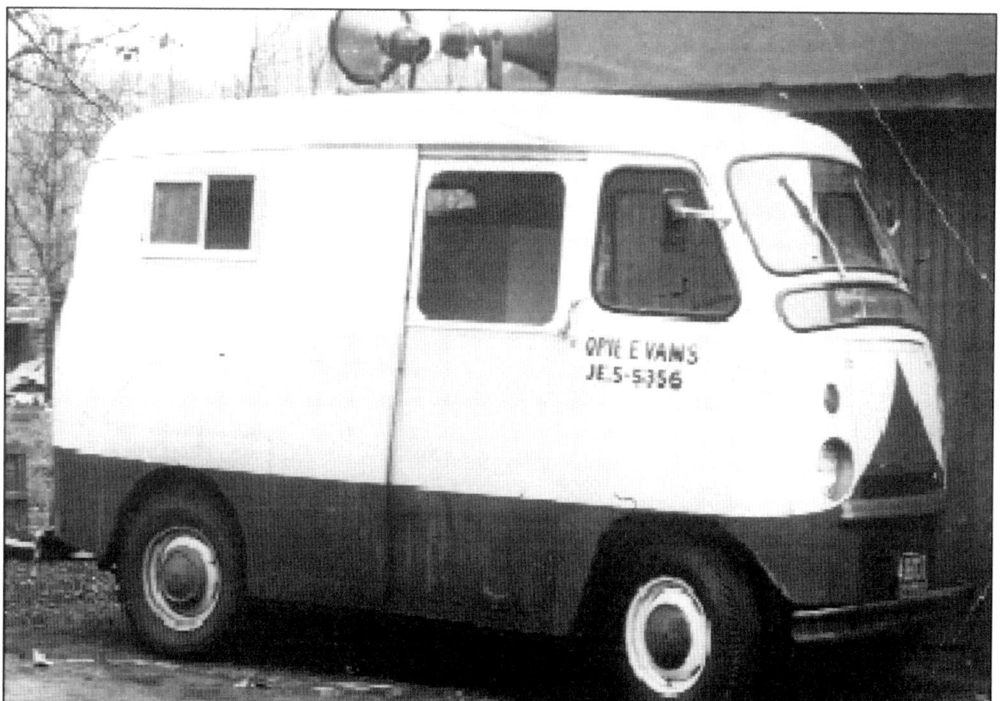

African-American photographer Opie Evans operated this van, which he used to travel to places where pictures were to be taken.

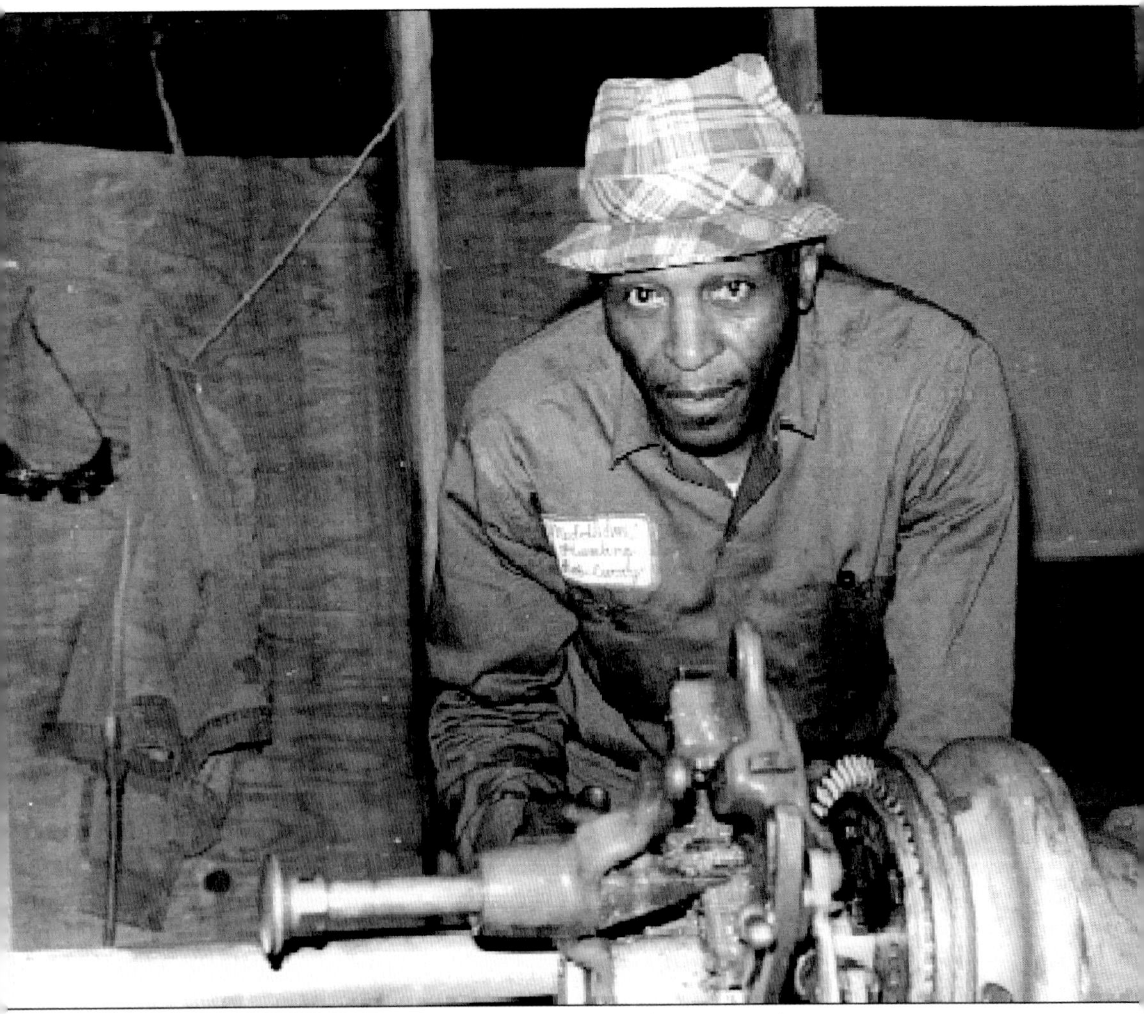

Robert Curry, a plumber, works on a project at a building site in Akron.

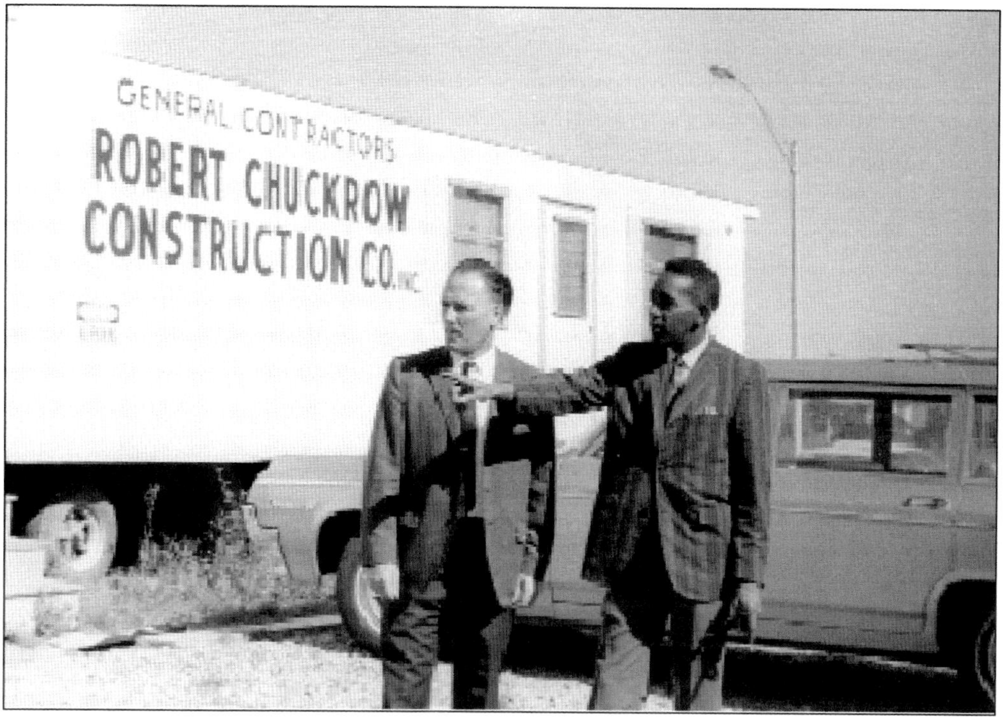

Sam Chambers (on right) and Don Worchester discuss work at a work site in Akron.

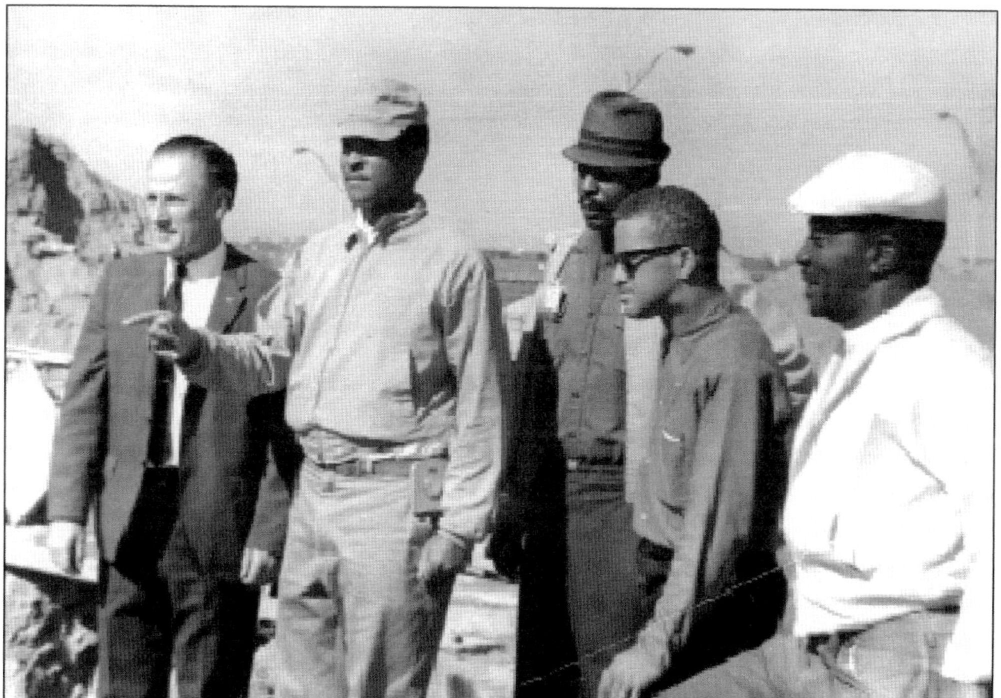

Don Worchester gets some information about the job Wilson, Logan, Jefer, and Logan are doing. (Their first names are unknown.)

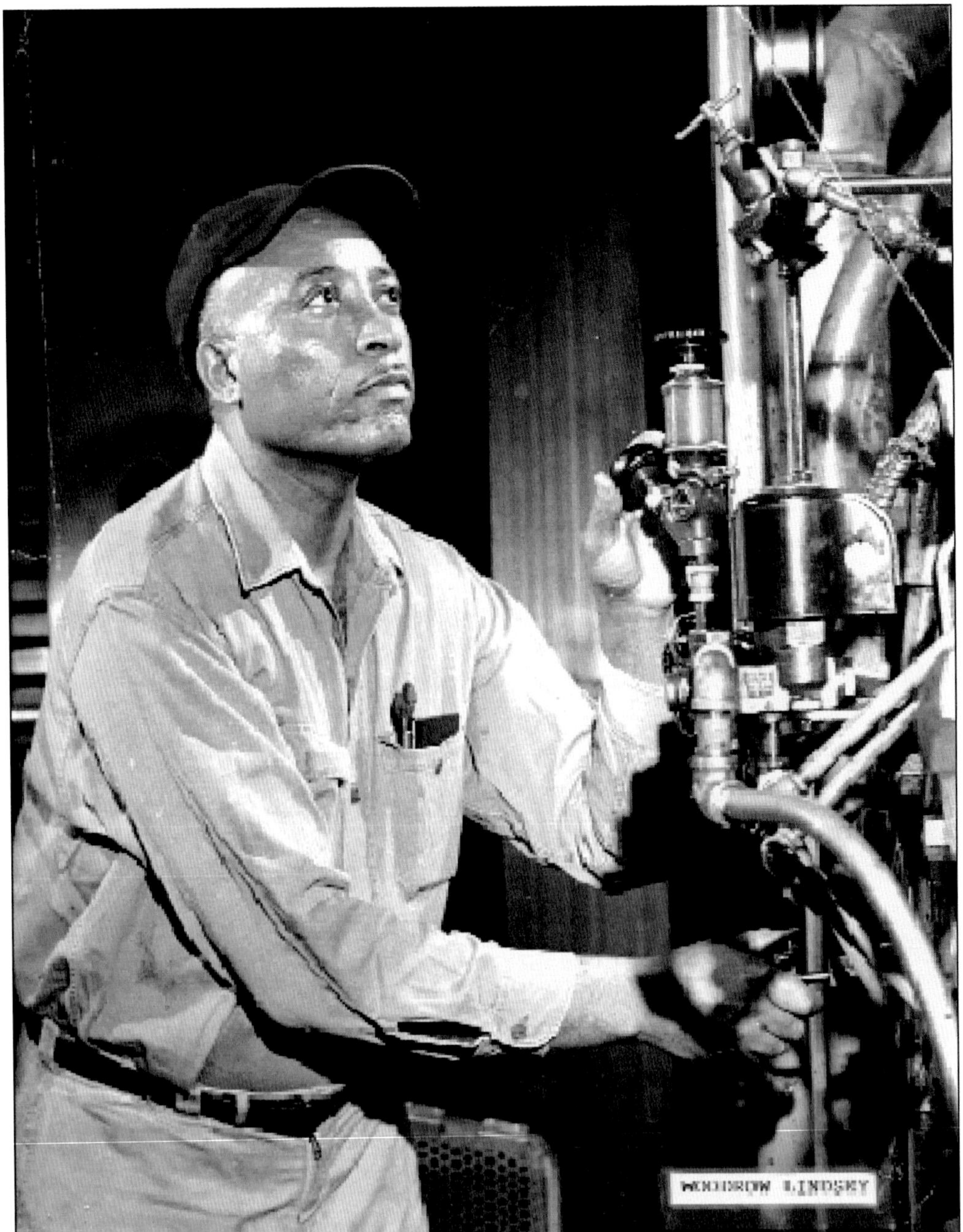

There were several African Americans who found employment in the rubber industry. They played a vital role in ensuring that Akron maintained its status as the rubber capital of the world. Woodrow Lindsey operates a machine while working in the rubber industry.

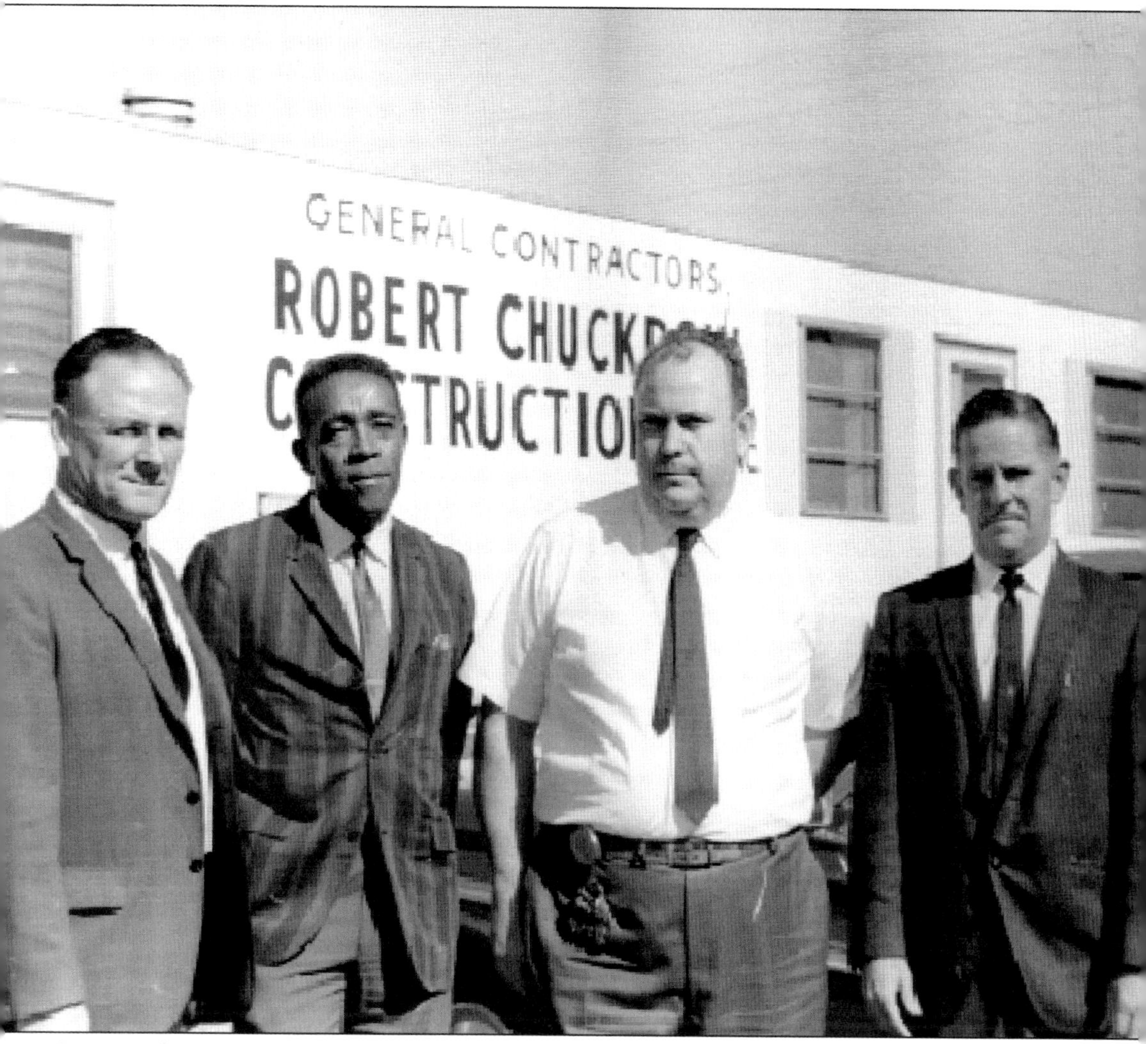

Don Worchester, Sam Chambers, Walter, and Wall discuss the progress of work at a worksite. (No first names were found for Walter and Wall.)

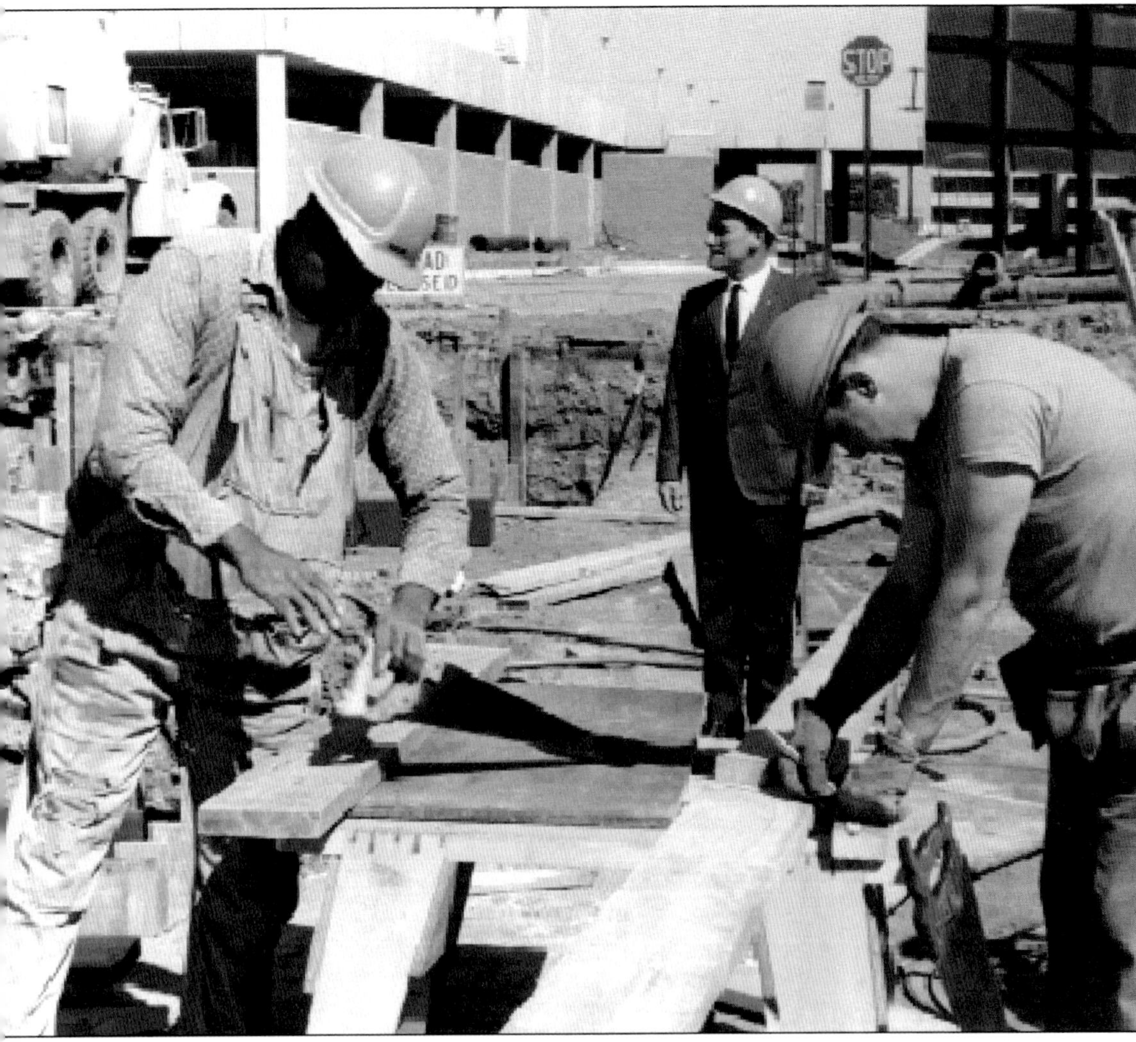

Woodrow Worthy, an African-American carpenter, works on a project at the University of Akron.

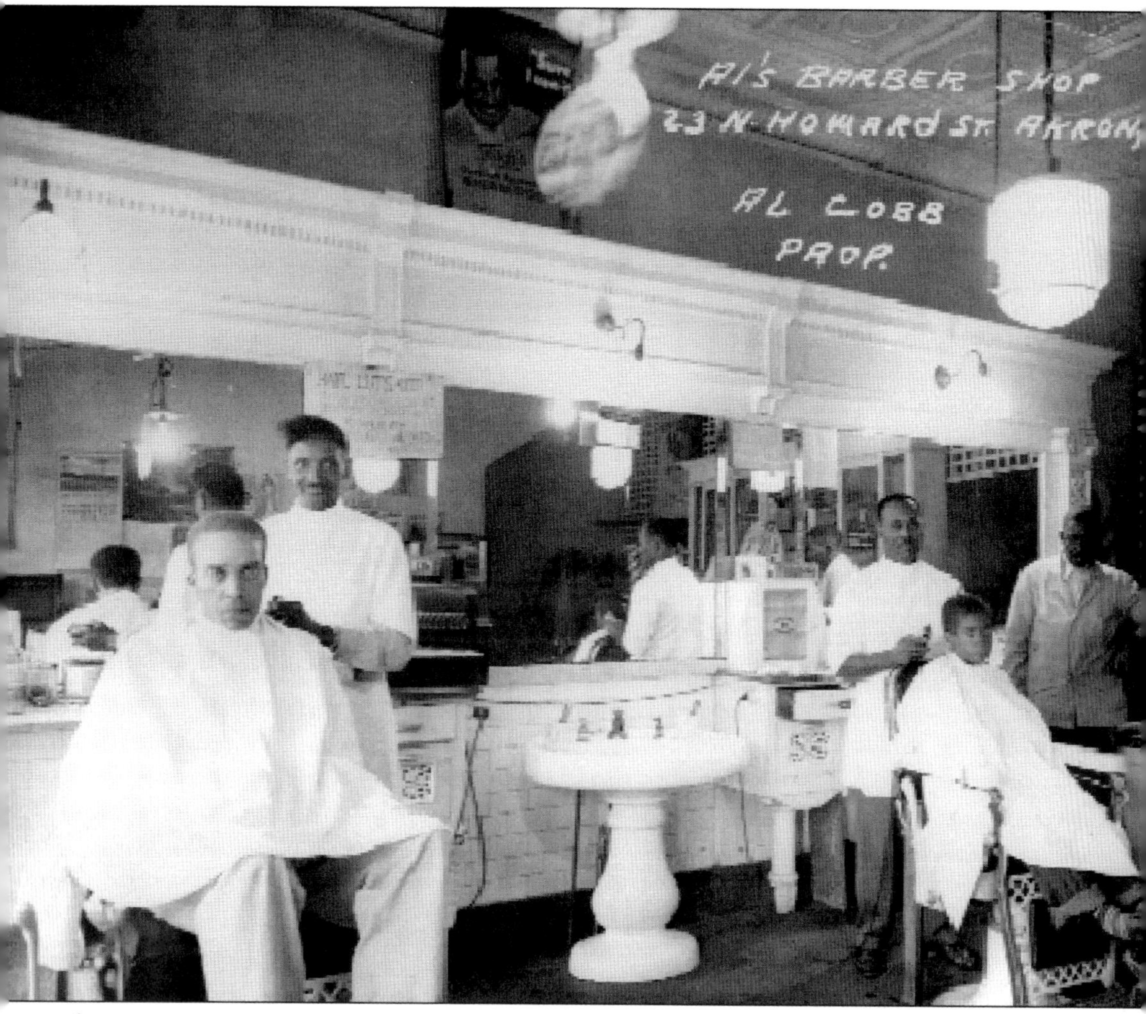

African Americans owned and operated a number of establishments in Akron. One of the many businesses that are prevalent in most African-American communities is the barbershop. They are meeting places and areas where men bond. This is Al's Barbershop, a mainstay in Black Akron.

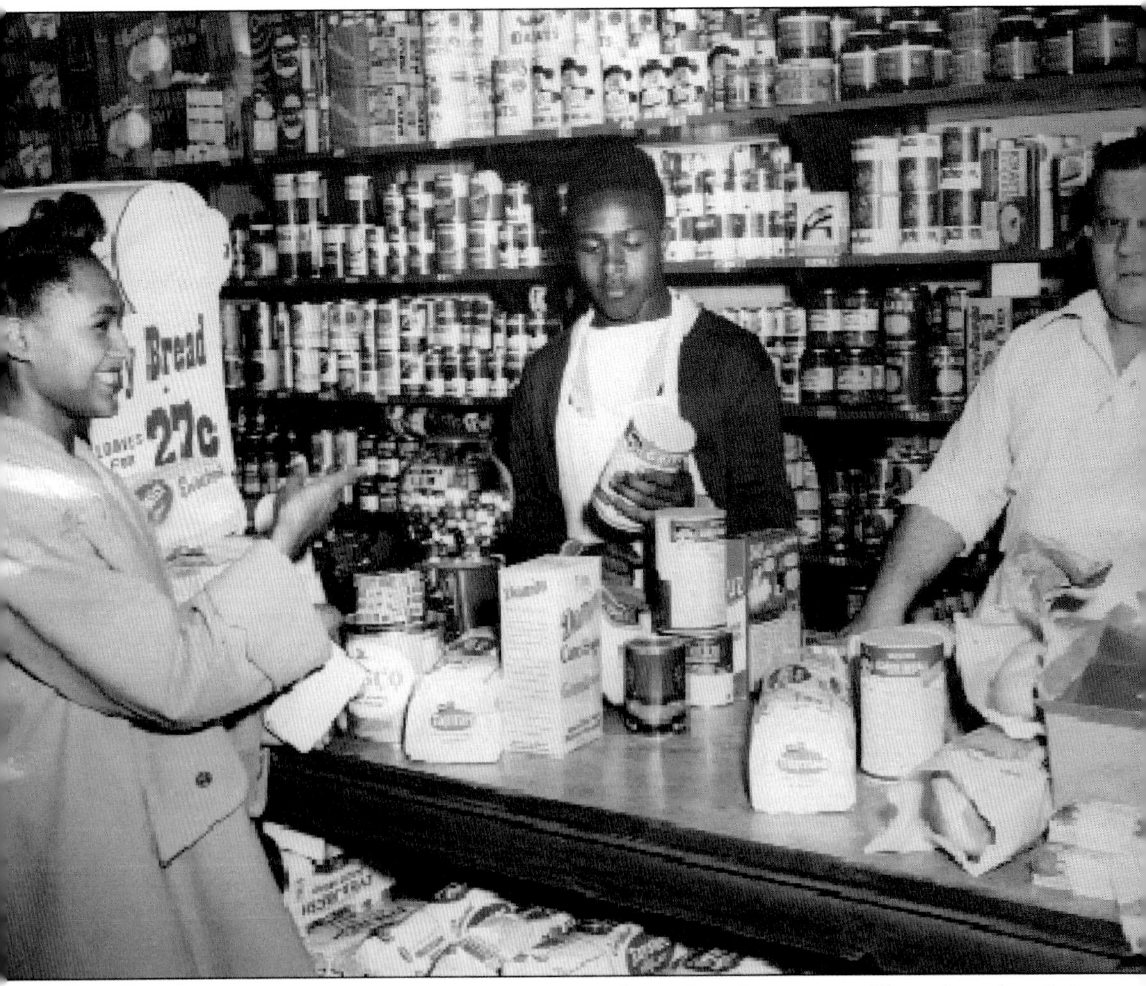

With the coming of the Civil Rights movement African Americans were able to broaden their opportunities and get jobs in different places. Here is an African-American clerk in David Drug Store.

Four

POLITICS

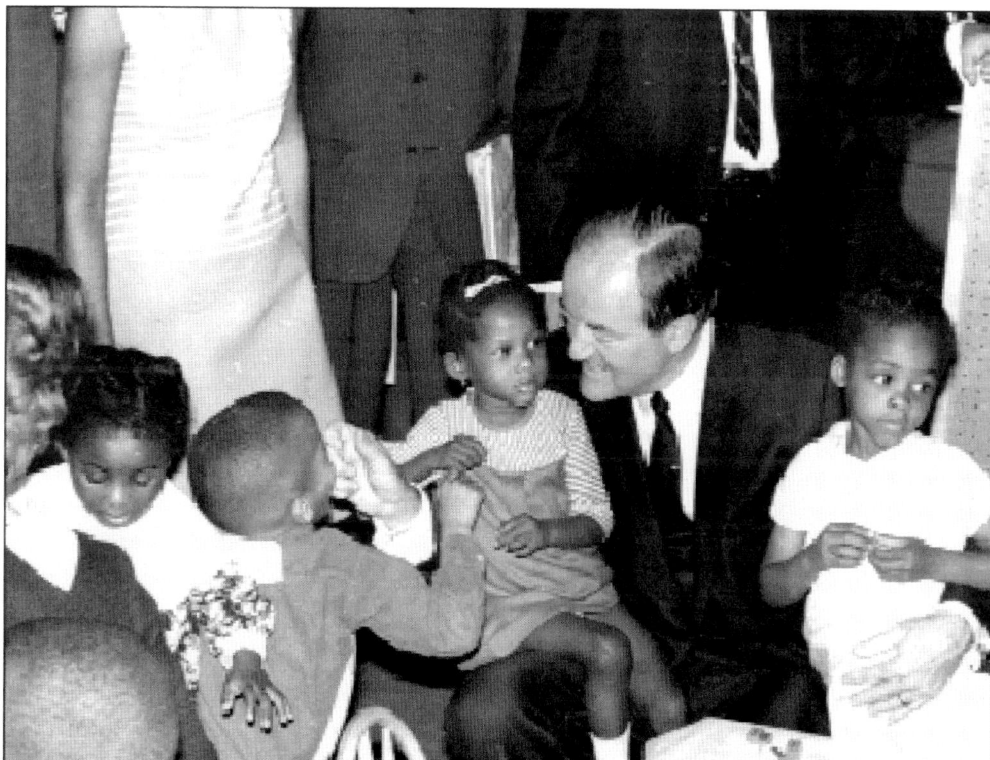

Politicians from all over the country came to Akron to help the city foster positive race relations. Hurbert Humphrey spends time with children at an Akron area public elementary school.

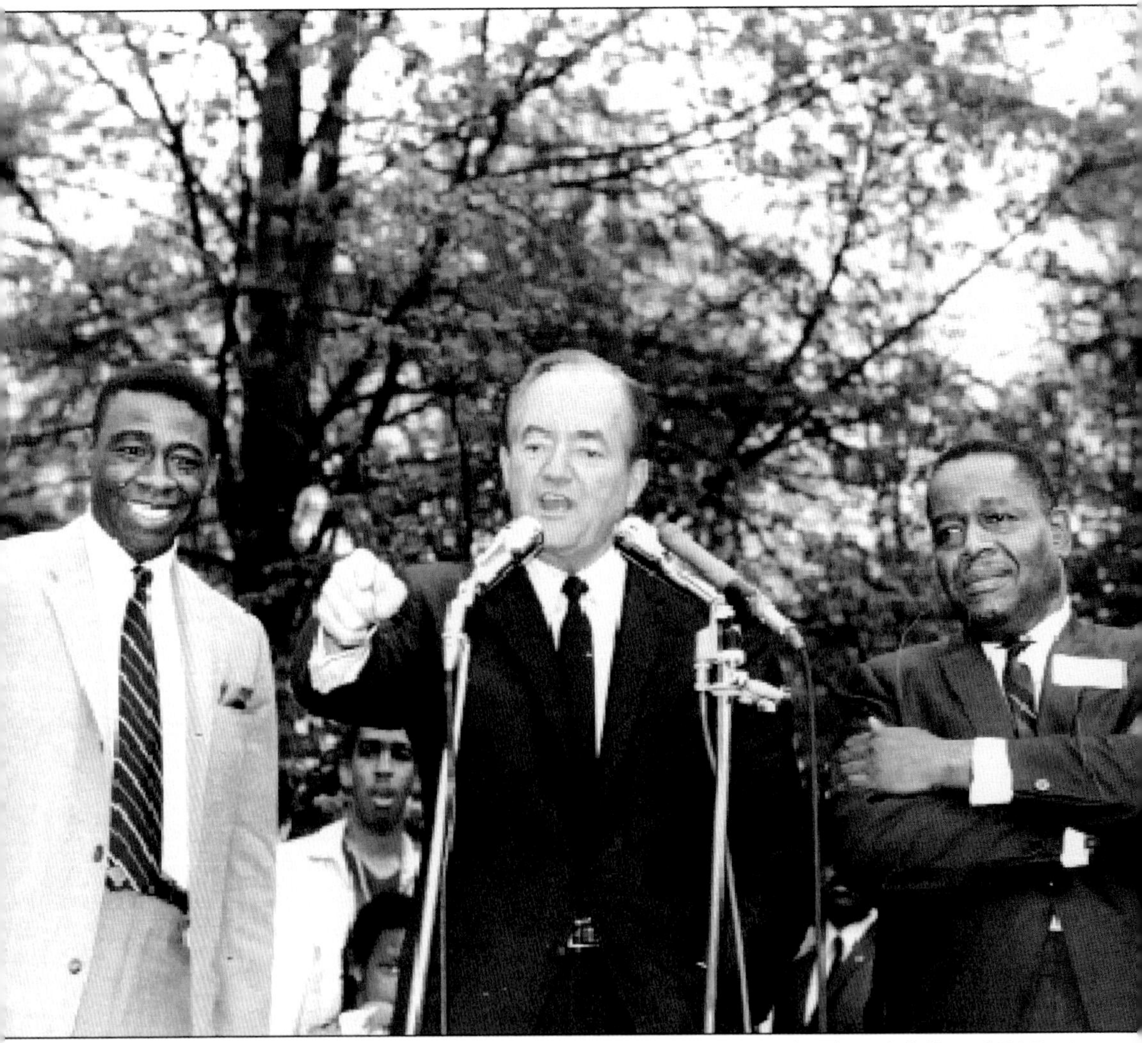

Hurbert Humphrey with Akron African-American local politicians Richard Neal (left) and Ed Davis (right) at a rally in Akron. Humphrey spent a great deal of time campaigning in Ohio during the campaign, and he made sure to court the African-American vote.

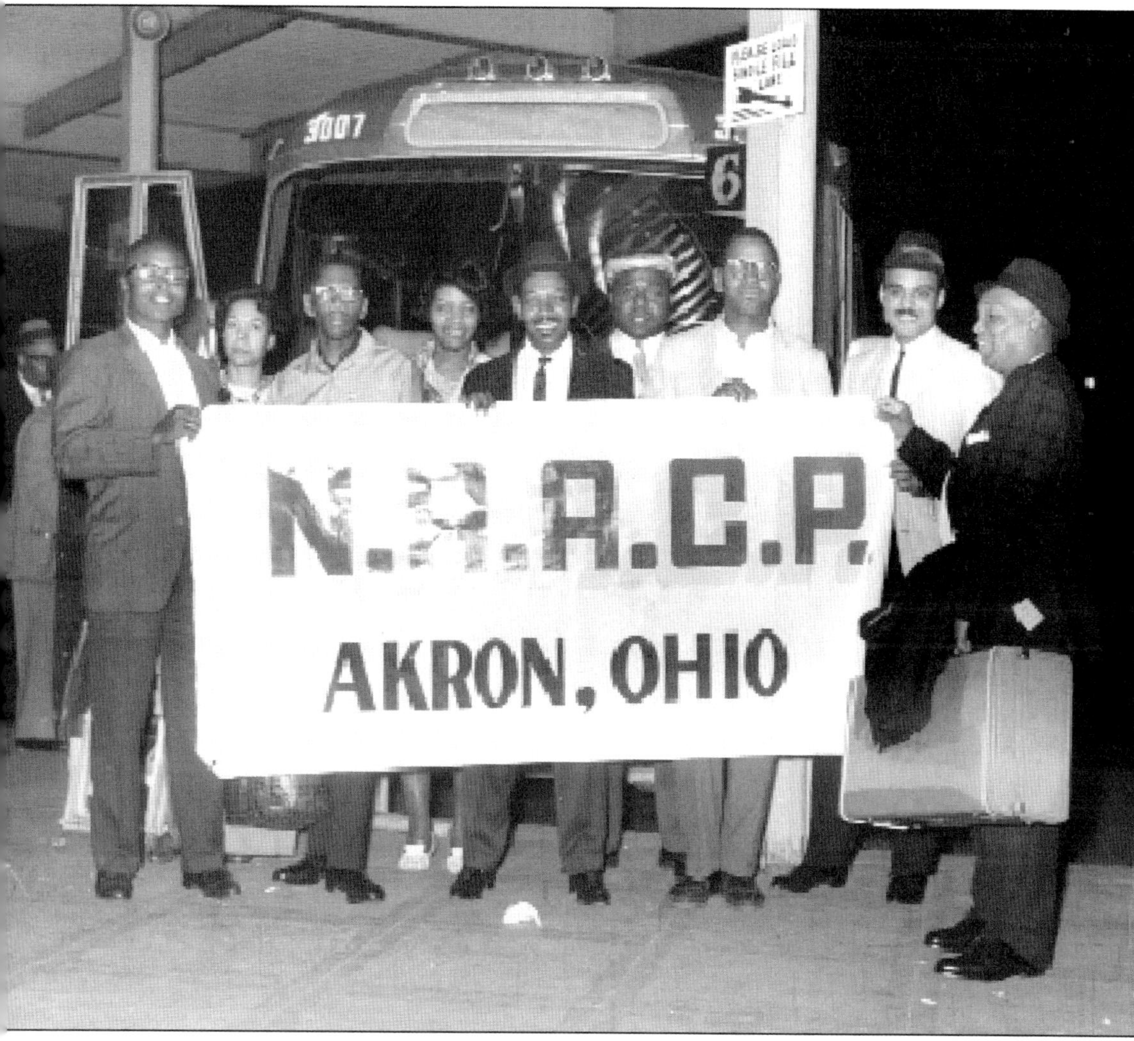

Proud African-American Akronites hold a banner to celebrate their participation in the 1963 March on Washington. In the picture are, from left to right, Robert Brown, Rite Eldridge Sharpp, Edwin Parms, Priscilla Sanders, unidentified, Delbert Sanders, Henry Munford, Harvey Anderson, and Marlon Dixon.

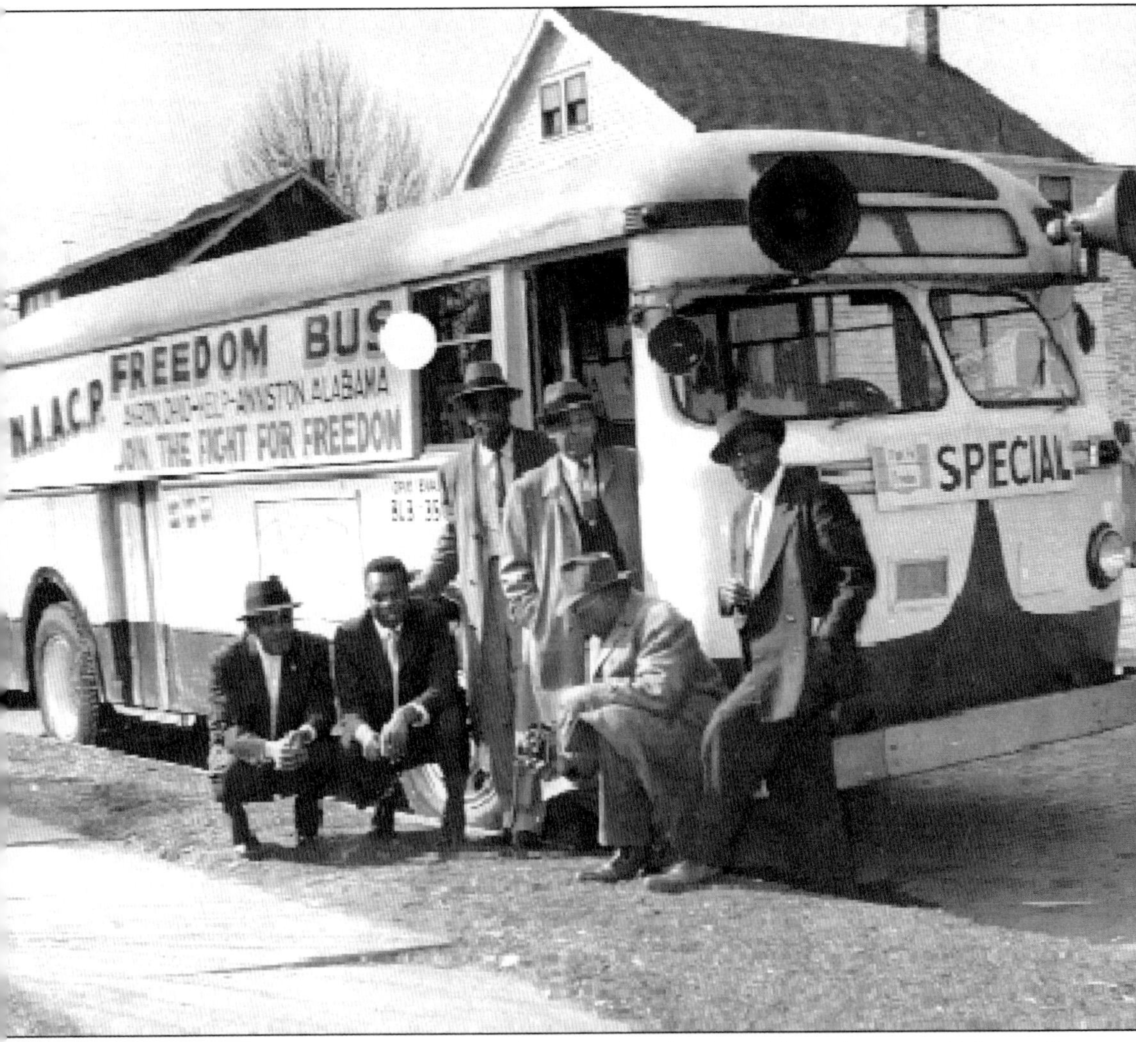

Several Akron NAACP activists sign up Akronites for a freedom ride to Anniston, Alabama: Mrs. Lancaster, unidentified, Pastor, unidentified, Mr. Davis, Allen Killings, Evans, and C.O. Stewart.

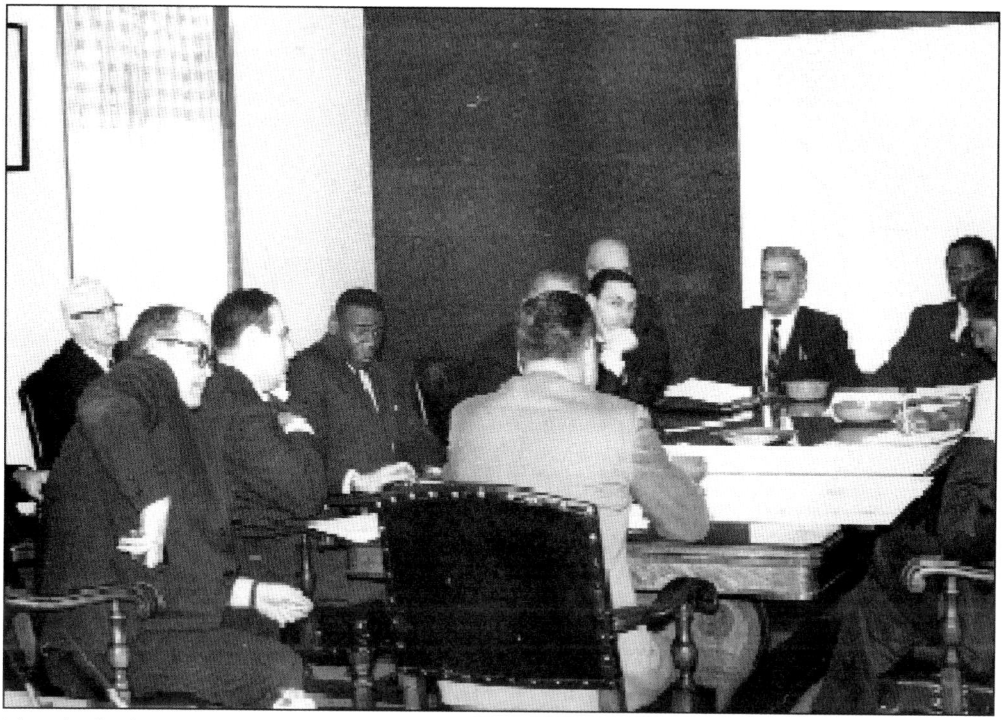

The Elizabeth Park Gym committee meets to discuss an important issue. Seated at the table are two very influential African Americans. They are Richard Neal on the left and Frank Lomax on the right.

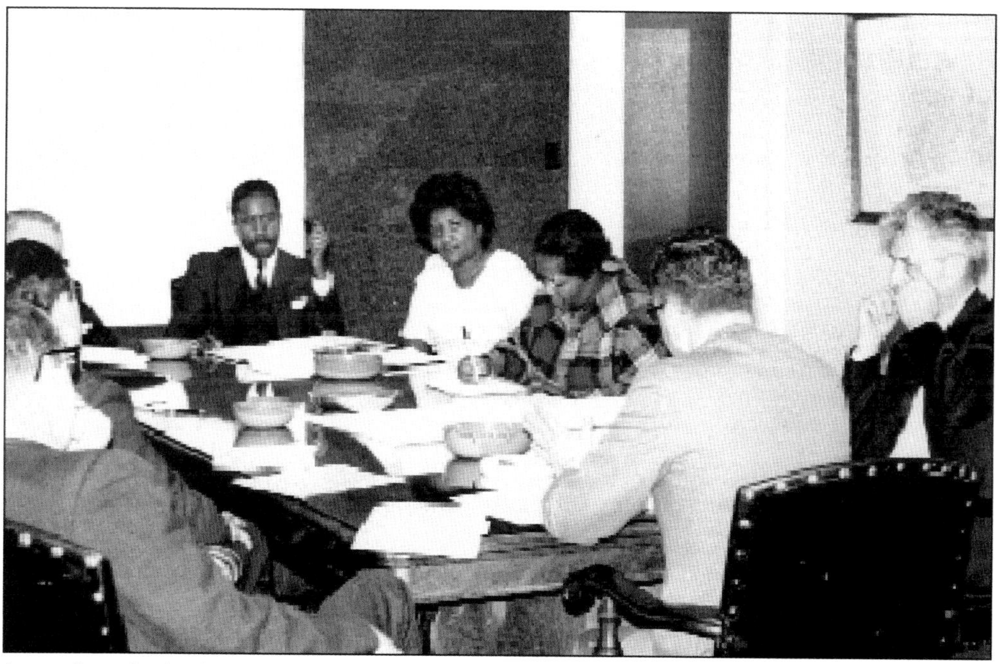

At another Elizabeth Park Gym meeting Frank Lomax plays a very significant role in ensuring the meeting is run well.

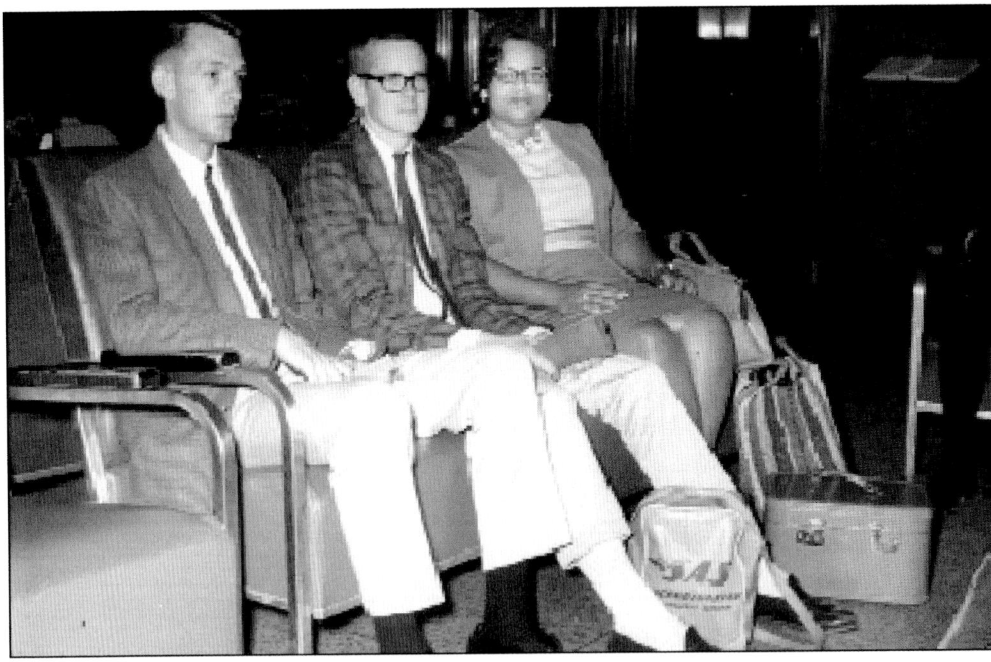

Three unidentified NAACP members, two white and one African American, await a bus to the March on Washington, displaying the interracial spirit of the day.

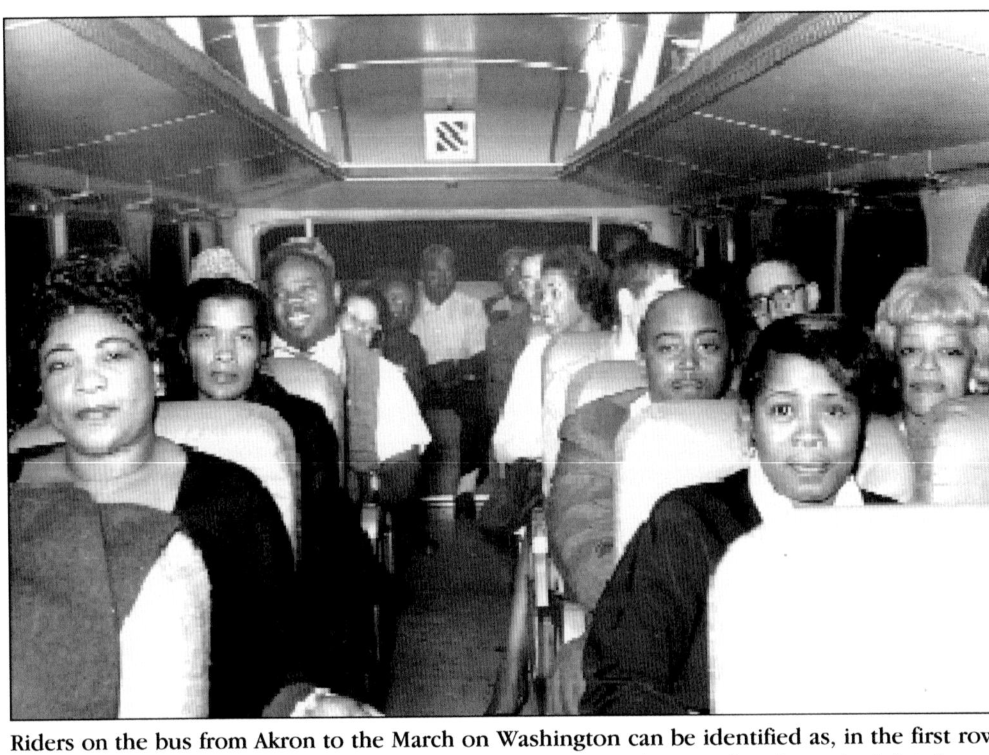

Riders on the bus from Akron to the March on Washington can be identified as, in the first row on the right, Collie Green, and on the left, Polly Jackson. In the row, fourth on the left is Leona Wright Farris, and on the right aisle seat, Madge Mapp.

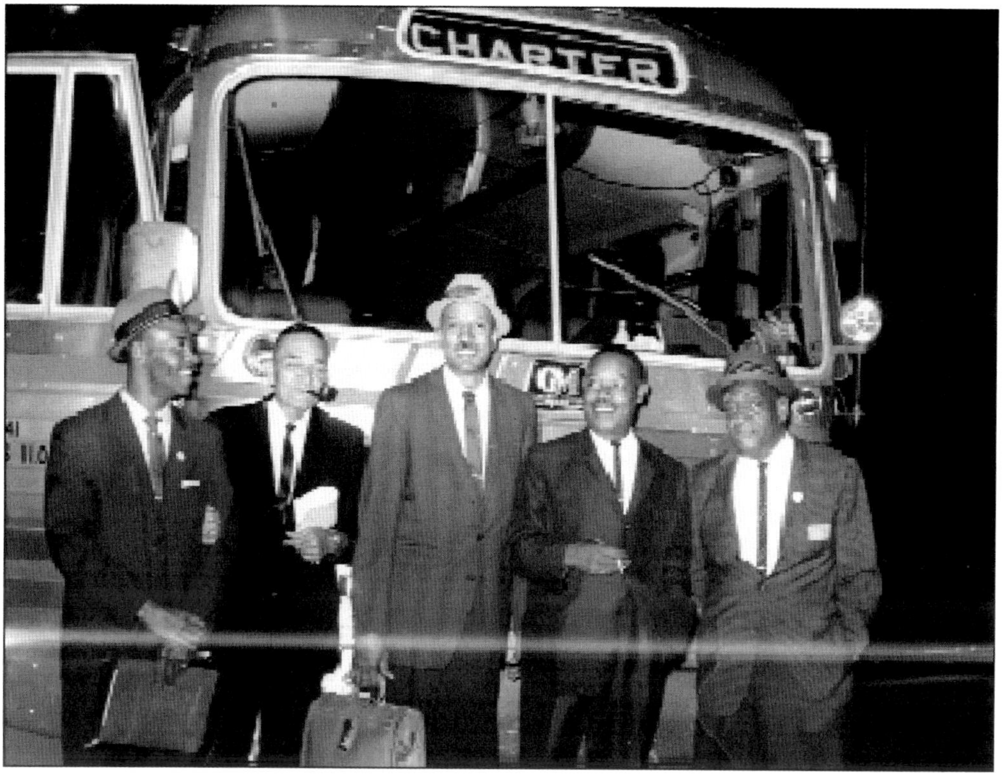

From left to right, an unidentified man, William Fowler, Willis Shaw, Jimmy Turner, and Ed Davis pose for a picture in front of a bus, before the March on Washington.

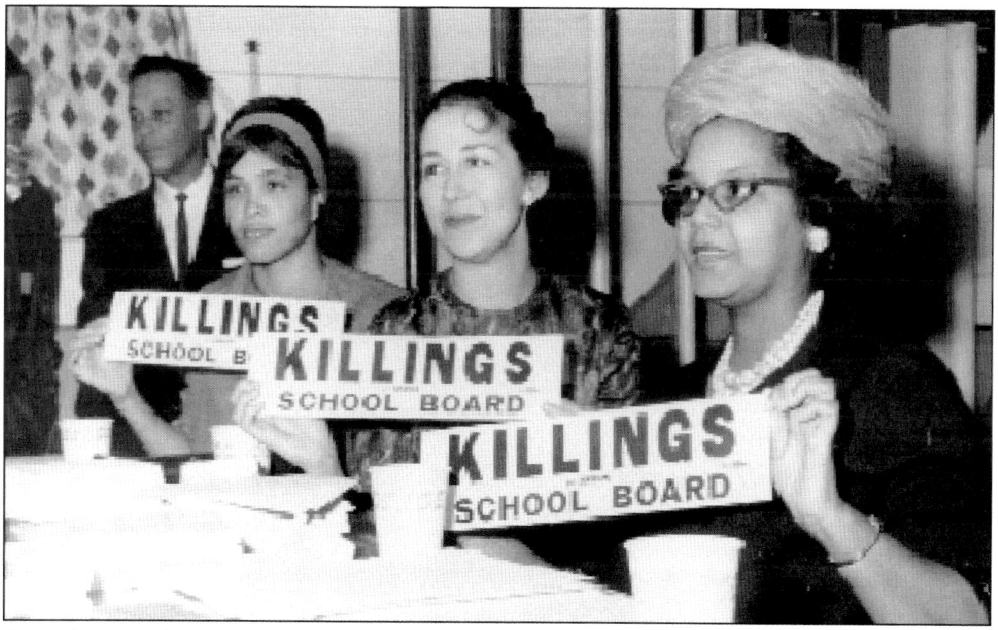

Several people demonstrate their support for a candidate running for school board. In the picture are, on the far left, George Miller, Shirla McClain, unidentified, and Maxine Blake.

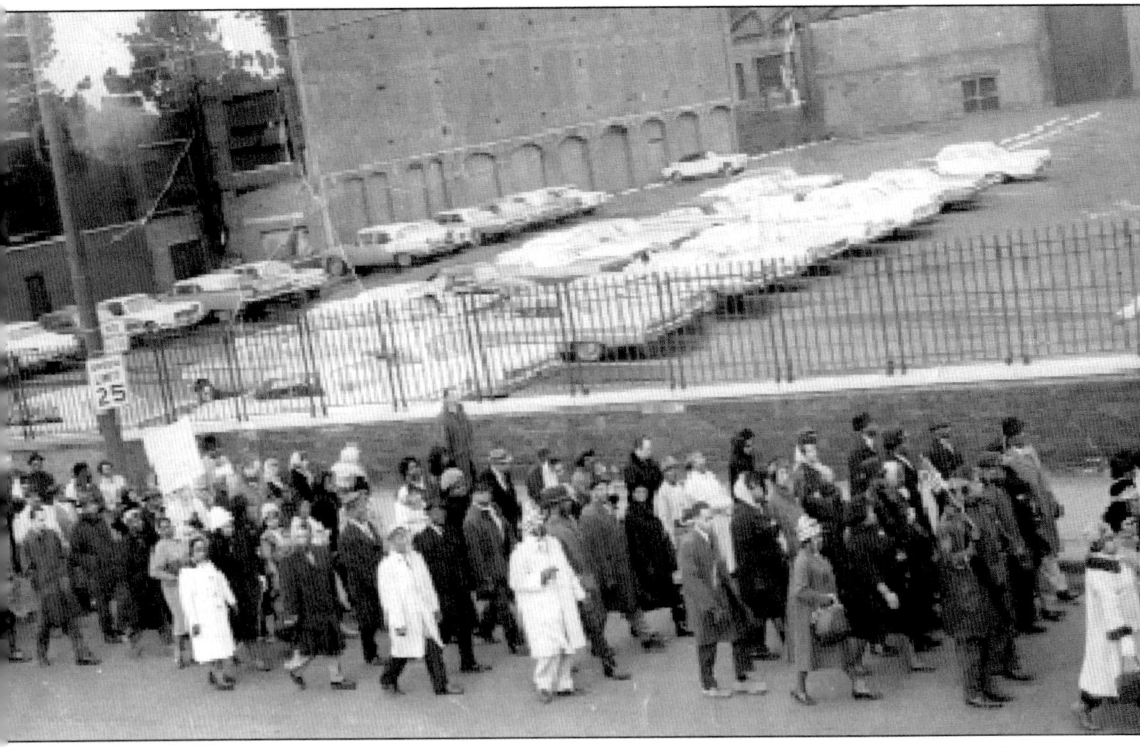

African Americans in Akron participated in a sympathy march for the people of Selma, Alabama.

Students protest at the University of Akron, demanding a culturally relevant educational experience.

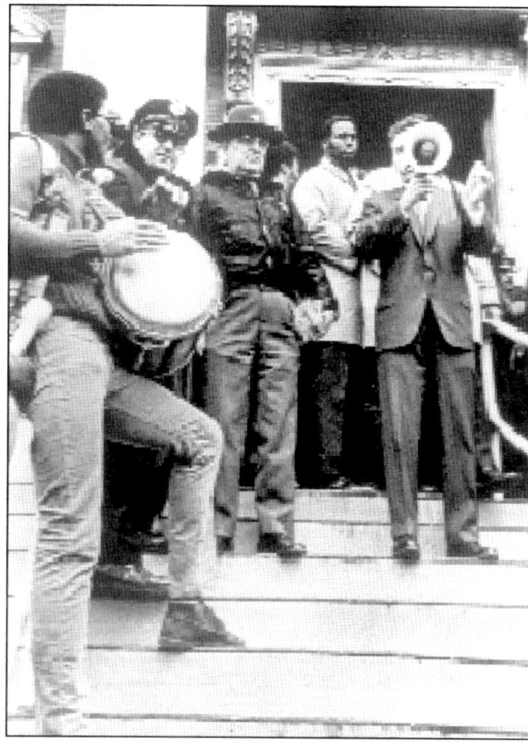

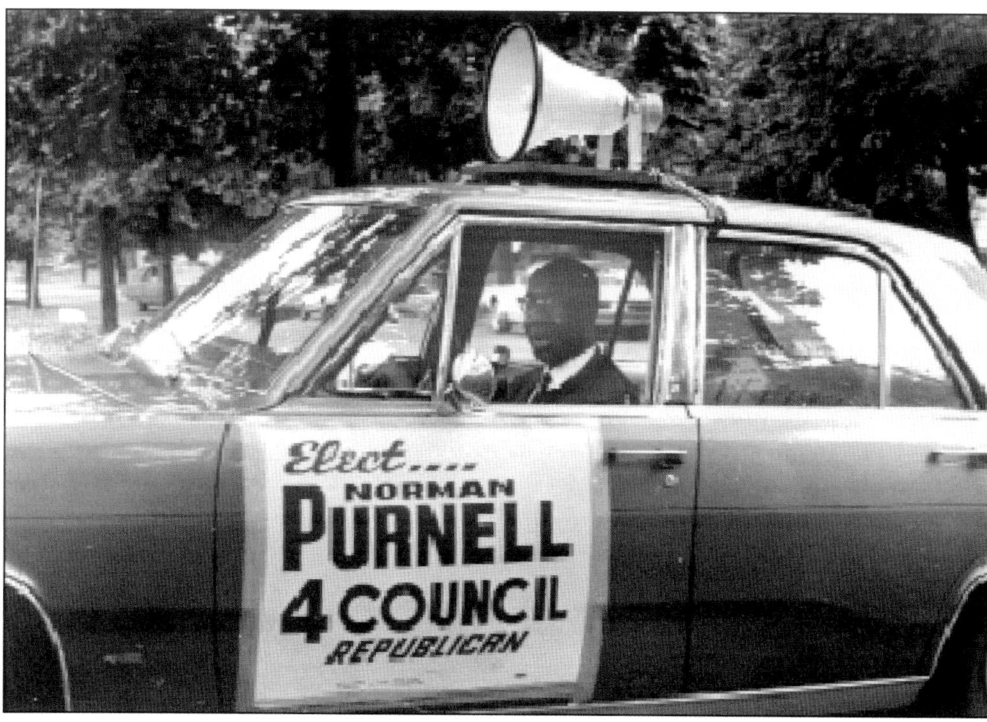

African Americans have been active in politics for quite some time. Norman Purnell ran for city council in Akron.

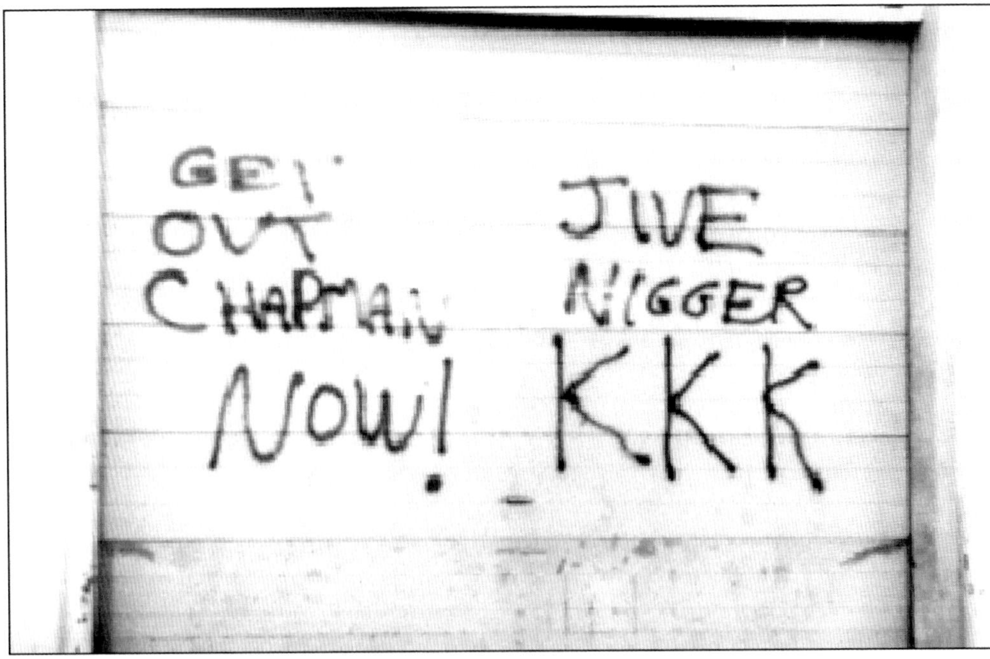

Not everyone was impressed with the progress Akron Americans had made in Akron. There were several white people who opposed African Americans integrating into their neighborhoods. This photograph shows graffiti written by the Klan on Martin Chapman's garage after he moved into a new neighborhood.

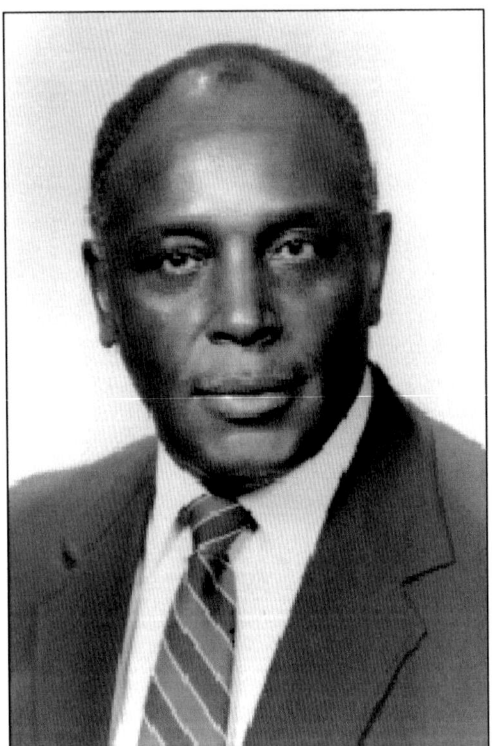

Henry Flowers was an activist African American who fought for more African-American political participation.

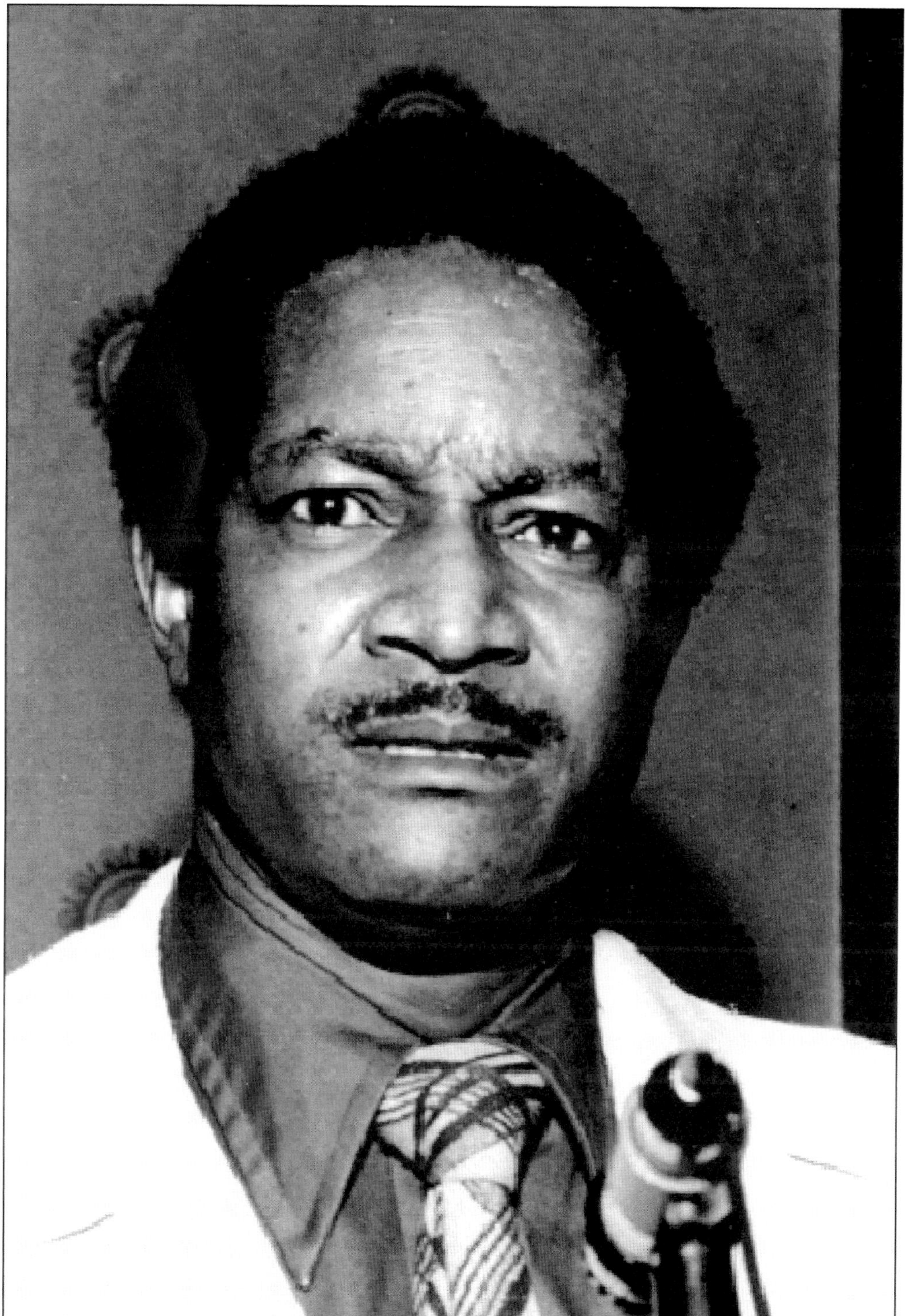

Ambrose Brazelton was a gym teacher in the Akron Public School system. He would eventually serve in the state education department.

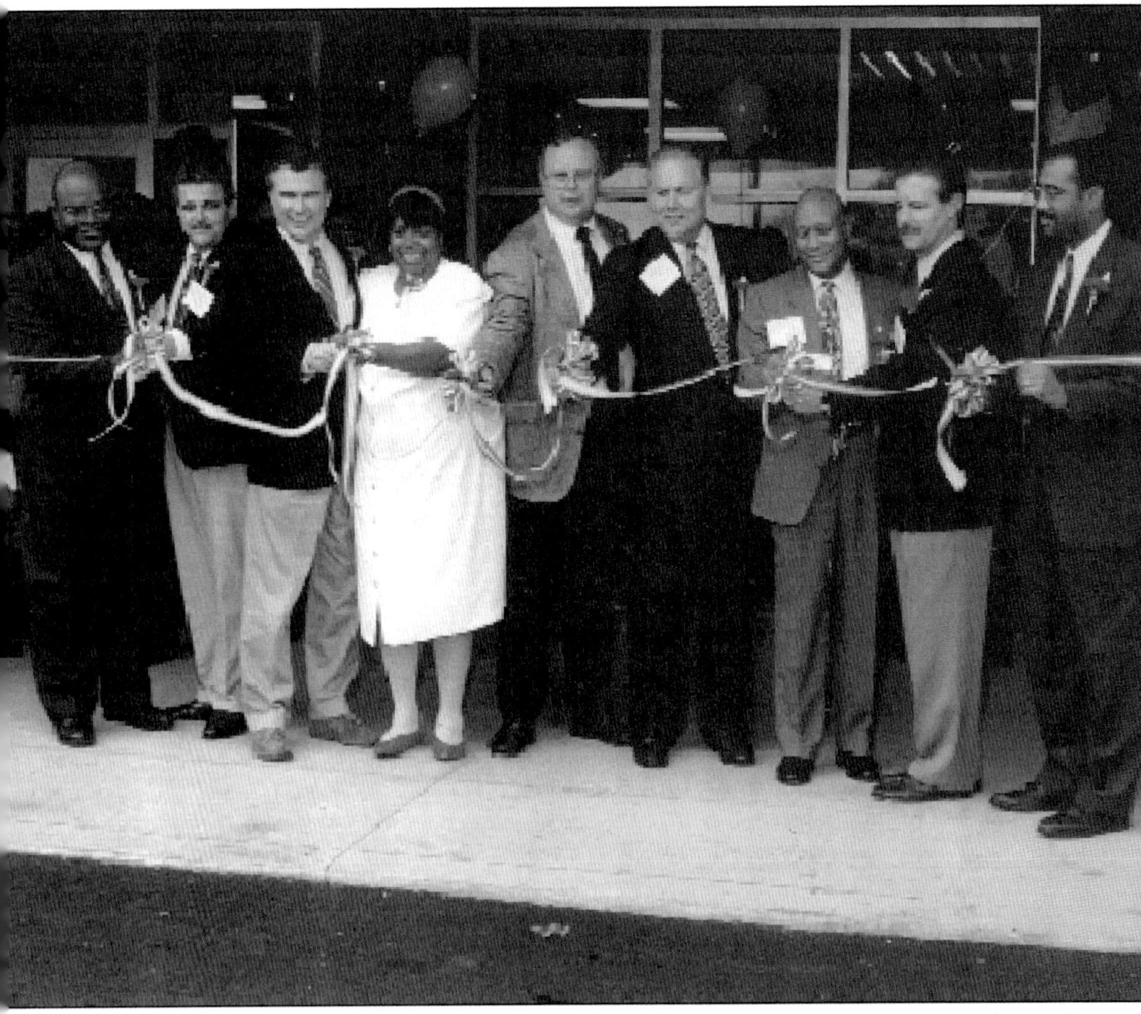

Several Africans Americans participate in a ribbon-cutting ceremony. This picture shows the level of cooperation between African American and white leaders in Akron. Pictured are some of the best-known politicians in the city: from left to right, Samuel Deshazior, unidentified, U.S. Representative Tom Sawyer, Akron Mayor Don Plusquellic, businessman Malcolm Costa, and State Representative Vernon Sykes.

Five

Leisure

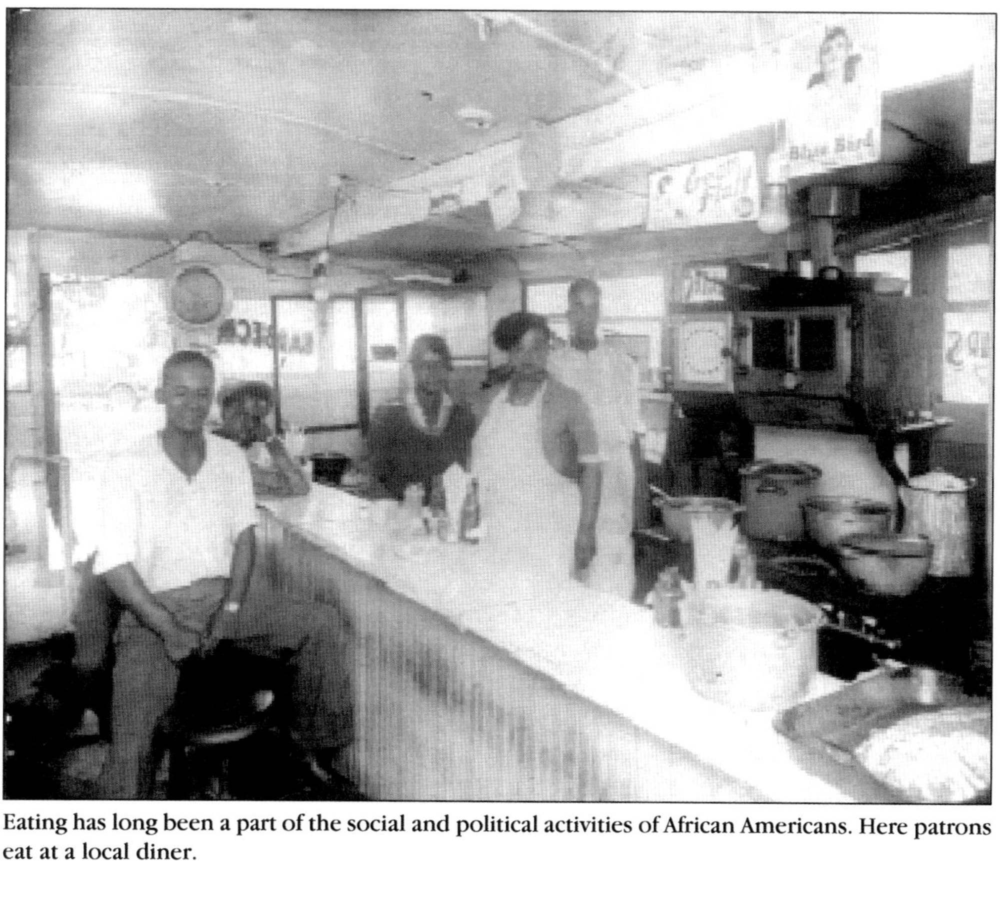

Eating has long been a part of the social and political activities of African Americans. Here patrons eat at a local diner.

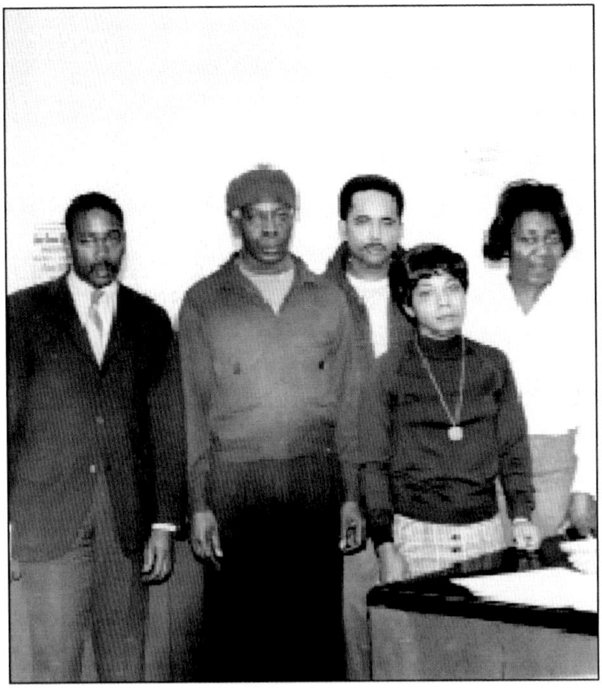

This is a picture of a group of African-American Akronites who planned activities for the neighborhoods.

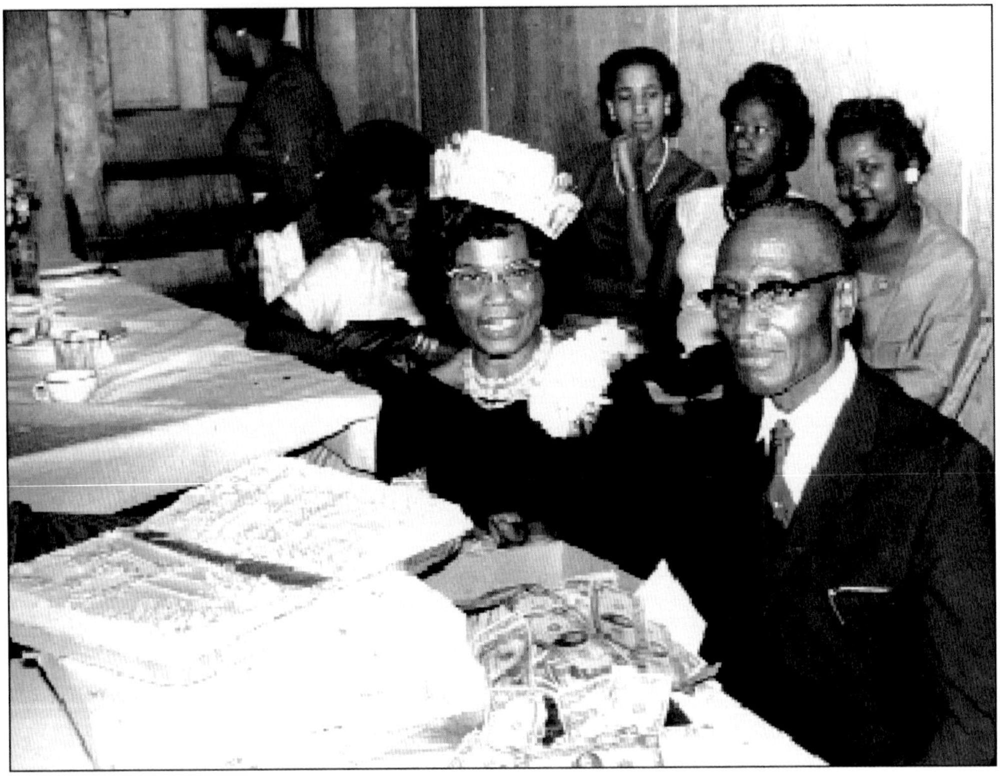

Reverend John H. Wheeler, pastor of the Providence Baptist Church, celebrates his anniversary at a church function.

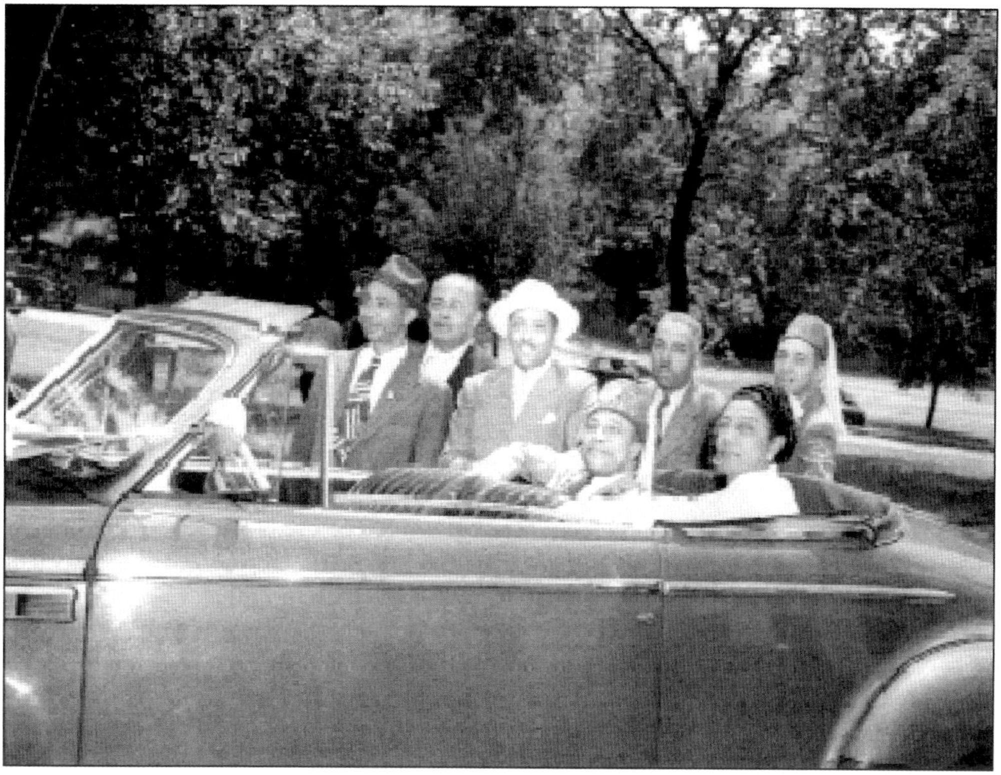

African-American Elks attend a Thanksgiving picnic in Akron, June 1946. One of the attendees was Leon Gordon, president of the Akron Branch NAACP, the first person on the right with the dark hat on.

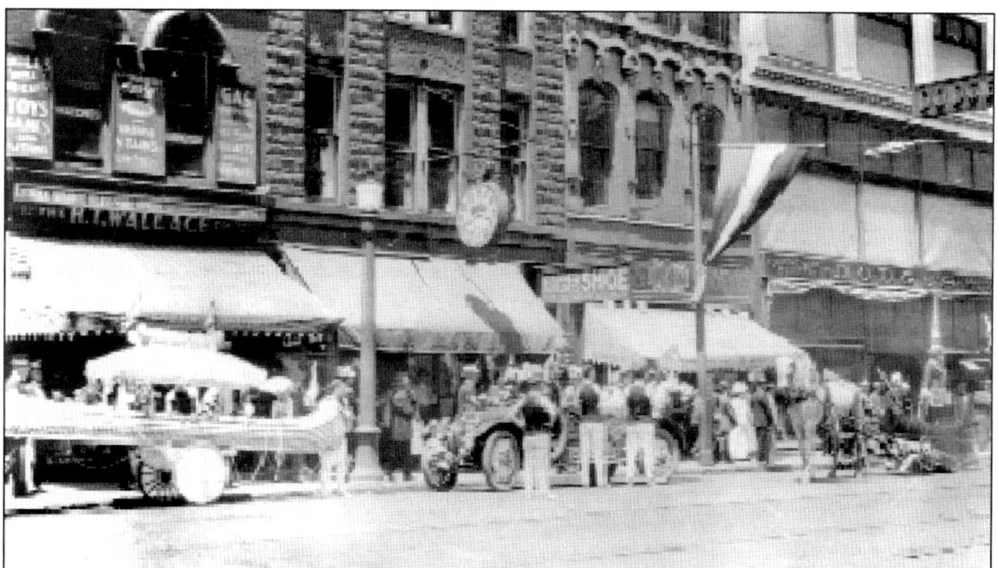

This parade is on Howard Street, a historical and important throughway in Akron, which housed many of the African-American businesses and entertainment venues.

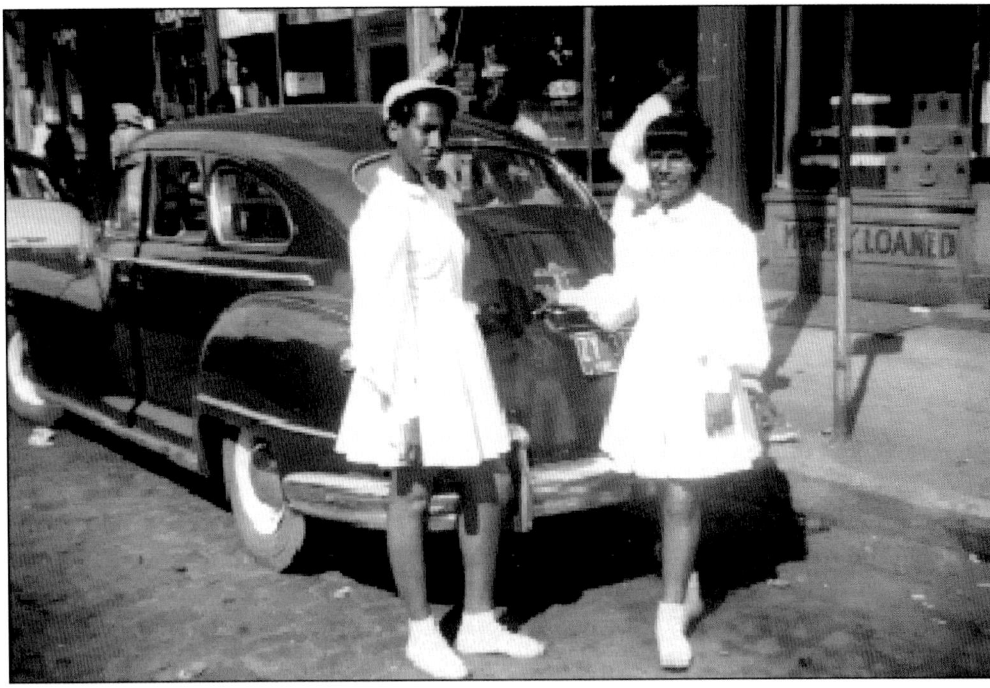

Two unidentified girls pose by a car on Howard Street.

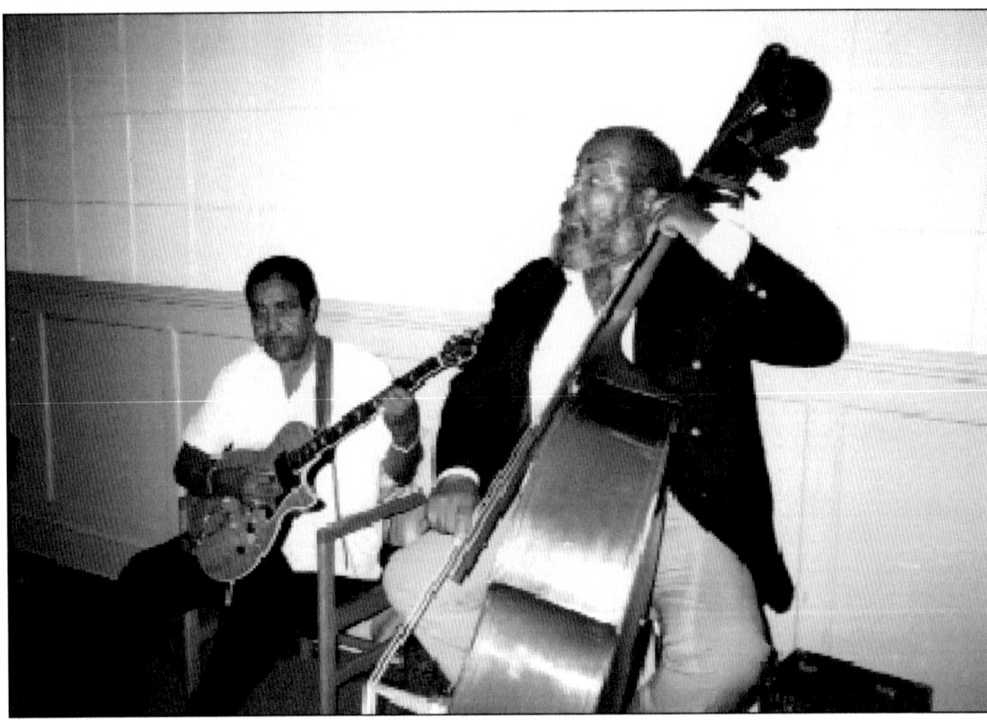

Dr. Lathardus Goggins plays his cello with an unidentified performer.

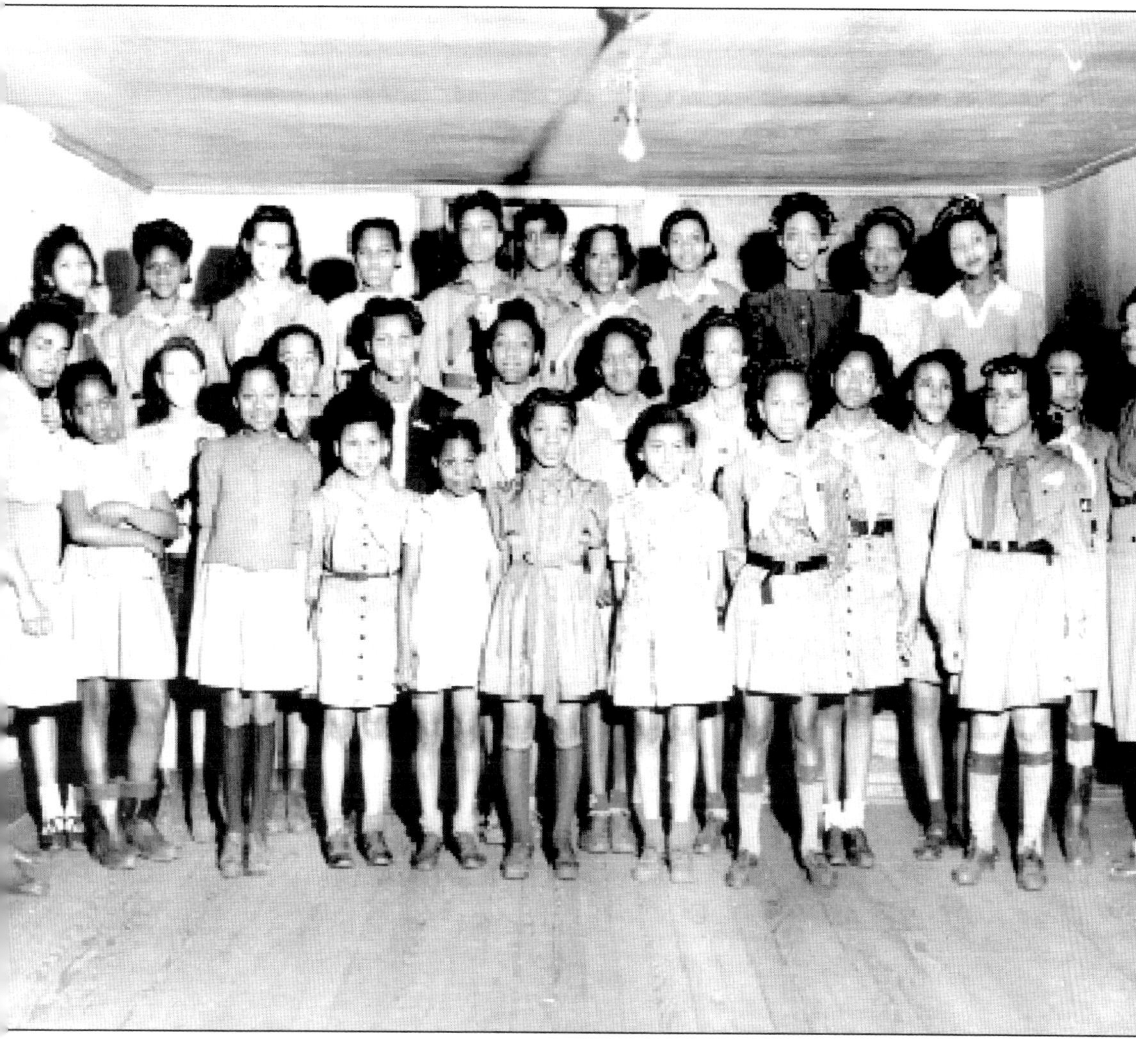

Mary Hogan Smith, first row far right, was the leader of the Akron Campfire girls. Here the girls pose for a picture. This was one of the many youth organizations created to help direct young people in Akron.

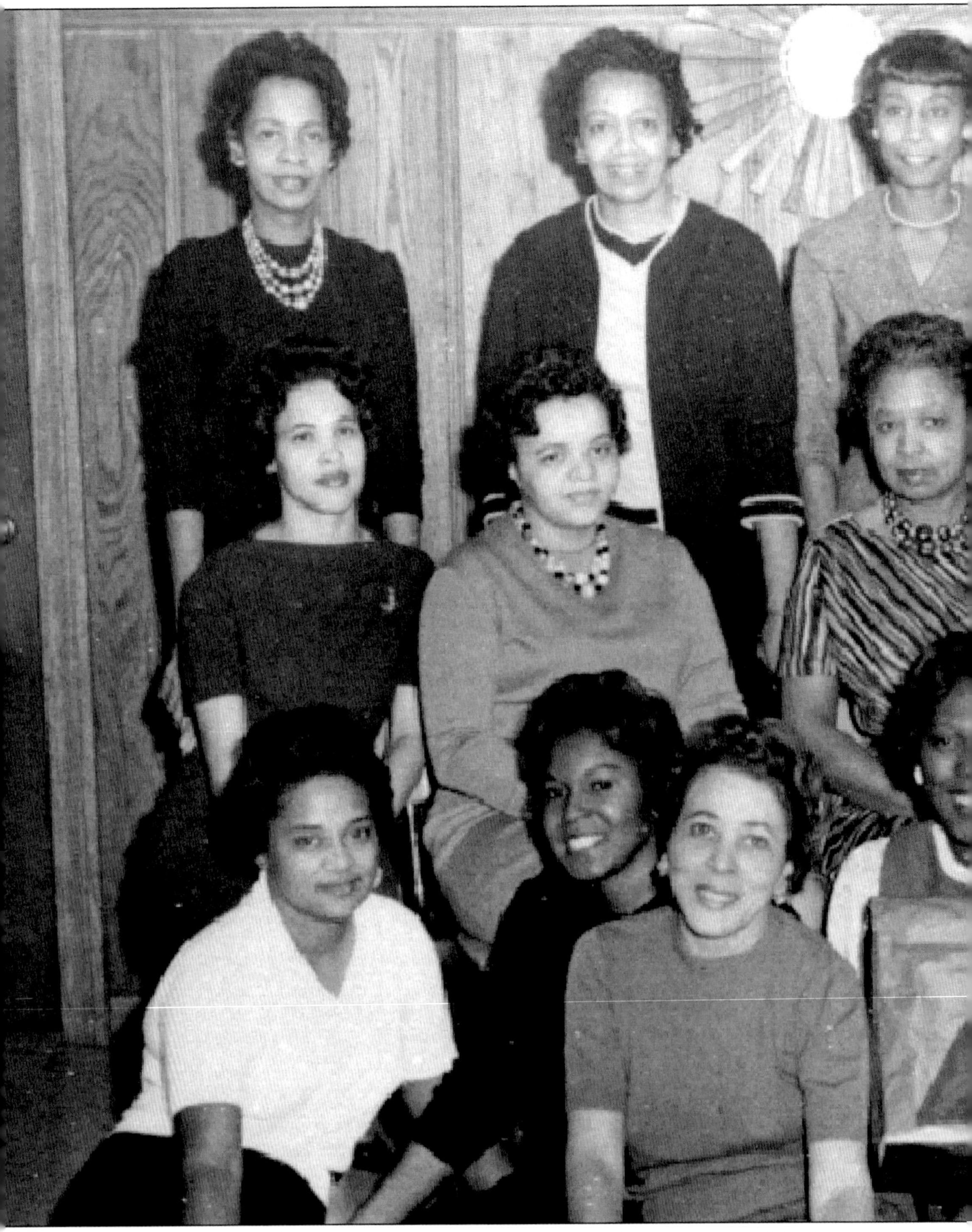

Women of the Phi Delta Kappa Sorority pose for a picture: first row left to right, Mae Bradley, Catherine Martin Butts, Beatrice Neeley, Joyce Finley Jackson, Margaret Roberts, and Adell Lewis; second row left to right, Dr. Shirla McClain, Doreen Fitzpatrick, Margaret McClain, Ester Spruill,

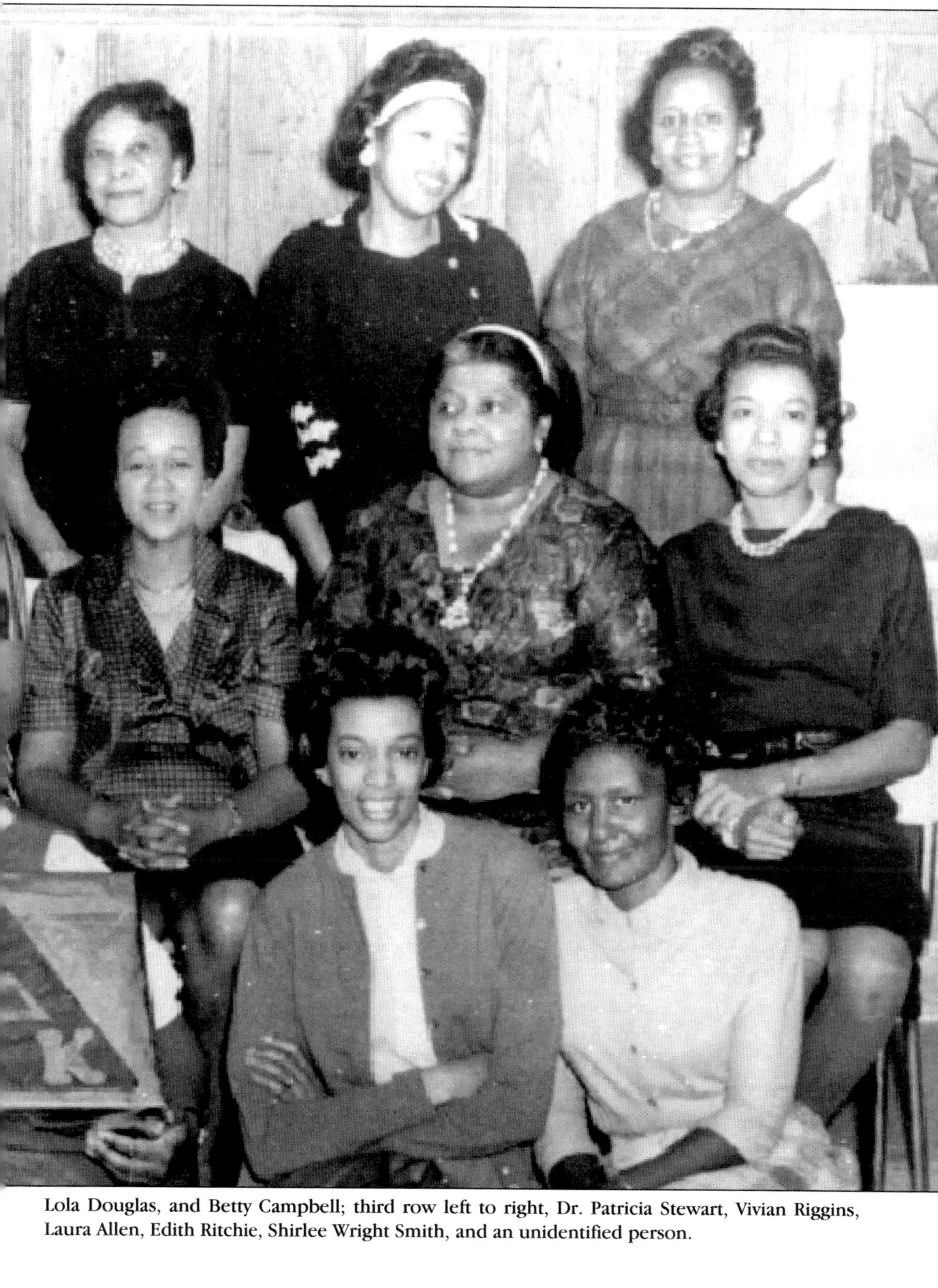

Lola Douglas, and Betty Campbell; third row left to right, Dr. Patricia Stewart, Vivian Riggins, Laura Allen, Edith Ritchie, Shirlee Wright Smith, and an unidentified person.

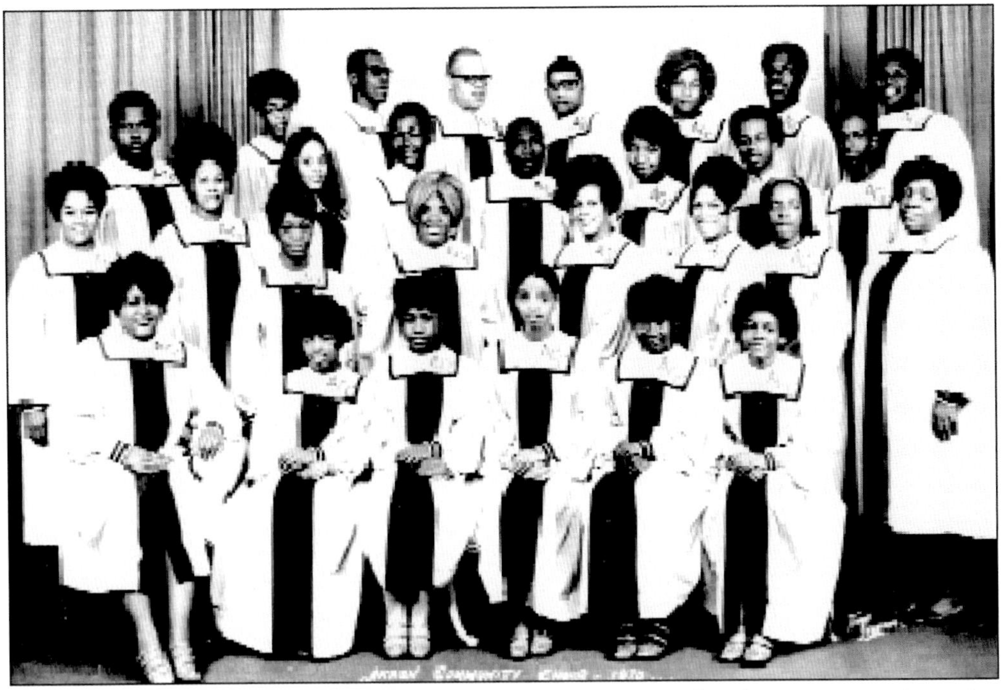

Akron's African-American community has continuously expressed a devotion to projects that cross racial boundaries. A good example is the 1970 Akron Community Choir seen here.

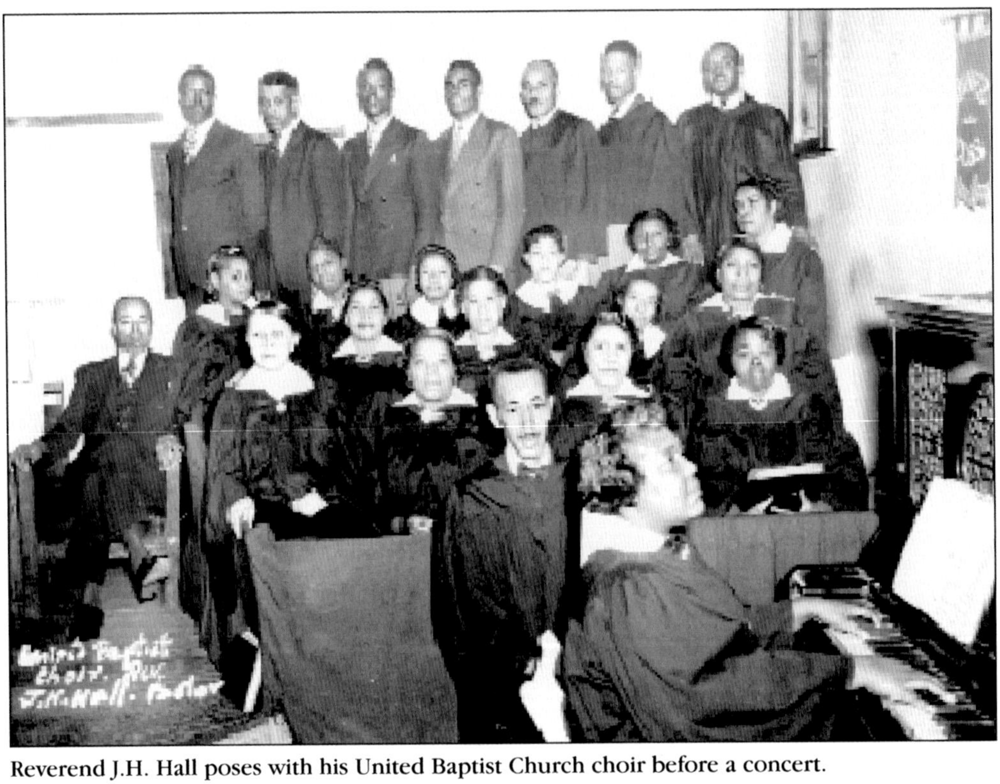

Reverend J.H. Hall poses with his United Baptist Church choir before a concert.

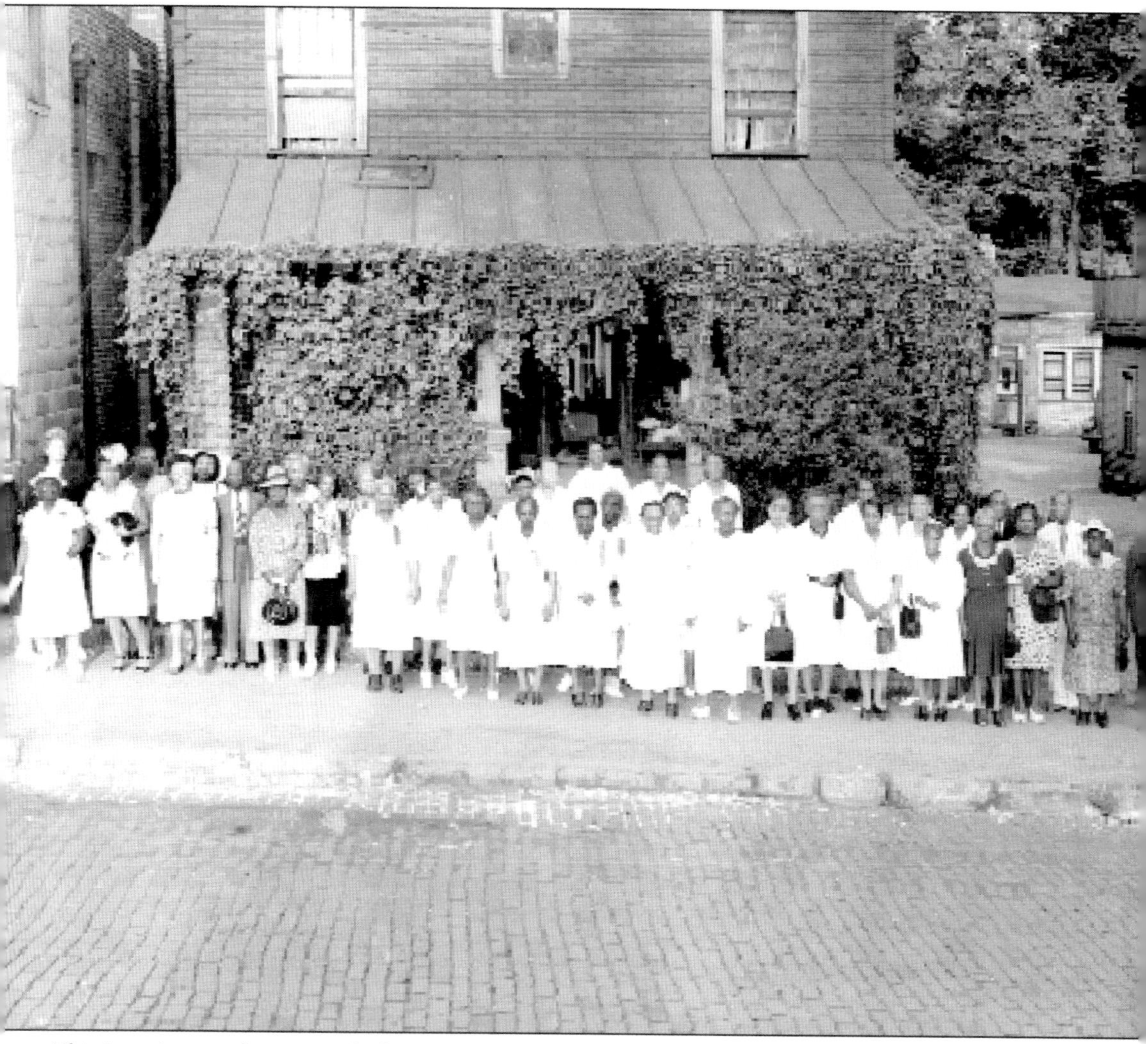

This is a picture of a group of African Americans posing in front of a house.

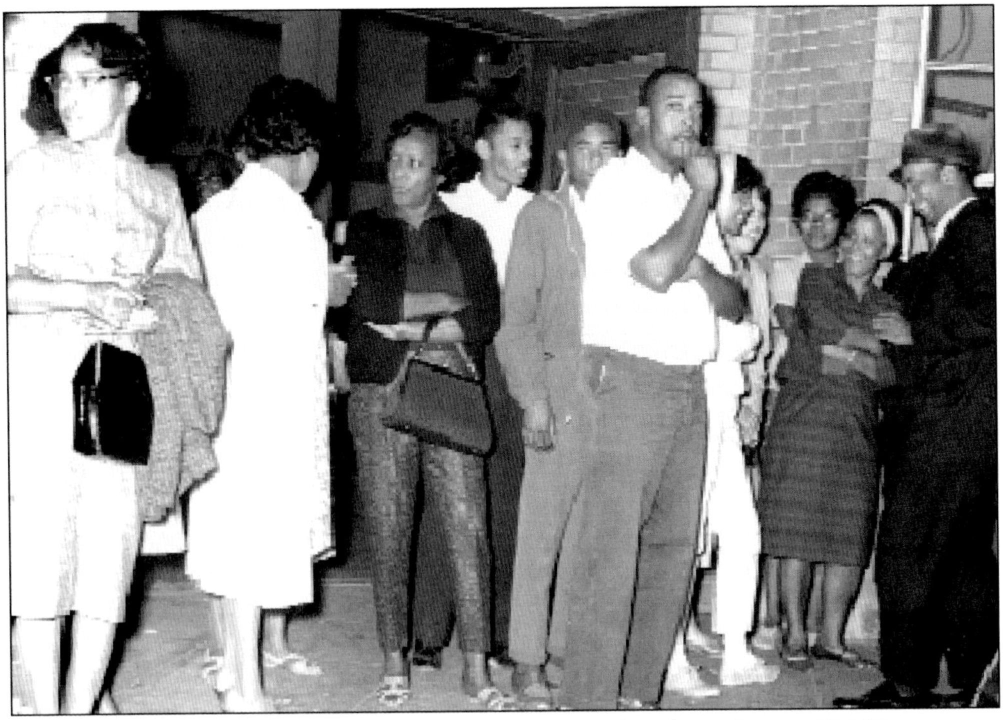

Attorney Jackson, on the far right in a suit, keeps the peace as he jokes with some NAACP protestors.

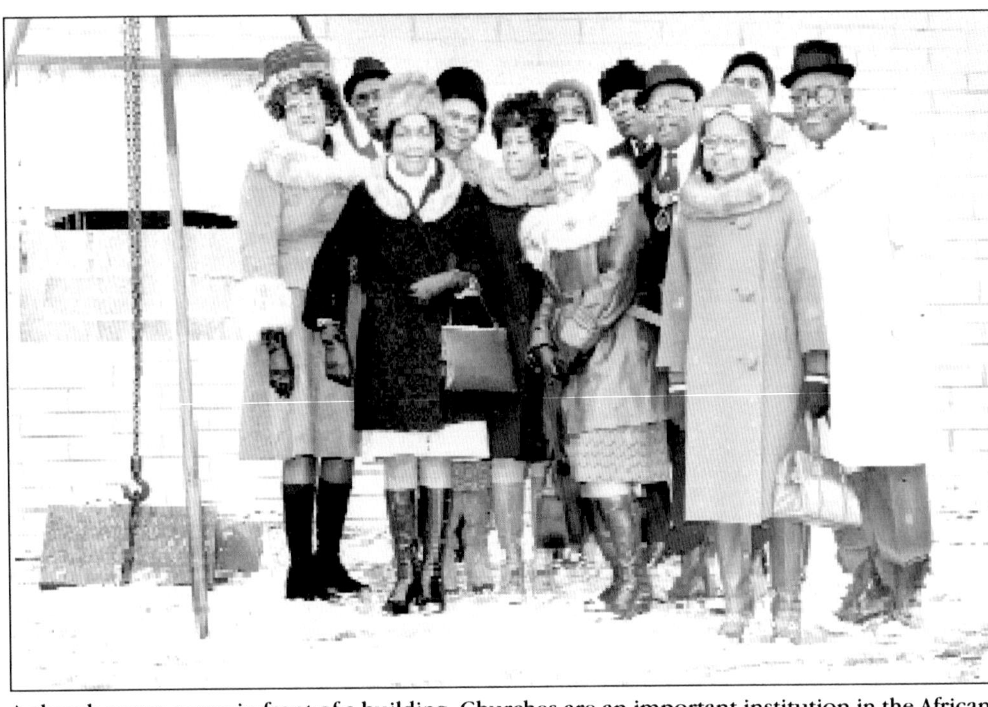

A church group poses in front of a building. Churches are an important institution in the African-American community, serving as unifiers of people.

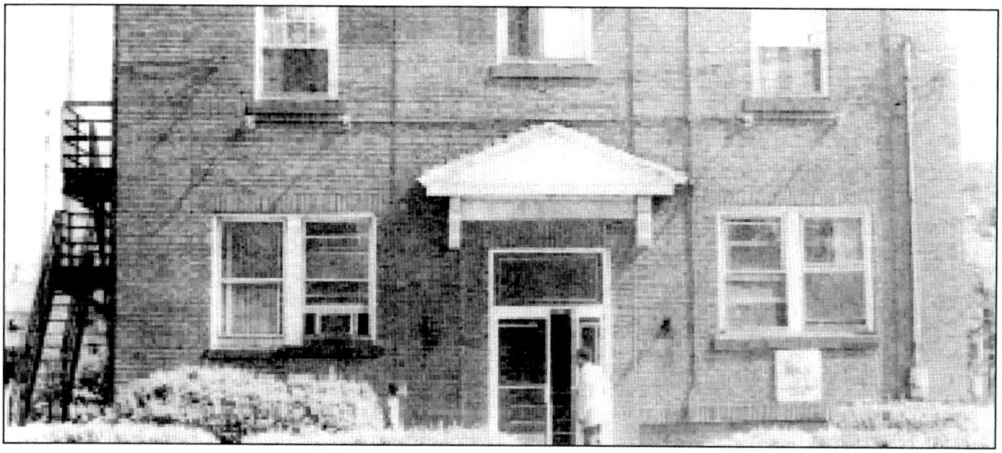

East Akron Community House was one of the most important gathering places for African Americans in the Akron community.

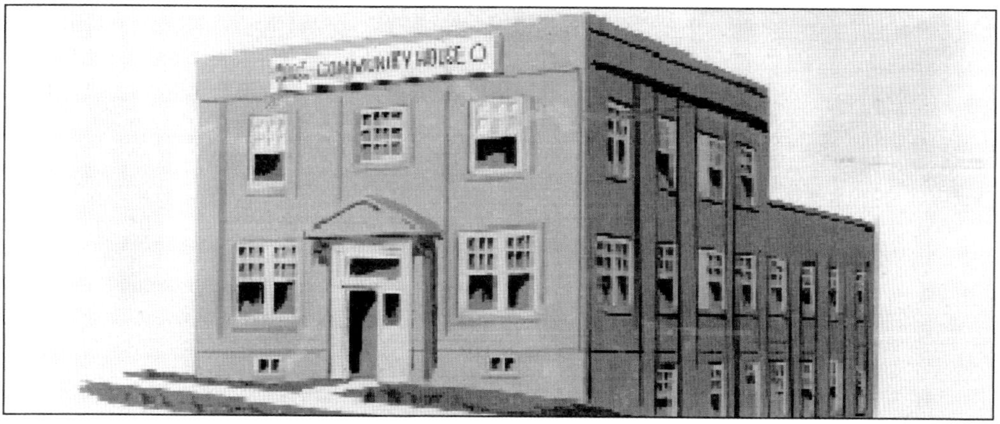

The East Akron Community House continues to play a vital role in the African-American community.

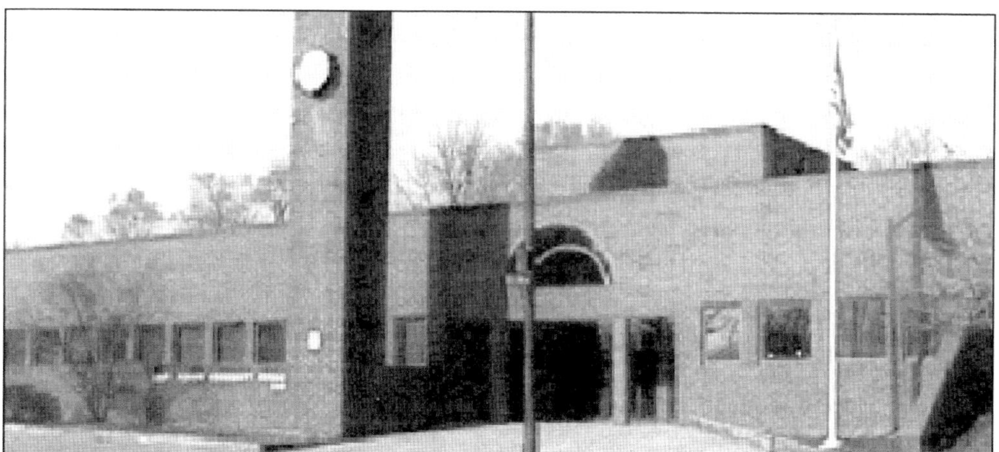

East Akron Community House was originally designed to play a role in the African-American community in Akron.

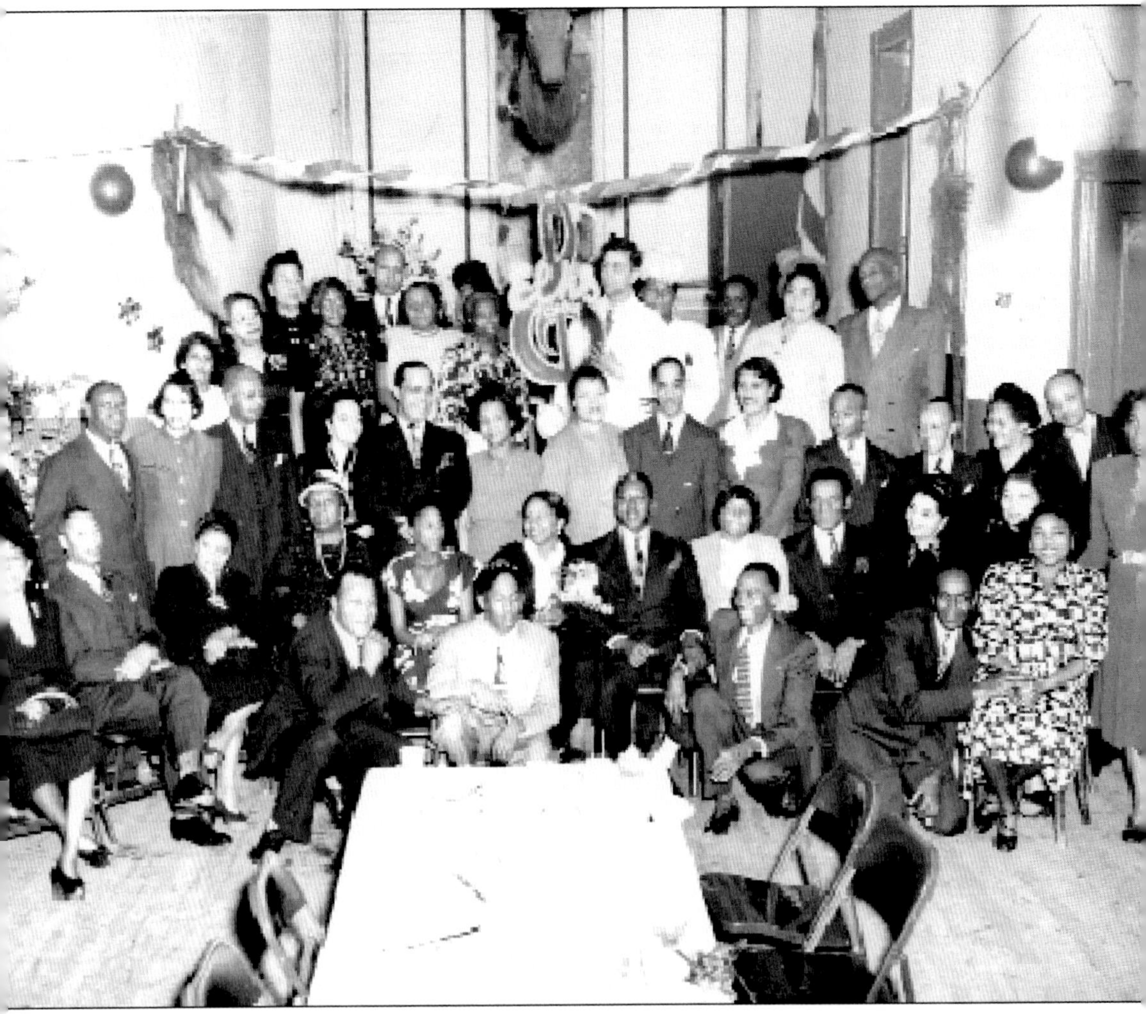

The area housed some of the most successful African-American schools, and the East Akron Community House helped organize the community to protect the neighborhood from government action to close schools.

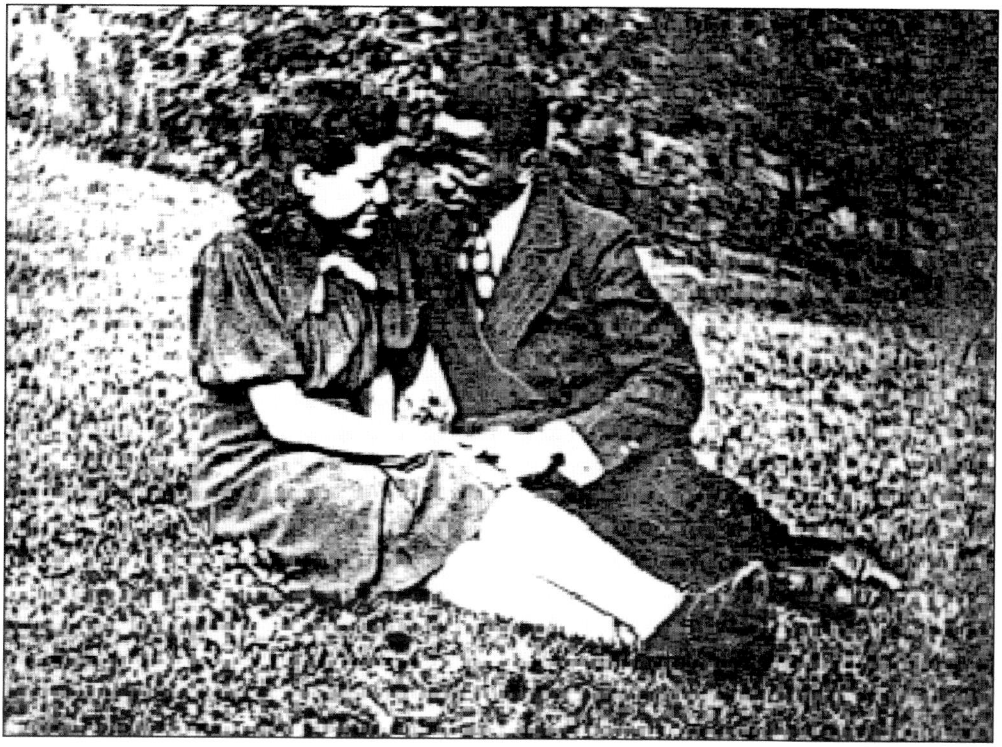

Leona Wright Farris and Melvin Farris celebrate a romantic moment while at Ohio State in 1939.

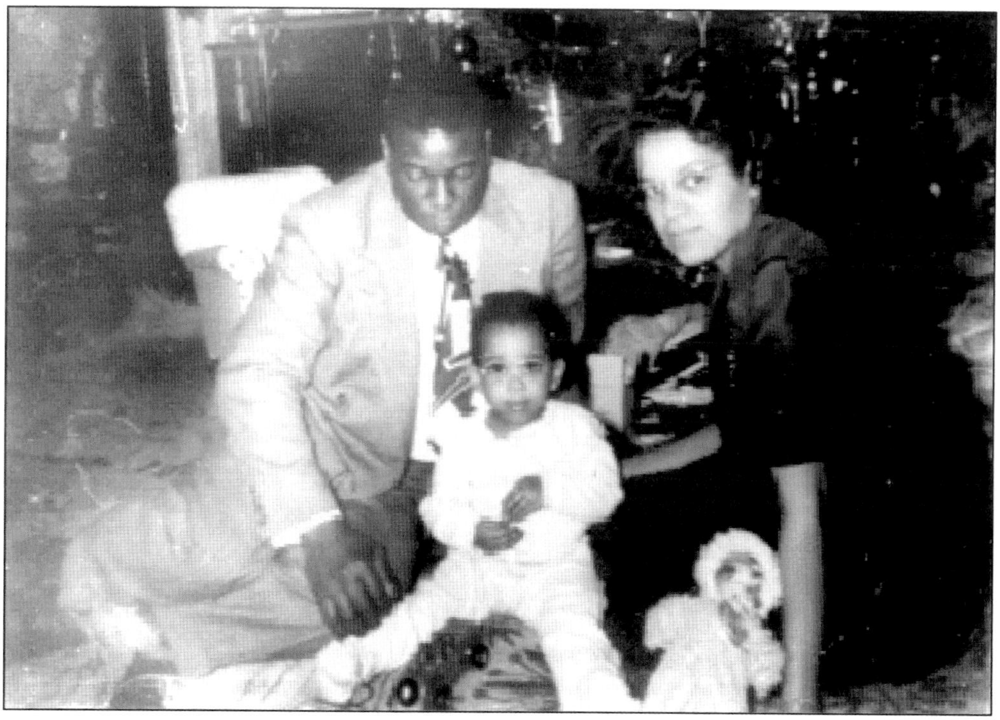

Dr. Farris celebrates Christmas with their daughter.

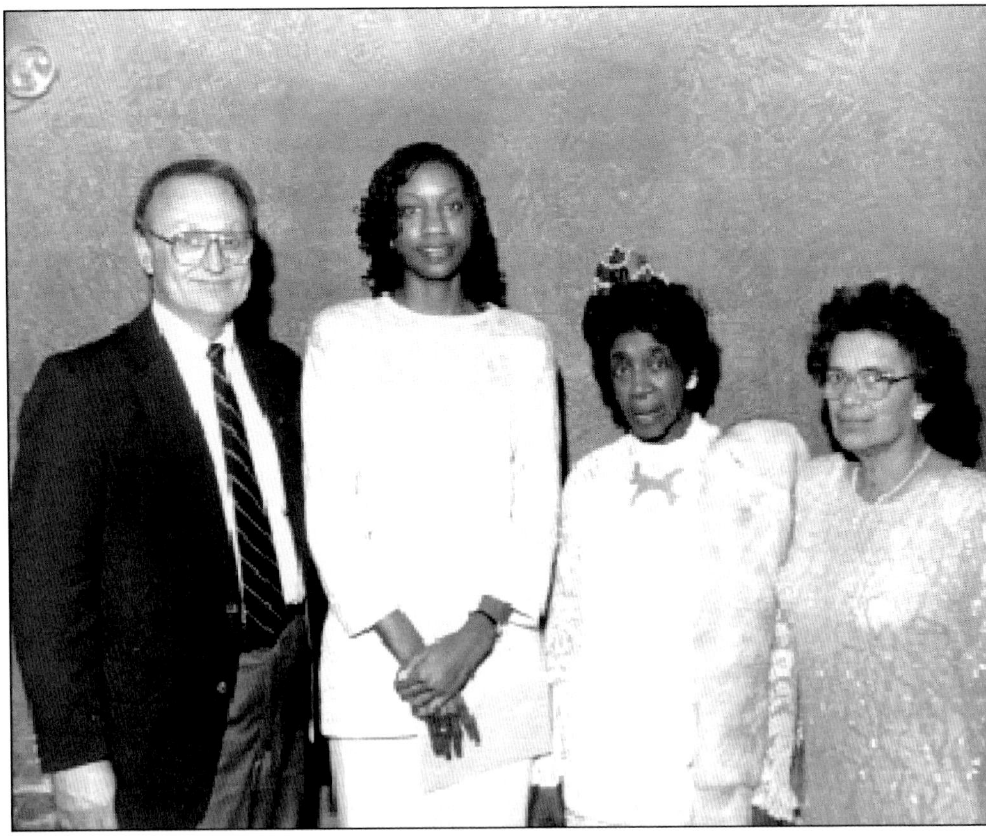

Former University of Akron President Muse, an unidentified student, Edith Delaney Mitchell, and Leona Farris participate in a scholarship program.

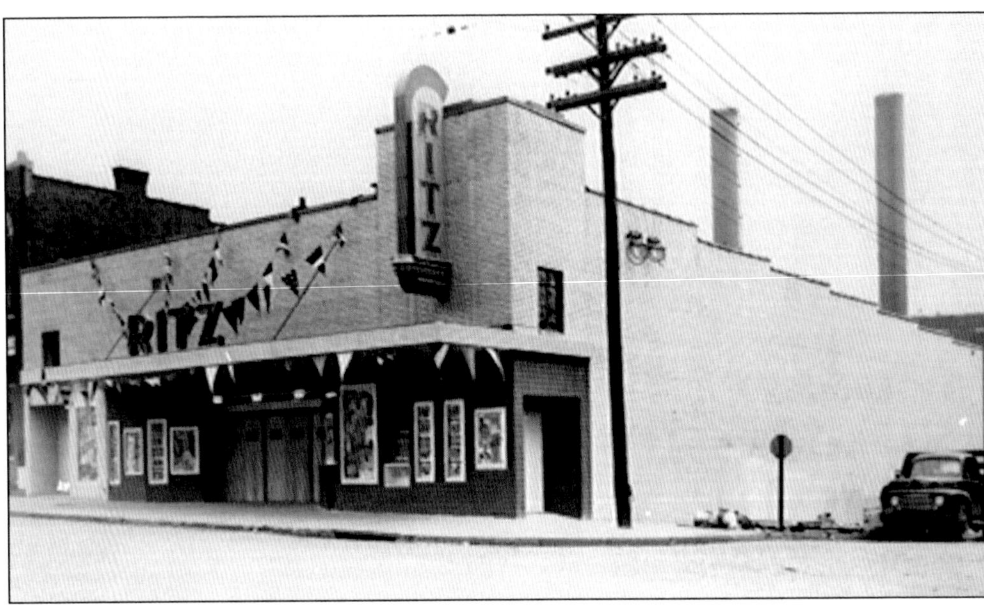

One of the many businesses located on Howard Street was the Ritz Theater.

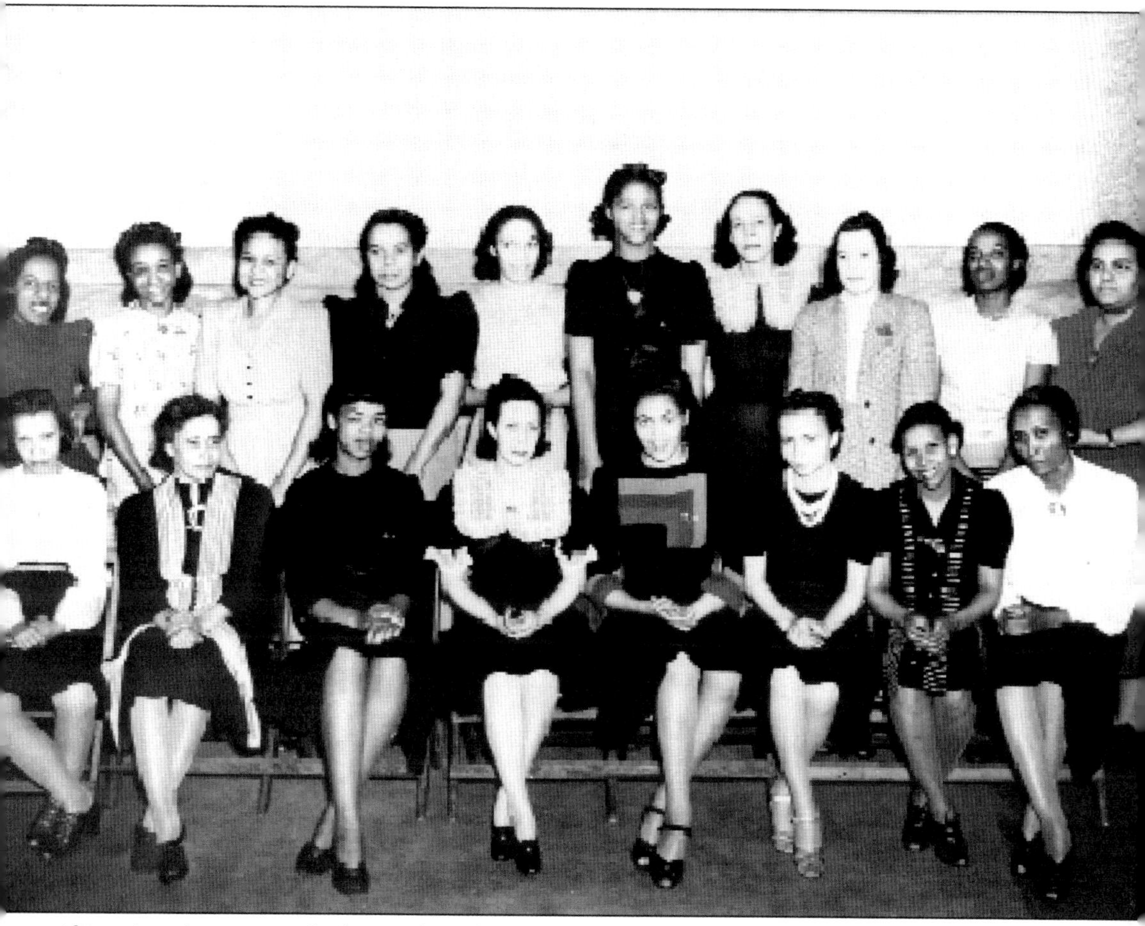

African-American women had a number of organizations, which helped form a sense of sisterhood.

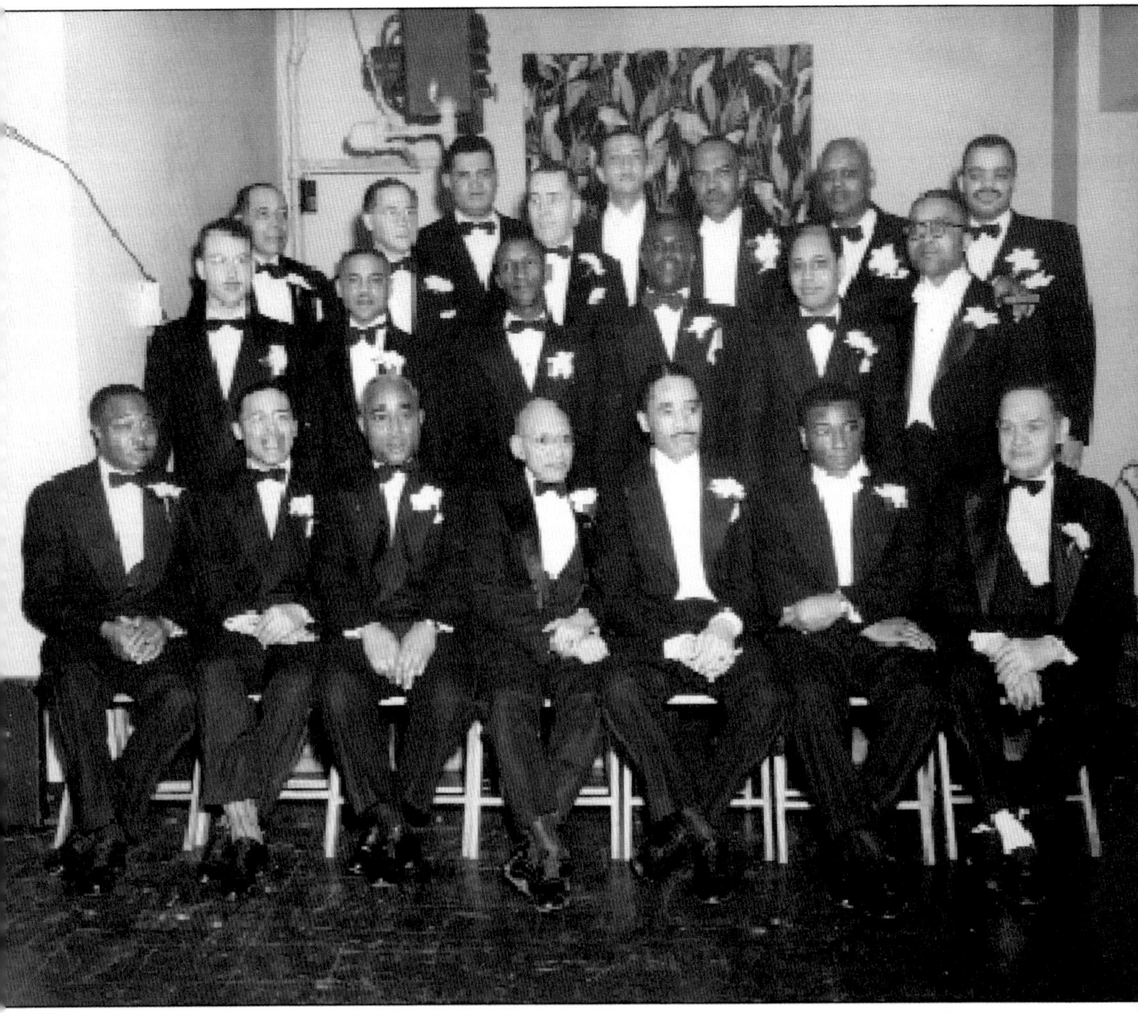

One of the most exclusive African-American men's groups was the Frontier's Club. This group picture has some of the most prominent African Americans in Akron. Included in the picture are Melvin Farris, second on the right, seated.

Six

Entertainment

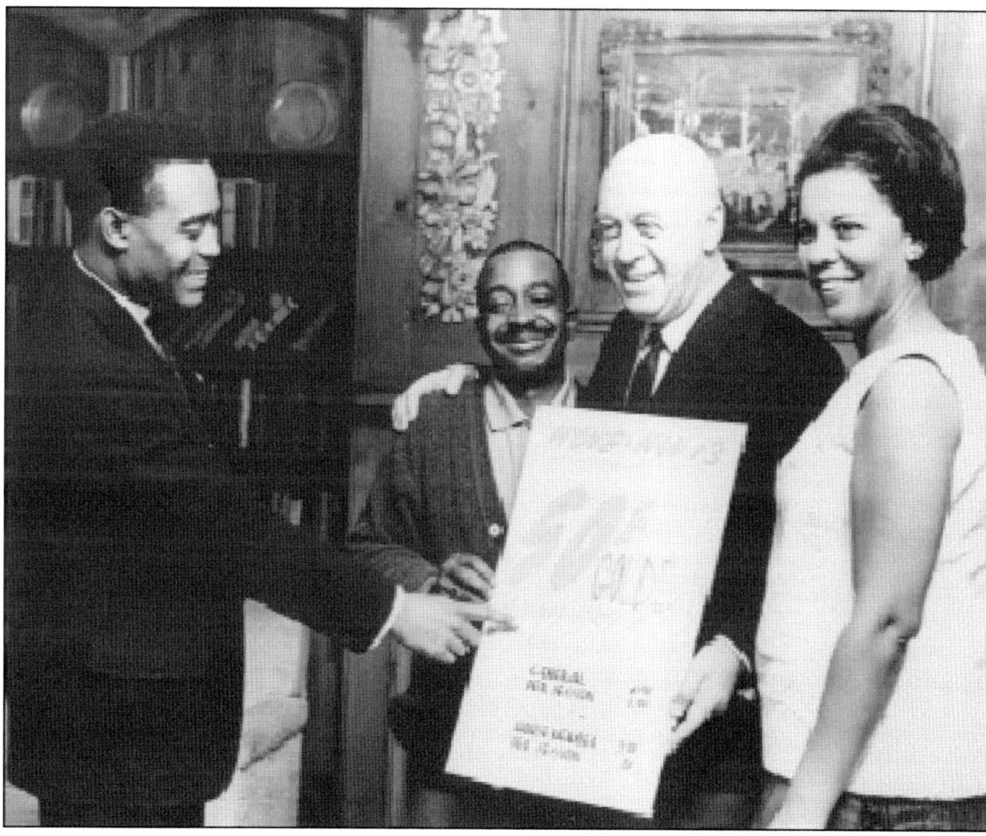

Otto Premiger helps open the Carmu House in Cleveland. Here Premiger holds a cut out of a ticket for the first production.

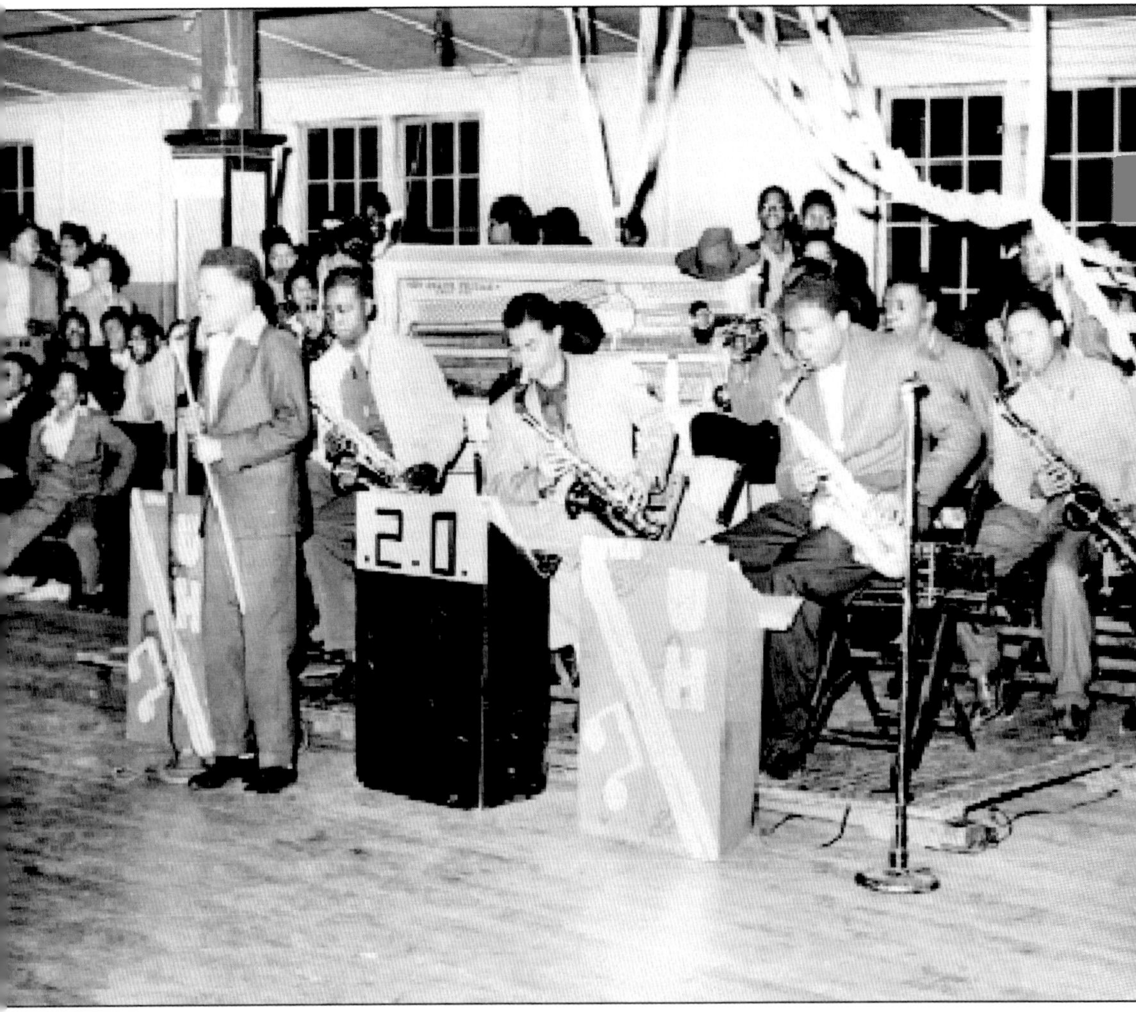

A band of young people plays during a community dance.

Charlena and Joel Fitzhugh pose for this picture. They were part of an entertainment group that started in Akron.

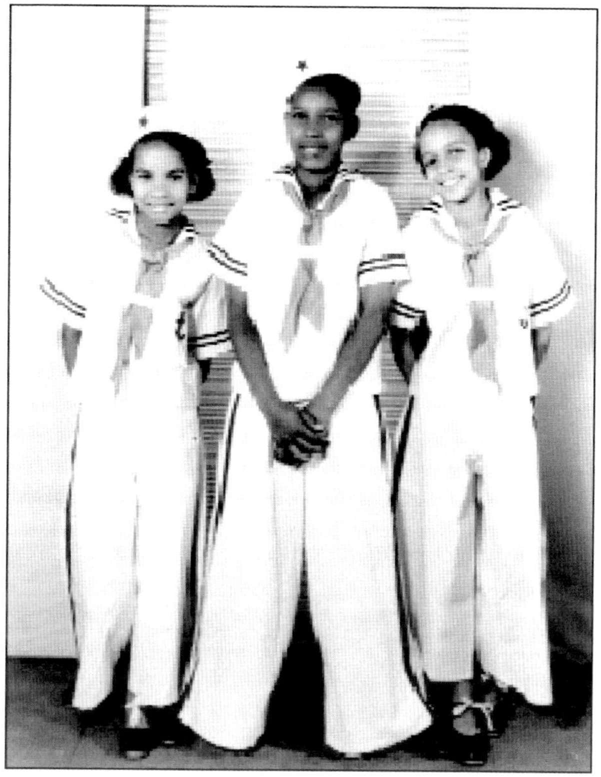

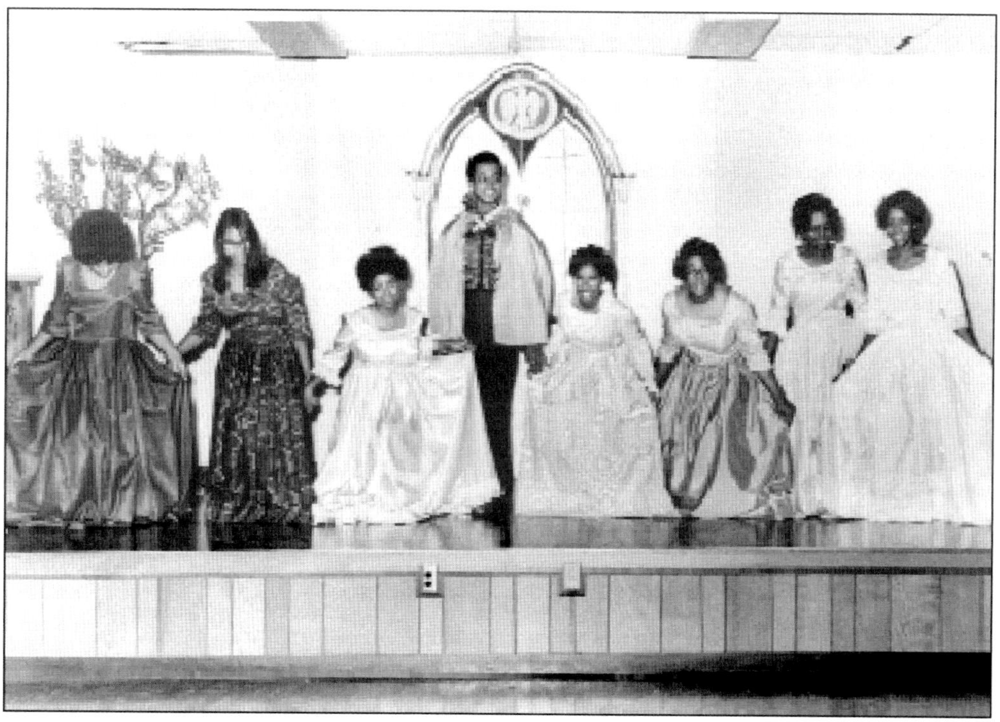

Students give a bow after a production of the *Soulful Cinderella*.

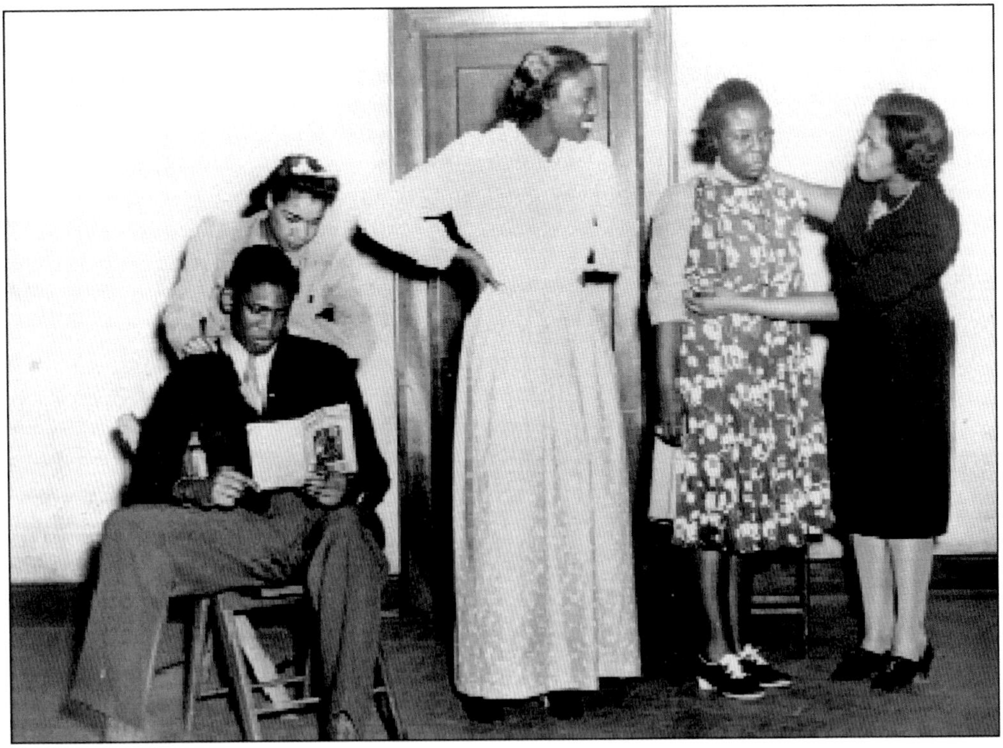

In this photograph the well-respected Dumas Players perform a play for the Akron community.

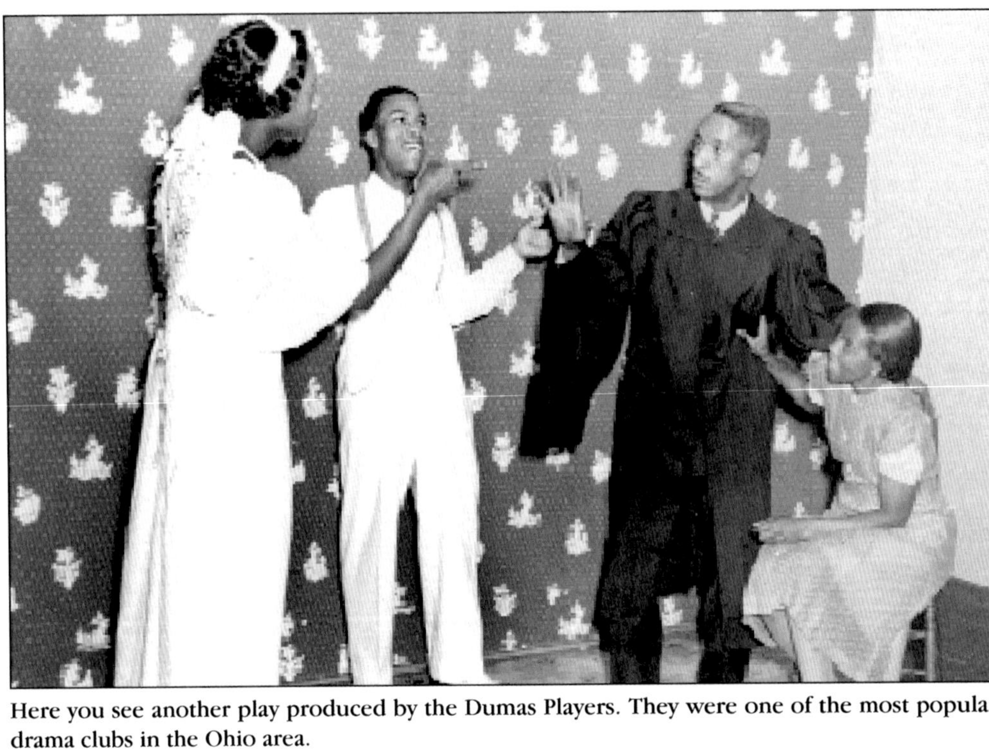

Here you see another play produced by the Dumas Players. They were one of the most popular drama clubs in the Ohio area.

Francine Murphy Taylor was a native of Akron who worked as a clothing, costume, and fashion designer who worked for several productions. She gained fame as a design artist.

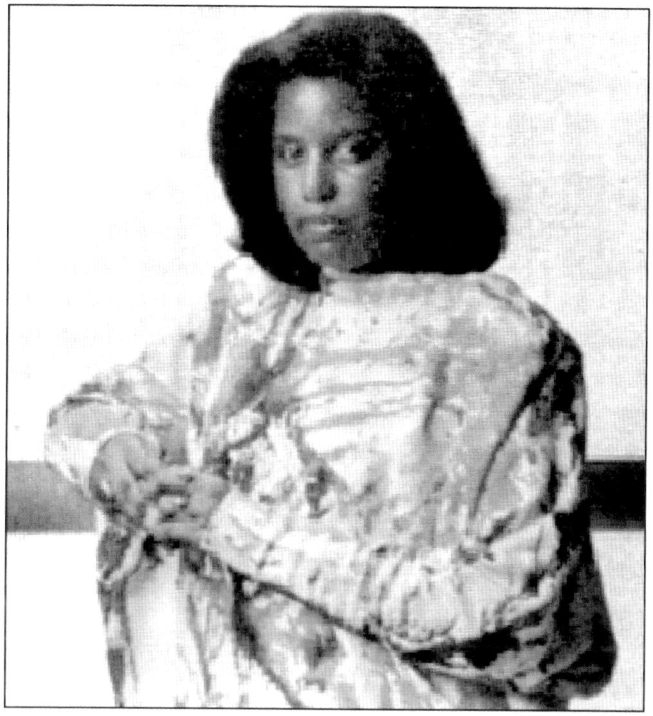

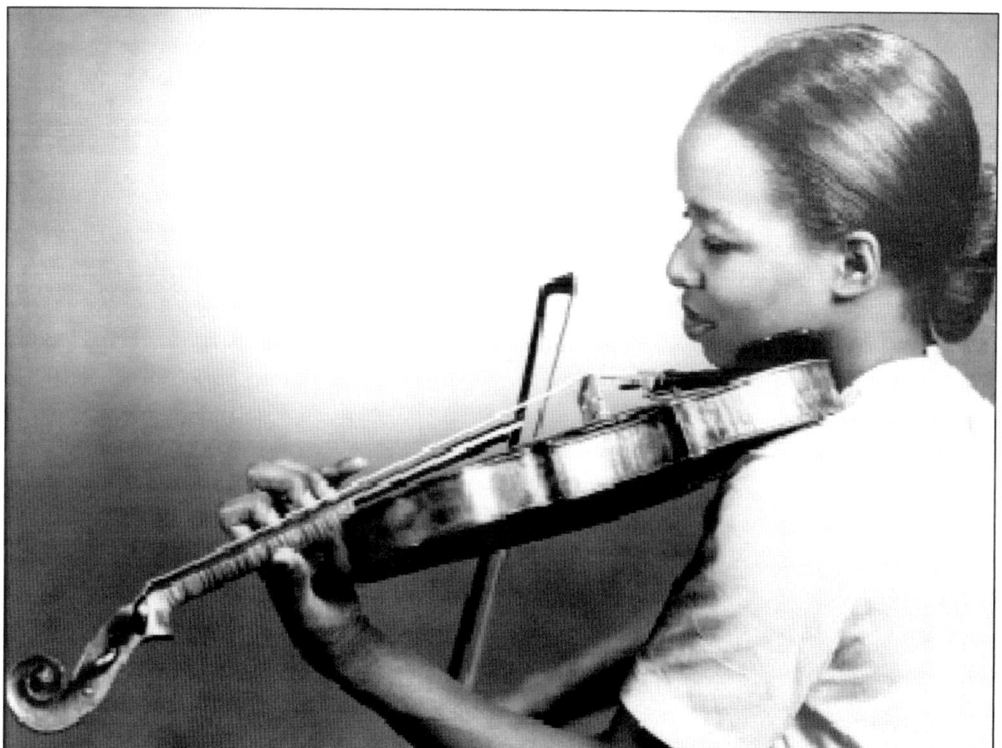

An unidentified young woman plays a violin during a concert in Akron.

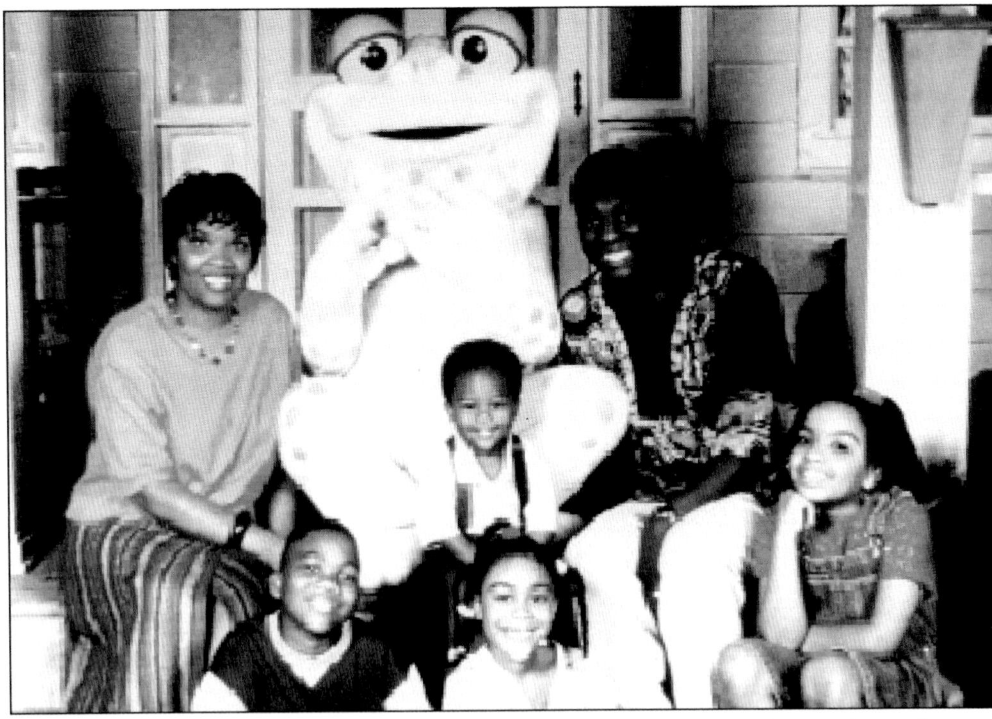

The *Gullah Gullah Island* Cast became popular with its appearances on *Sesame Street*. Some of the stars of this presentation were Akron natives. The *Gullah Gullah Island* Cast has produced several videos for kids that continue to sell.

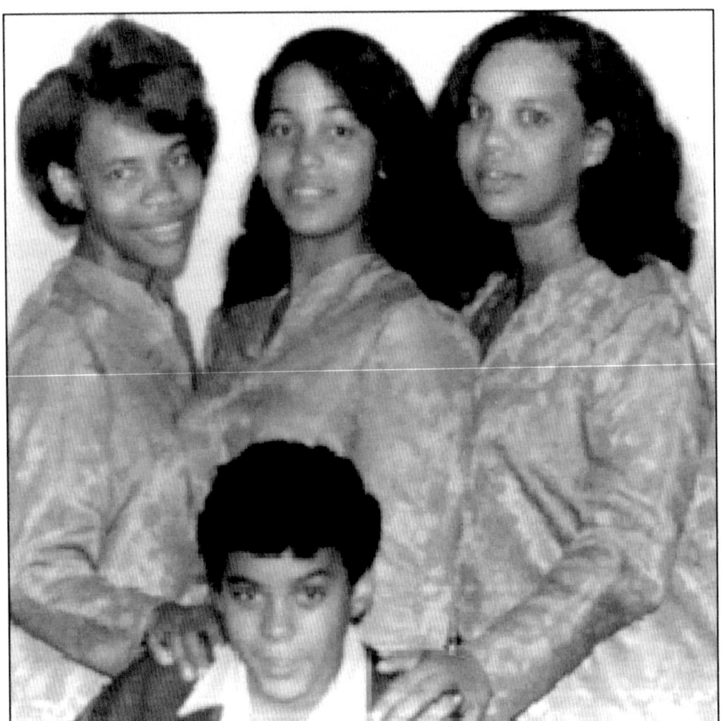

One of the most popular singing groups in Akron during this period was the Brown and Hewitt family singers.

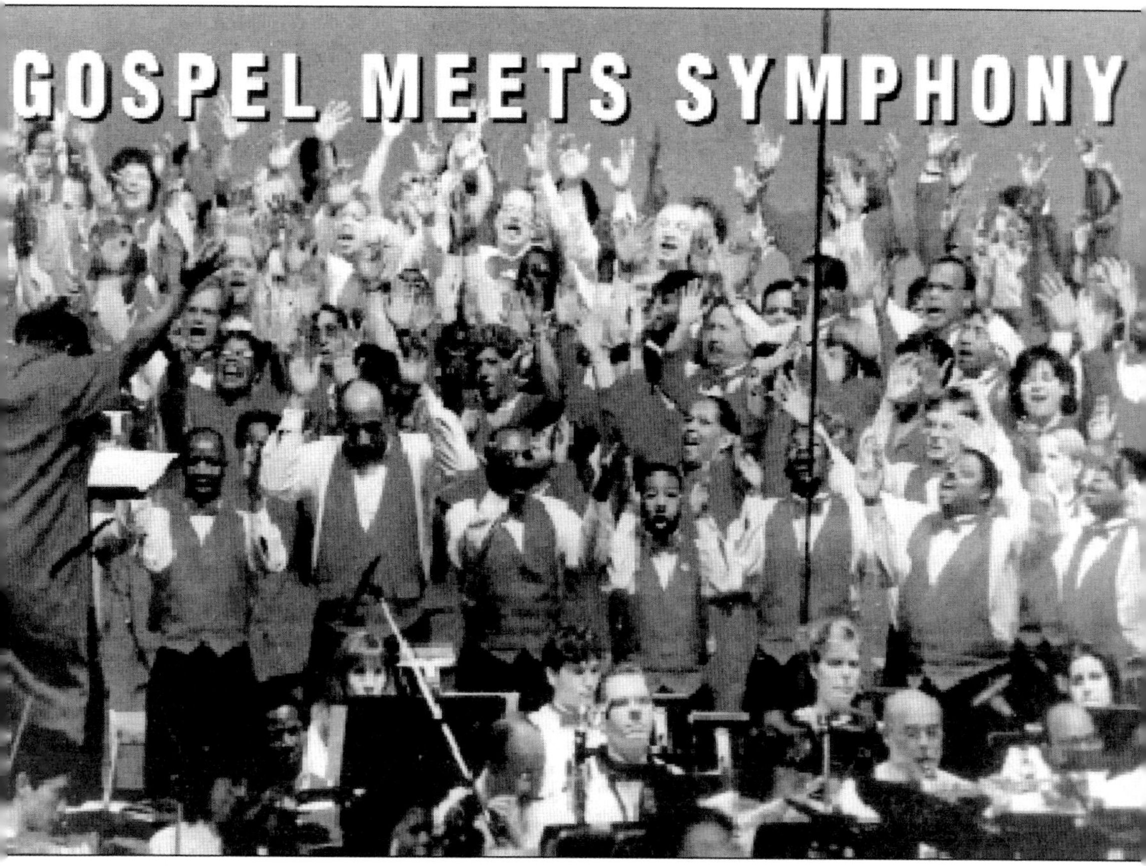

One of the most popular annual social events is the gospel-meets-symphony concert, which is held each year. This event brings people of all races and cultures together to enjoy varying musical styles.

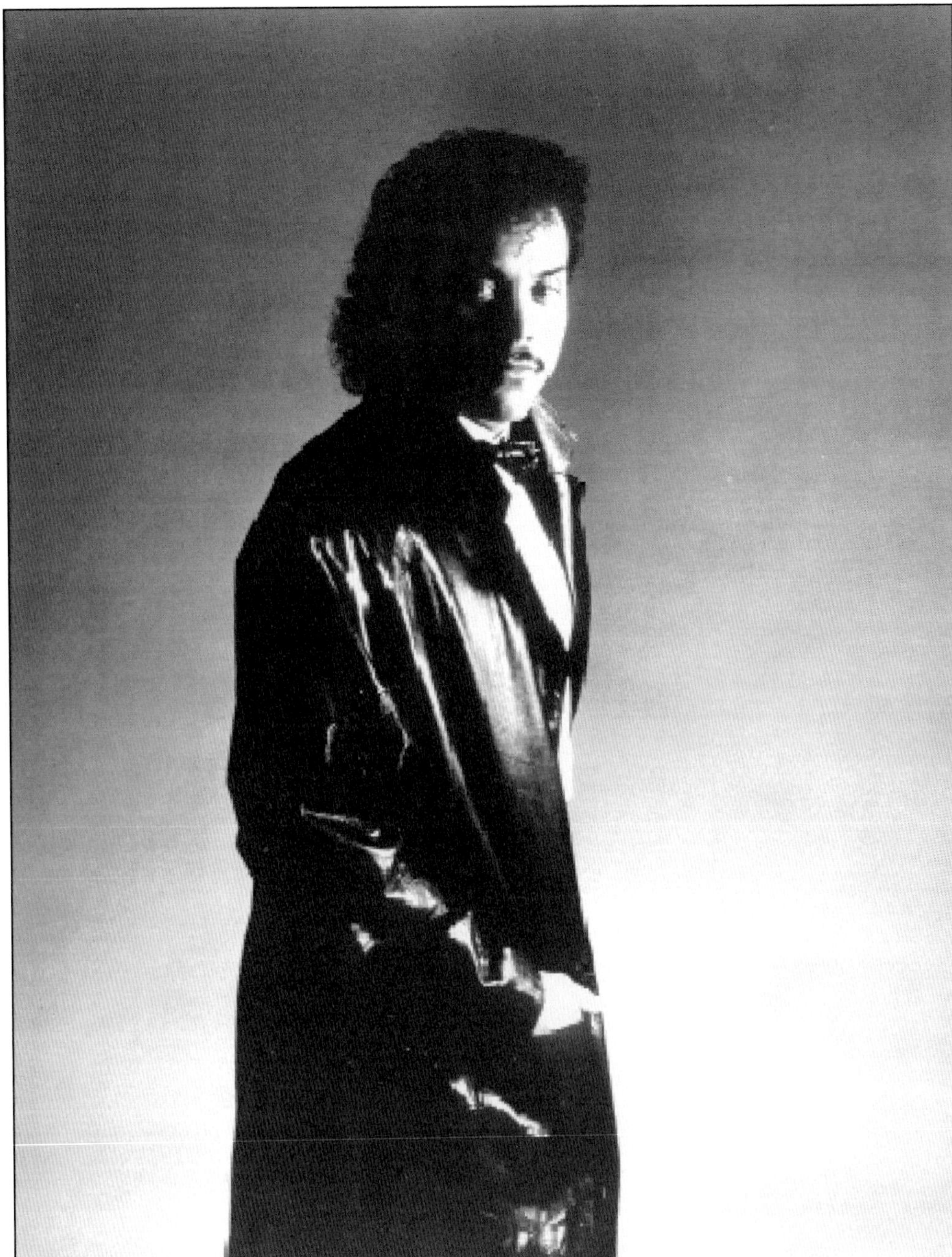

One of the most popular entertainers to hail from Akron was Howard Hewitt, who gained international fame as both a soloist and as part of the group Shalamar. Hewitt had a successful solo career recording such hits as "I am for Real."

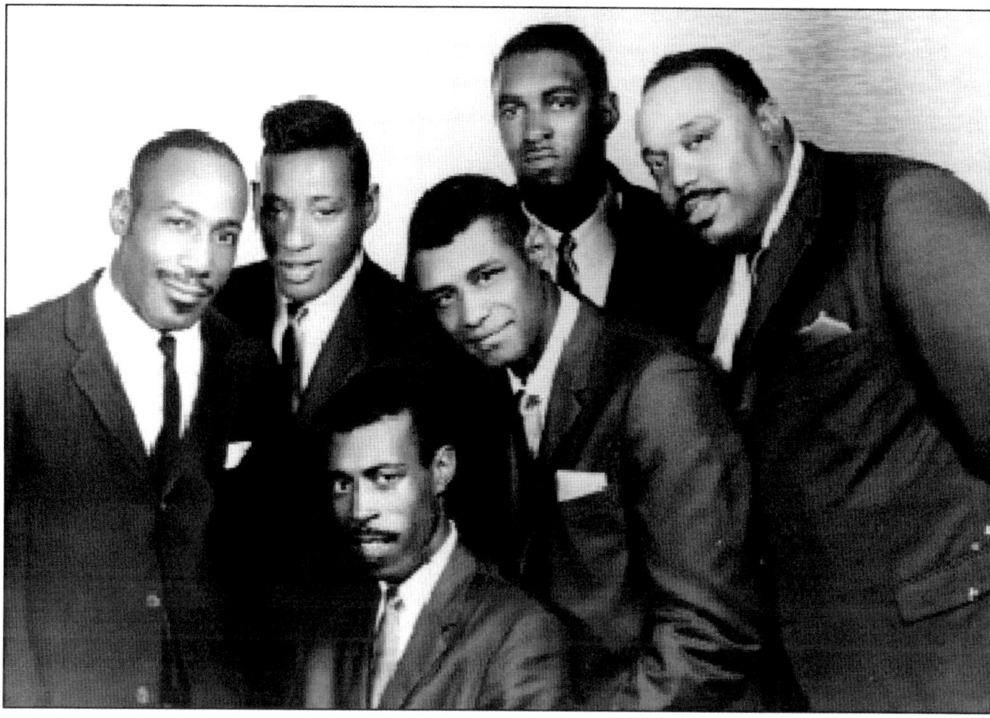

The Jackson quartet was a famous musical group that also came from Akron.

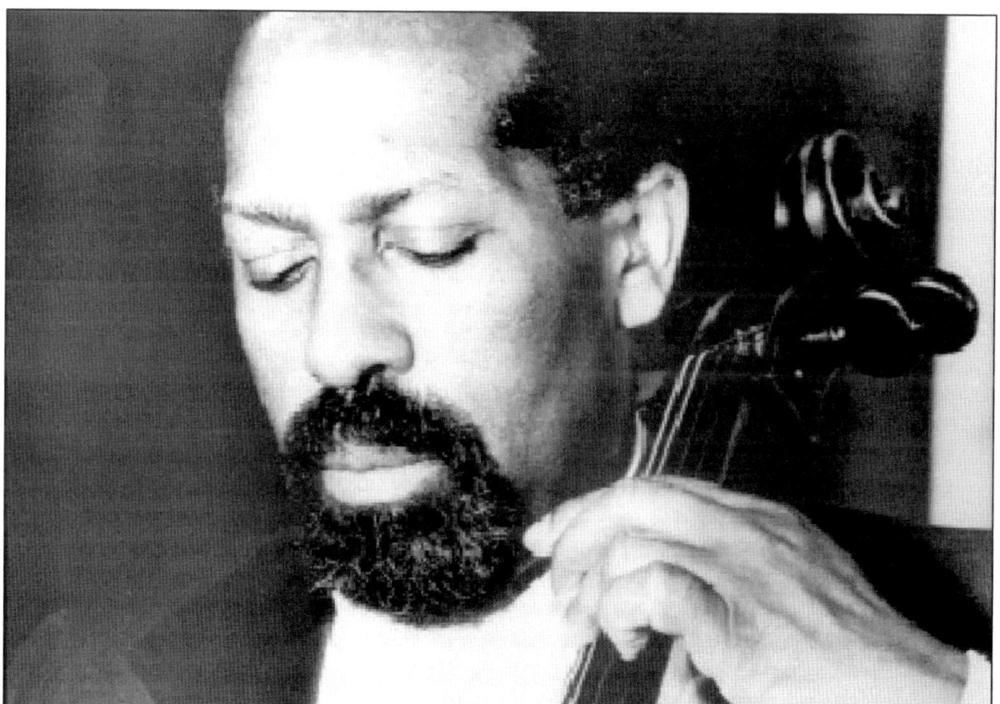

One of the most famous musicians of this era is Akron-native Kermit Moore. Here Moore plays in a concert.

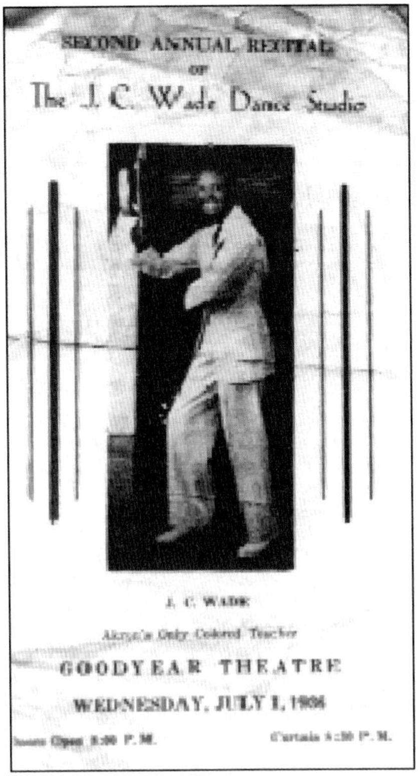

The J.C. Wade Dance Studio was a training ground for young dancers of all races. Wade was the only African-American dance teacher in Akron.

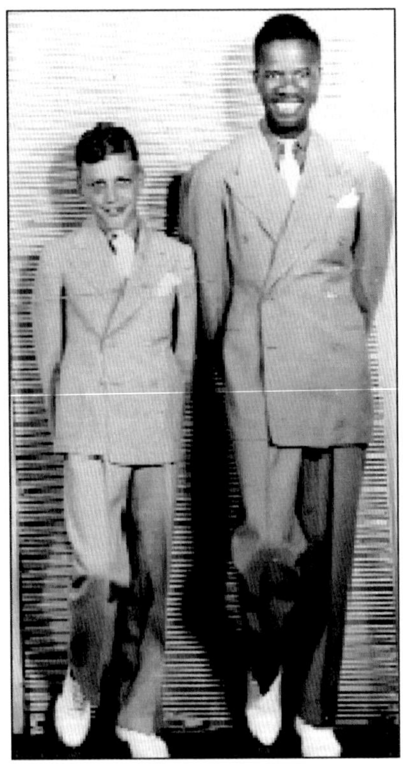

J.C. Wade and Billy Parson made a wonderful tandem when they did their dance routine. They traveled the country entertaining audiences.

Jessie C. Wade gained national prominence for his dance styles and was one of the most popular teachers of dance in the Akron area.

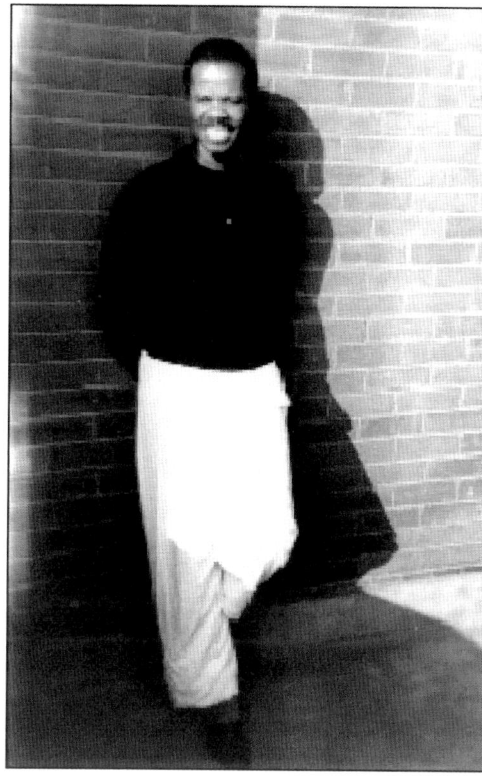

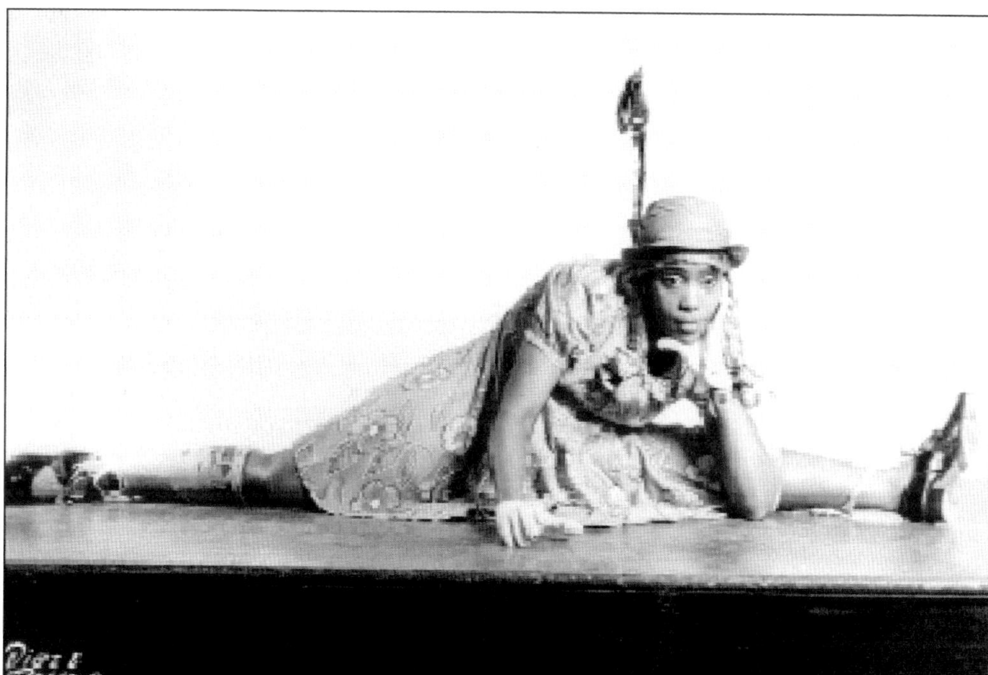

Merry Delaney, an Akron native, was a successful actress, starring in several productions that gained acclaim.

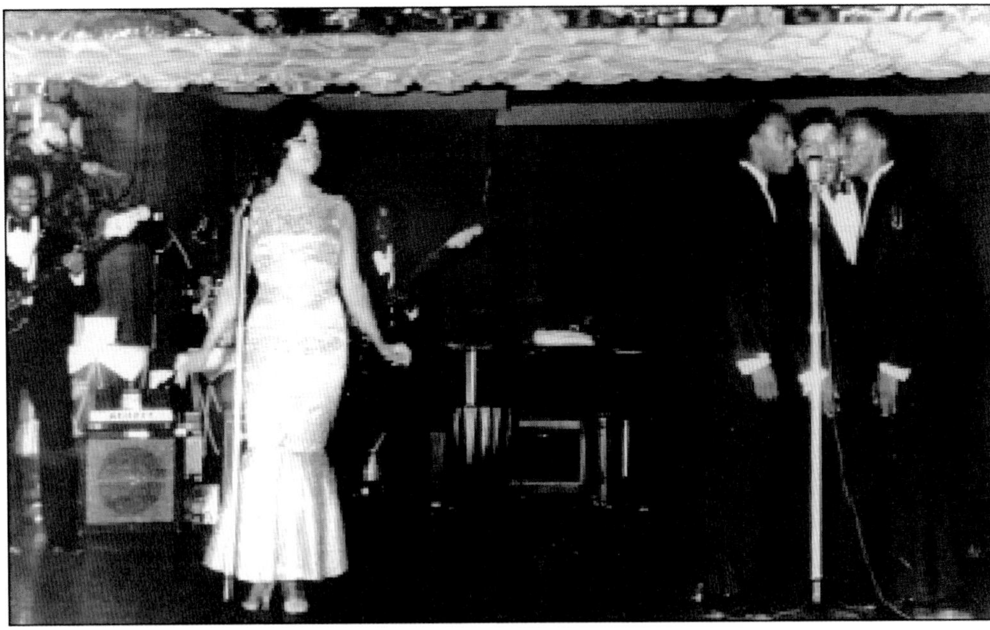

In this photograph Ruby and the Romantics, an Akron group, performs during a concert. This group had several hits during the 1960s. The group was originally organized in Akron in 1961 as the Supremes. The groups consisted of Ruby Nash, Ed Roberts, George Lee, Ronald Mosely, and Leroy Fann. They gained national acclaim with the single, "Our Day Will Come." This hit was followed by "My Summer Love" and "Hey There Lonely Boy."

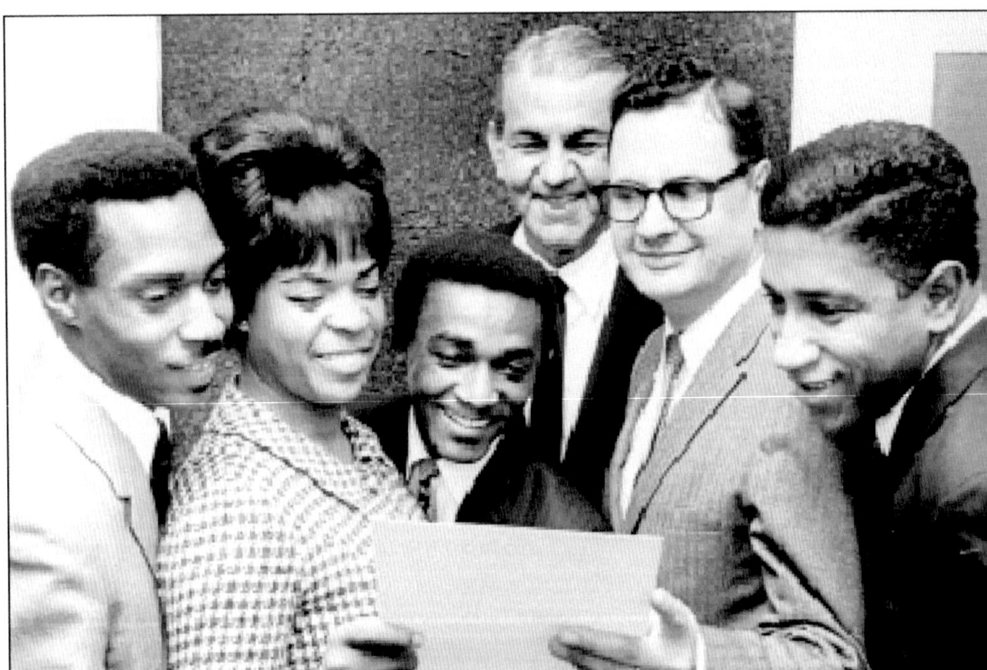

Ruby and the Romantics share an exciting moment with Akron Mayor John Ballard. The entire city shared in the success of this Akron group.

Akron was the hometown to several singing groups that gained fame during various periods. In this picture we see the Renowns.

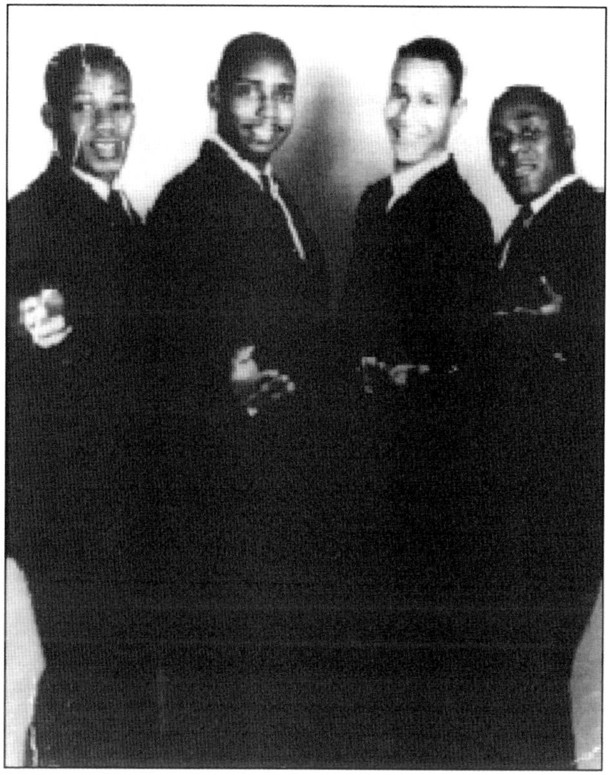

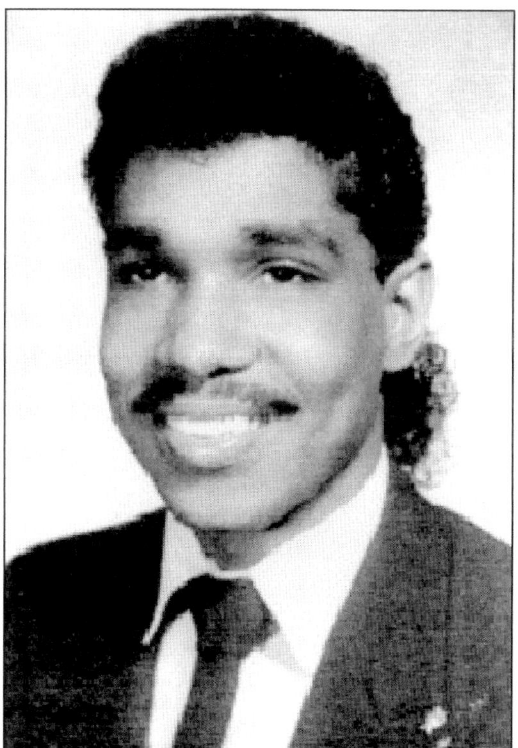

Bobby Jackson was an actor who starred in several plays and productions after graduating from the University of Akron. He also self-published a magazine that was highly acclaimed.

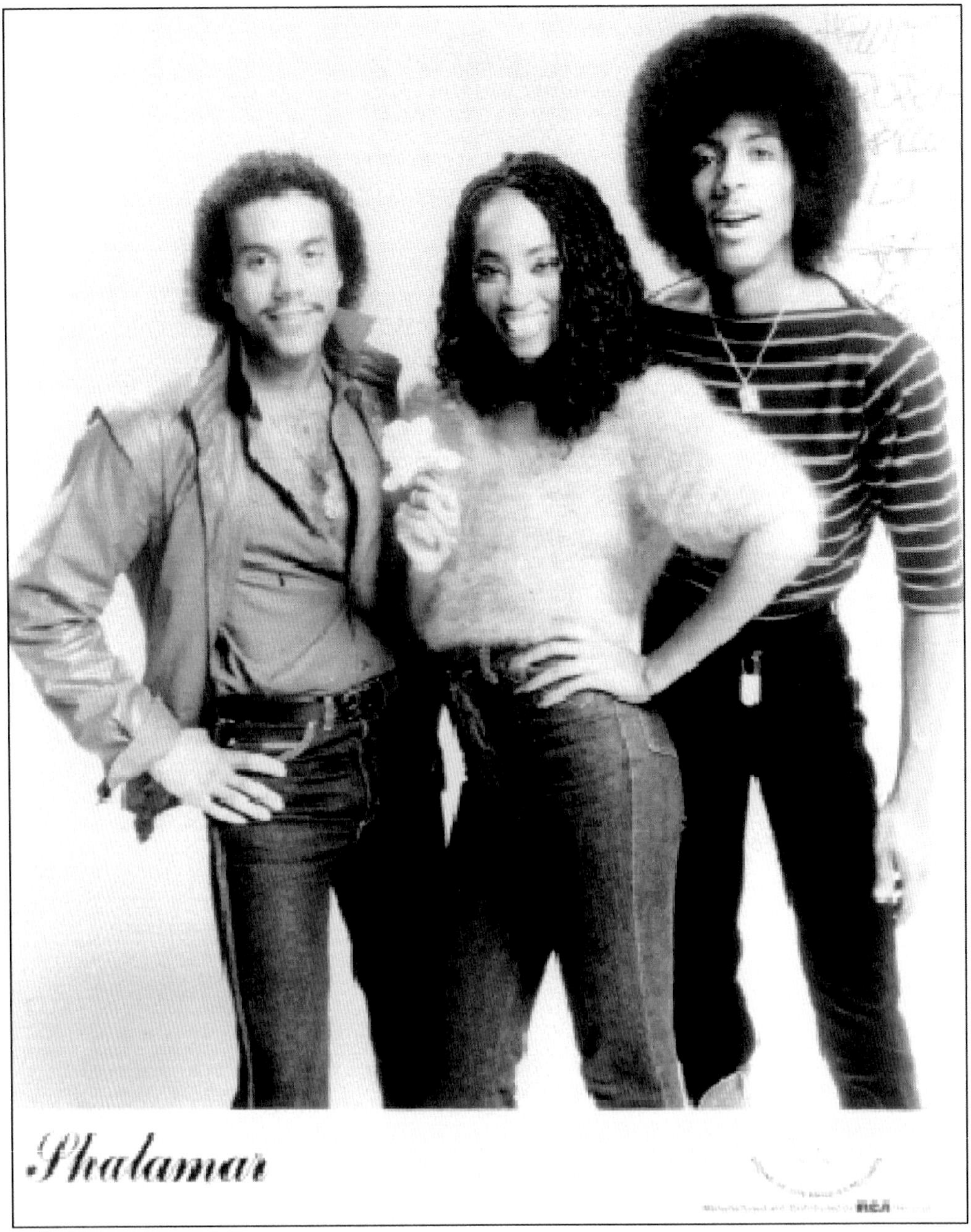

In 1979, Howard Hewitt joined the group Shalamar after another singer left the group. Shalamar, which consisted of Hewitt, Jody Watley, and Jeffrey Daniel, was an instant success with their album *Big Fun*.

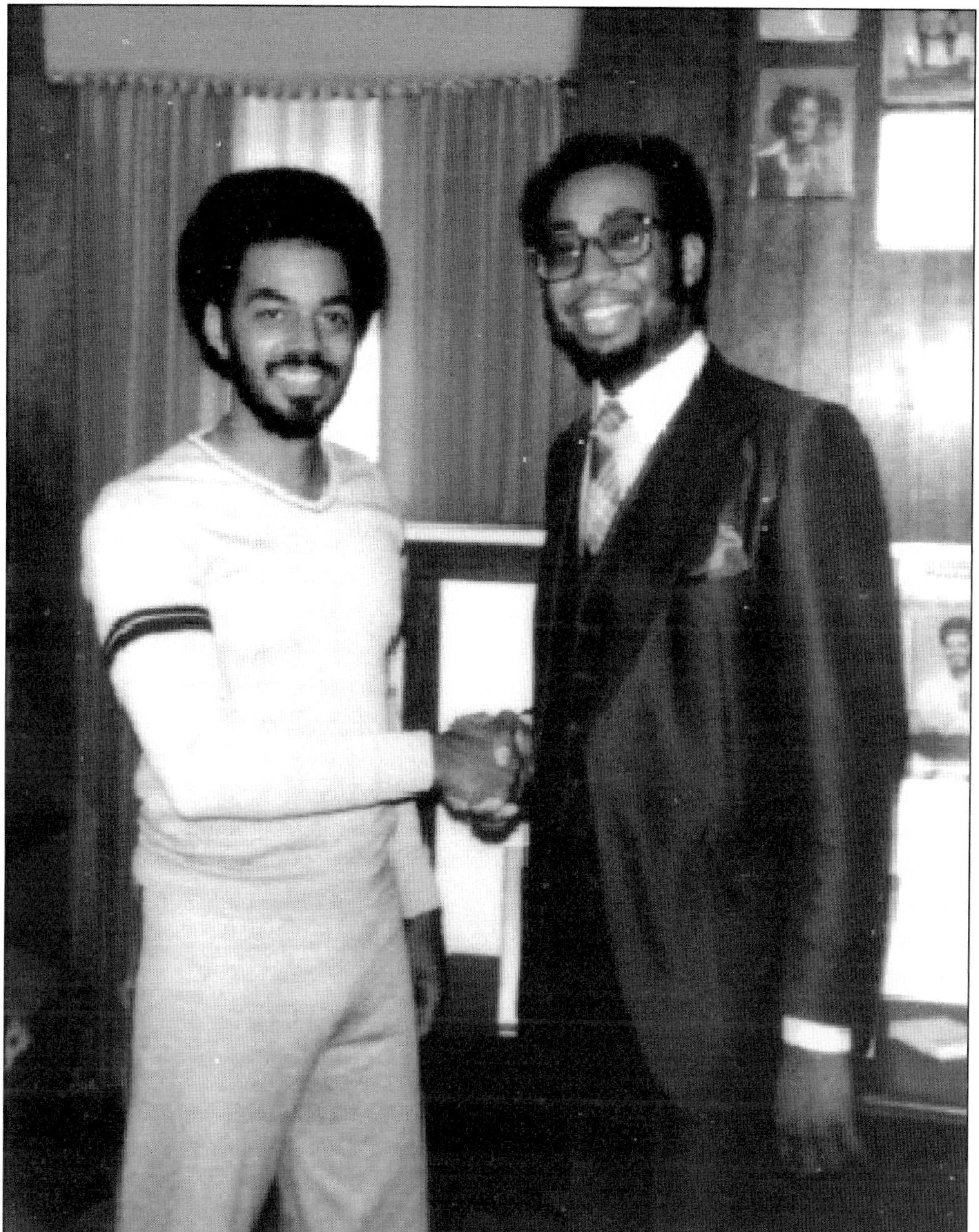

Two of the most recognized Akron musicians are pictured here. James Ingram and Eugene Sharpey shake hands after a meeting in Akron. James left Akron in 1973 to seek fame in the singing industry as part of the funk group Revelation Funk. He worked as a backup artist for several singers before gaining international fame and winning several Grammies for his music. In 1981 Ingram won a Grammy for his album *Just Once*. The album had several successful singles including, "Yah Mo B There," "One Hundred Ways," and others.

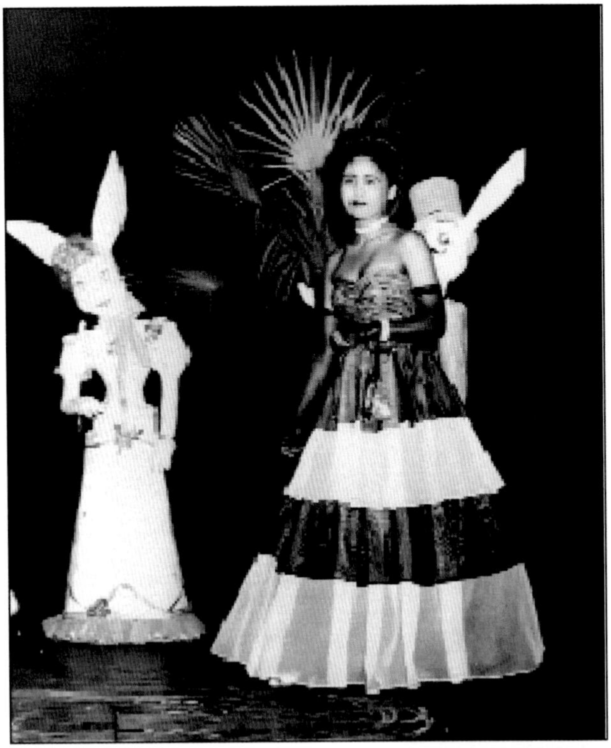

Valvane Robinson was an actress hailing from Akron who had modest success on the stage. She received acclaim for both her singing and acting.

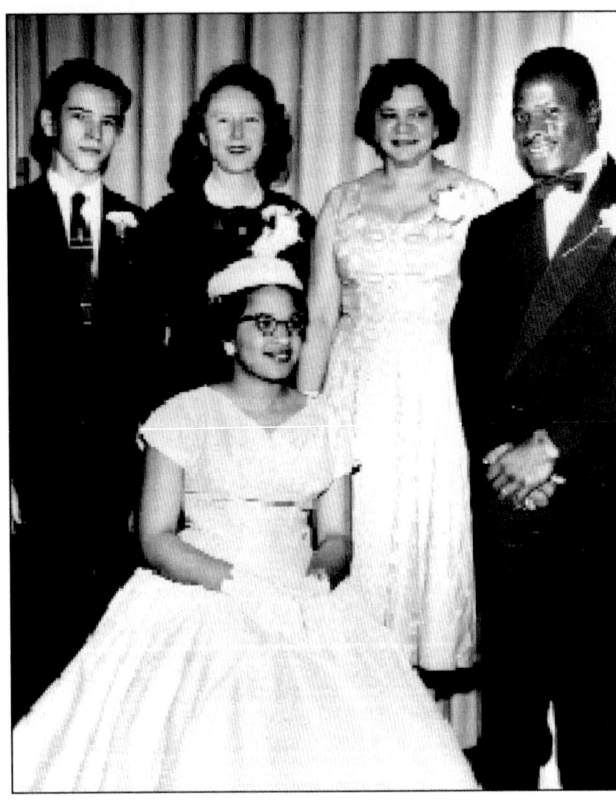

Loucelia Roy performs in a theatrical production in Akron.

Seven

SPORTS

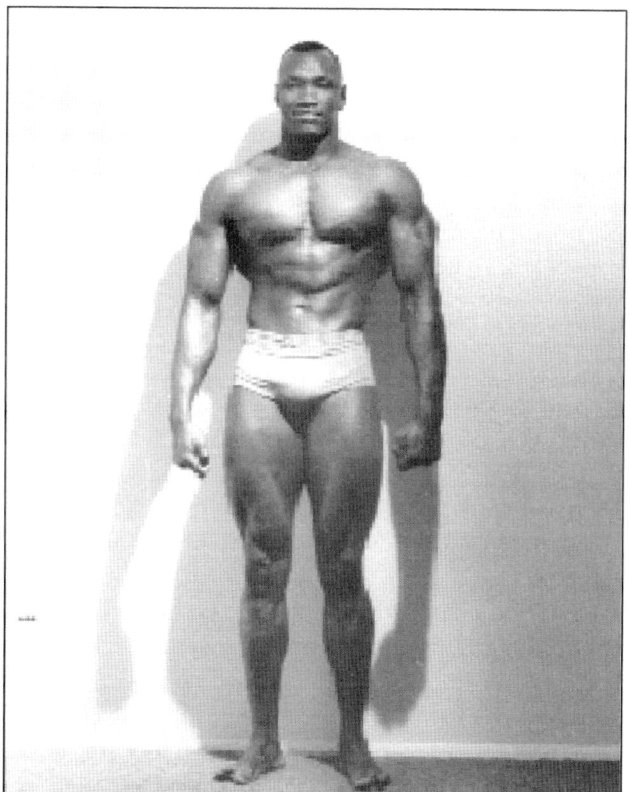

Health and fitness are very important for many young African Americans in Akron. An unidentified bodybuilder who worked out in Akron is shown in this picture.

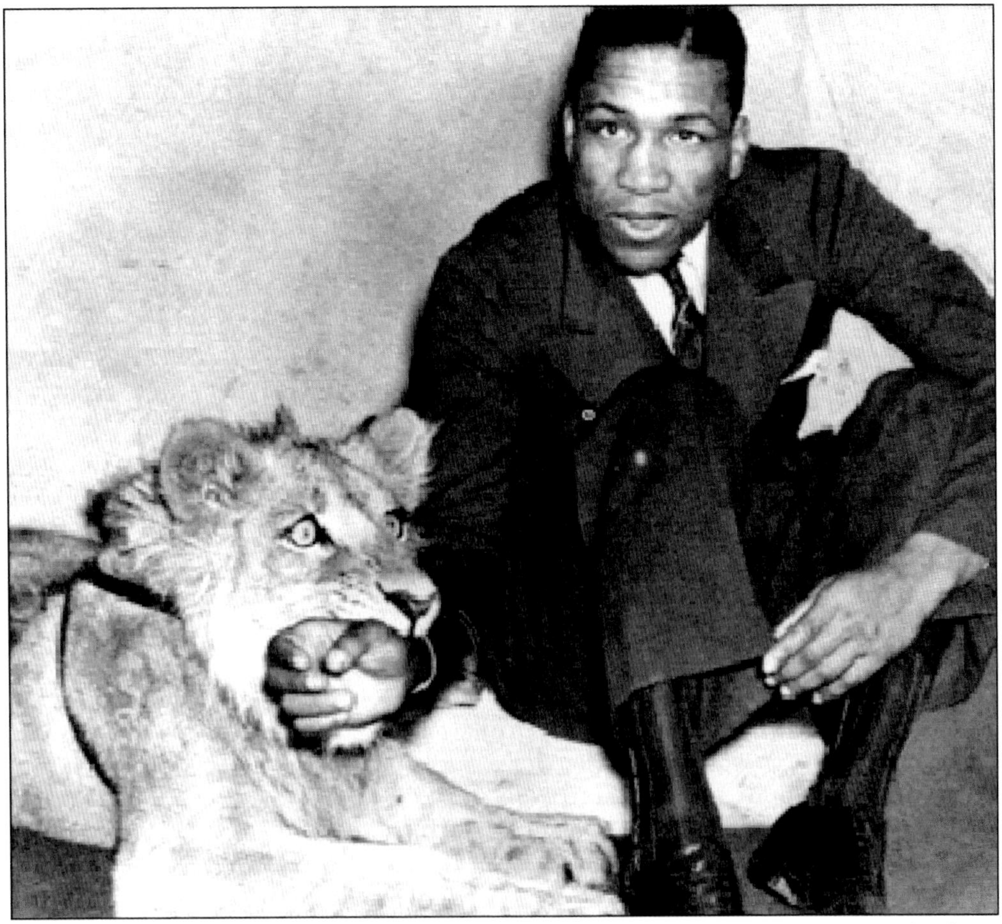

Gorilla Jones was one of the many boxers who hailed from Akron. Here Jones poses with a lion.

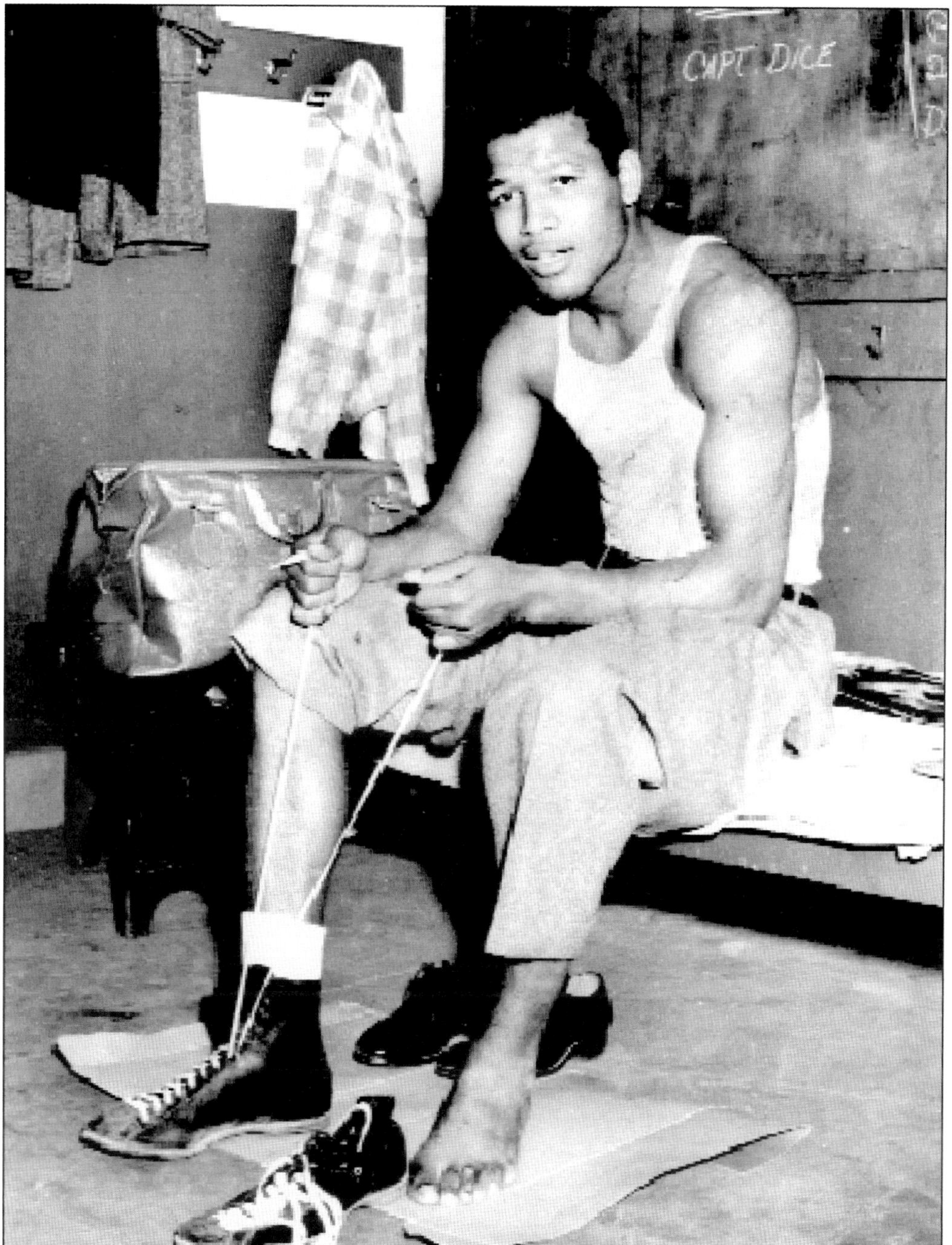

One of the boxers who spent time training in an Akron gym was a young Joe Louis.

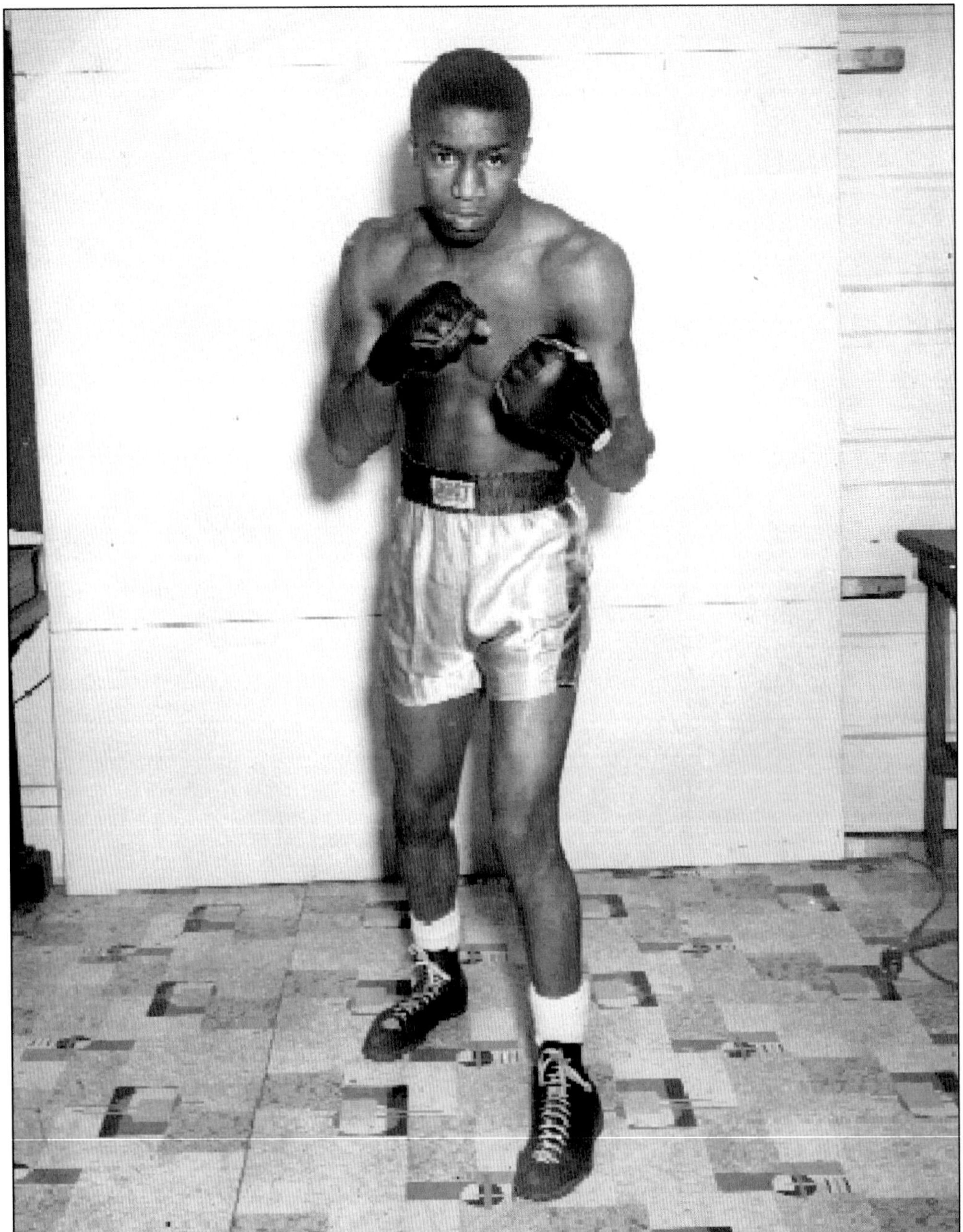

Ron Delaney received a great deal of acclaim as he rose up the boxing charts. Here are some pictures from an article on Ron Delaney in *Ring Magazine*.

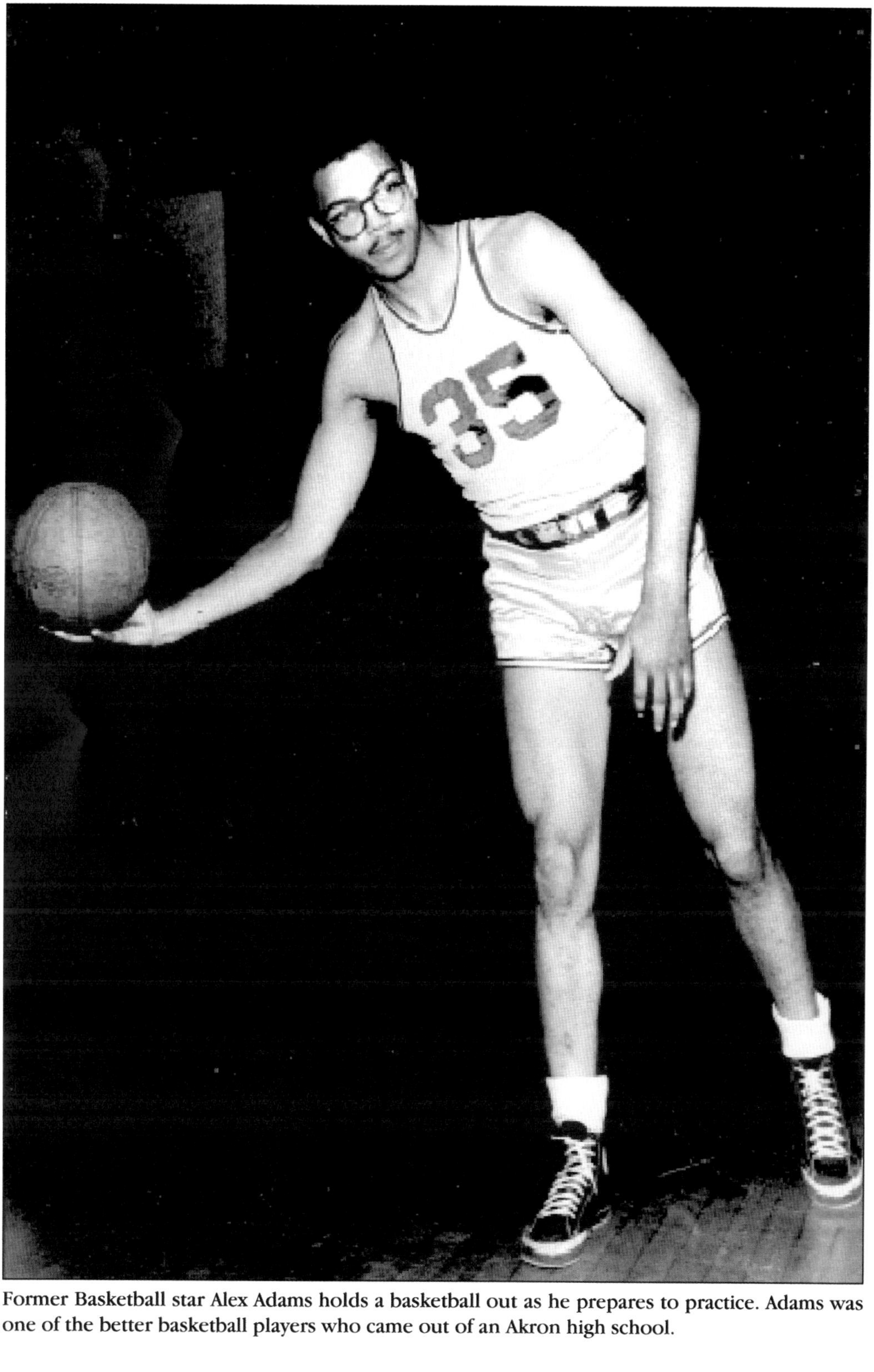

Former Basketball star Alex Adams holds a basketball out as he prepares to practice. Adams was one of the better basketball players who came out of an Akron high school.

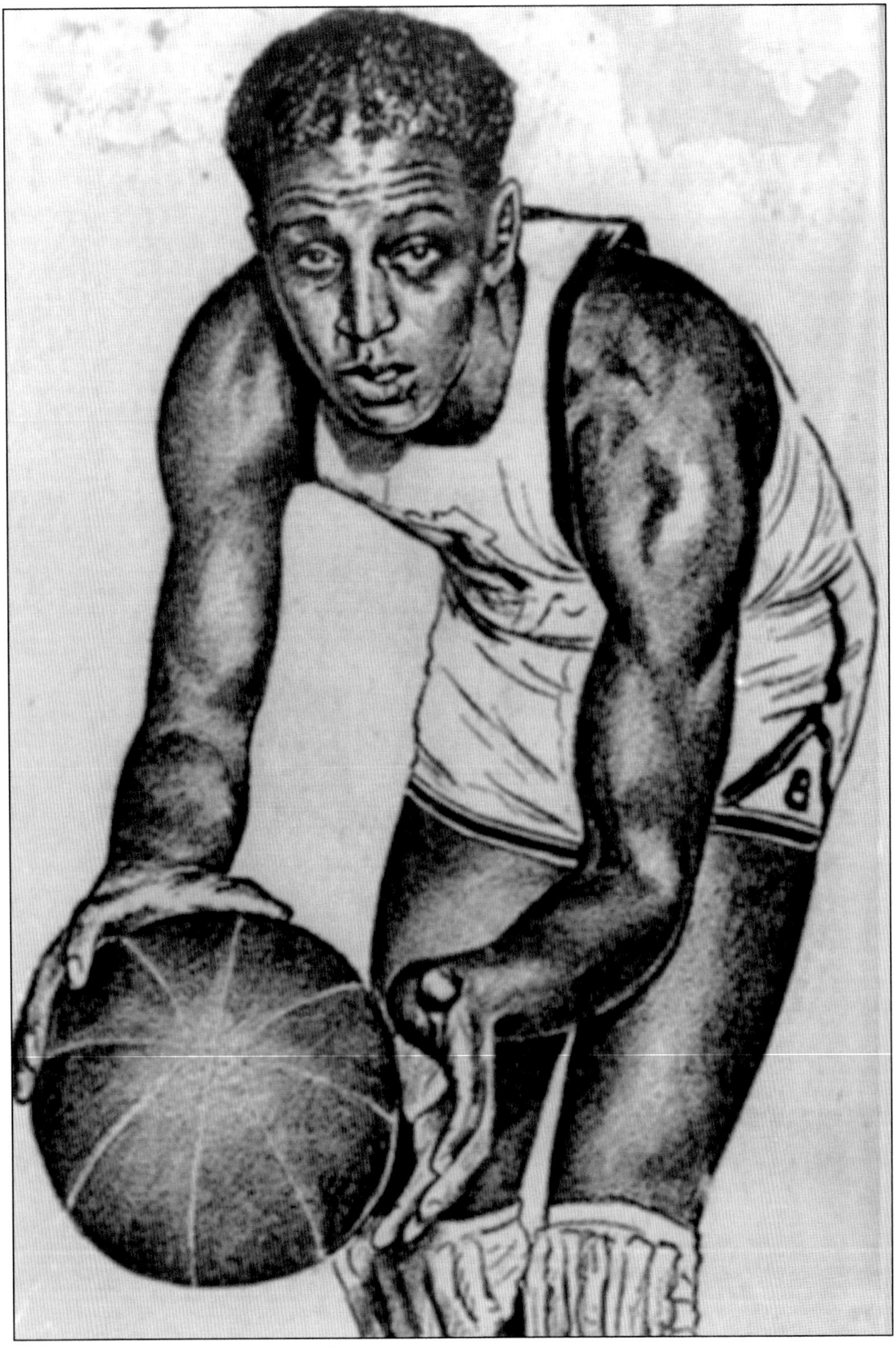

Andy Averitt poses with a basketball in this picture.

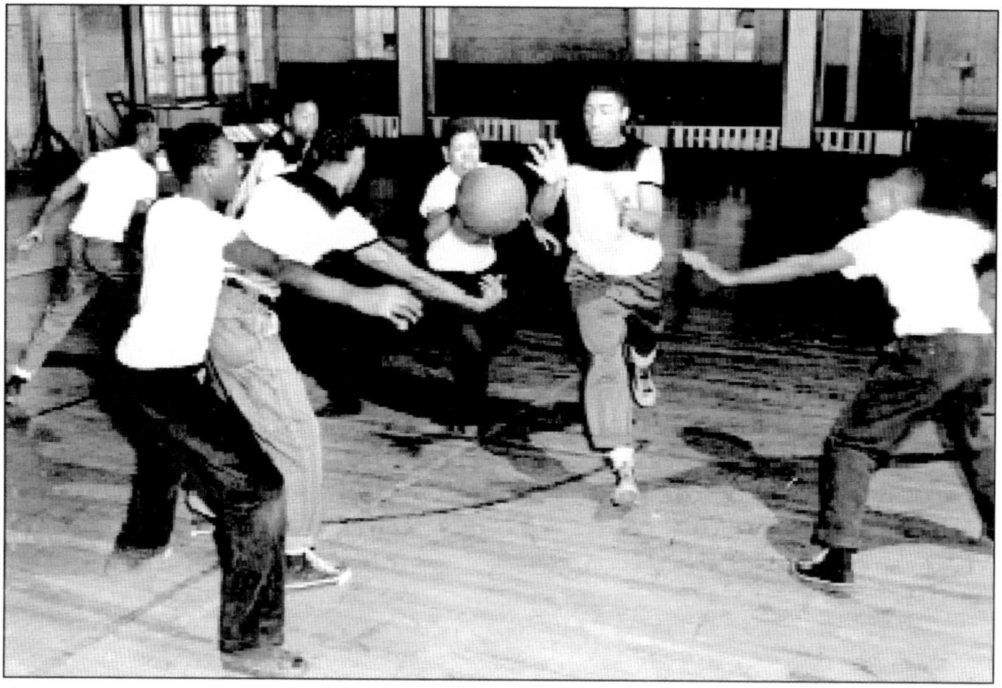

One of the many meeting places for youth in Akron was the community center. Here boys play an intense game of basketball at a local Akron community center.

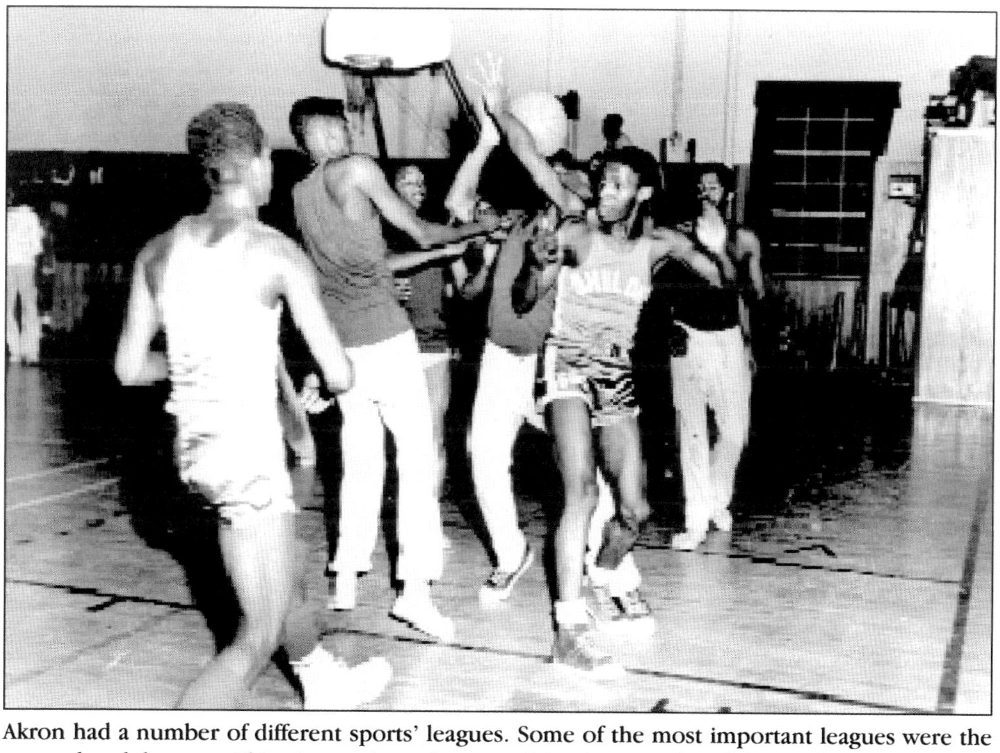

Akron had a number of different sports' leagues. Some of the most important leagues were the many church leagues. This picture shows boys participating in a church-league basketball game.

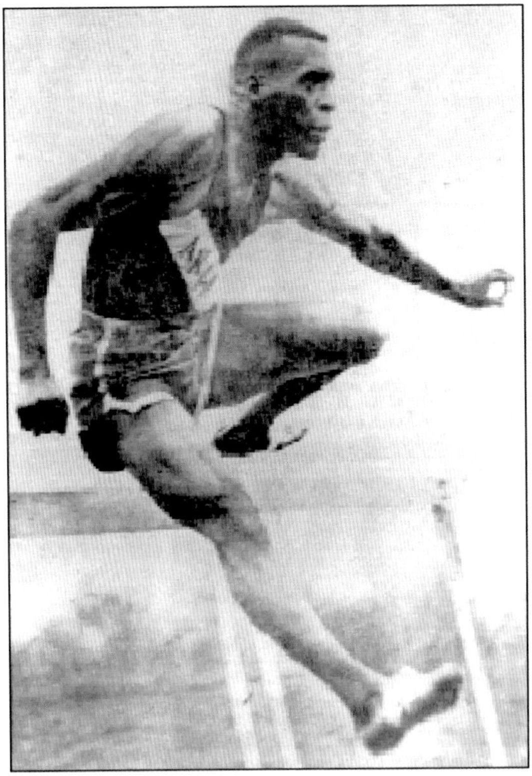

Former track star Climmon Lee was an Akron native. In this picture you can see the wonderful form that made Lee such a dangerous competitor.

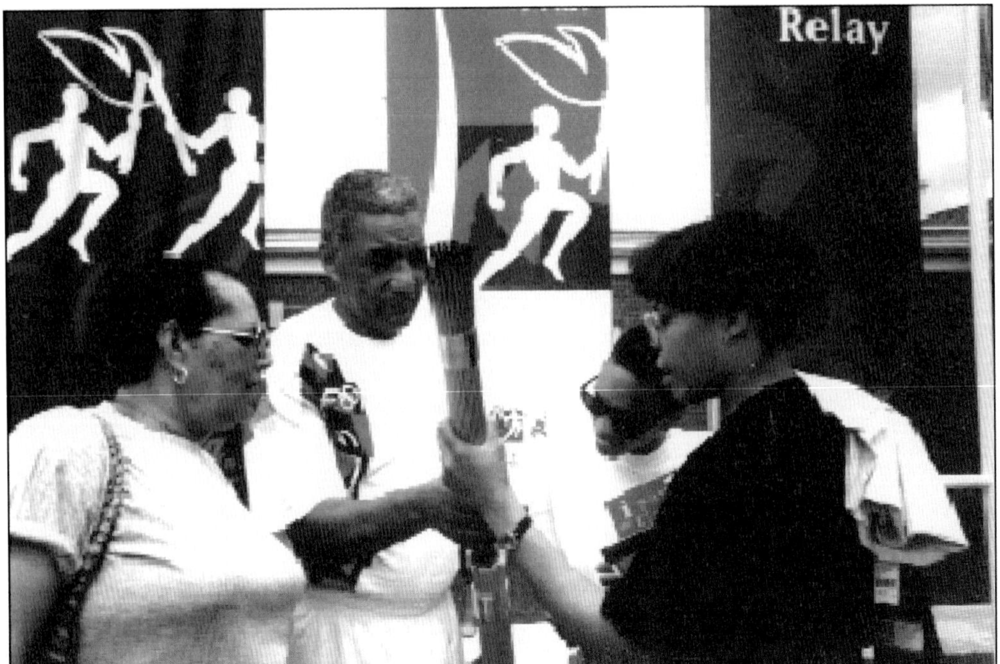

Former Akron Olympic-medalist Lester Carney prepares to carry the Olympic torch during a local track meet in held in Akron.

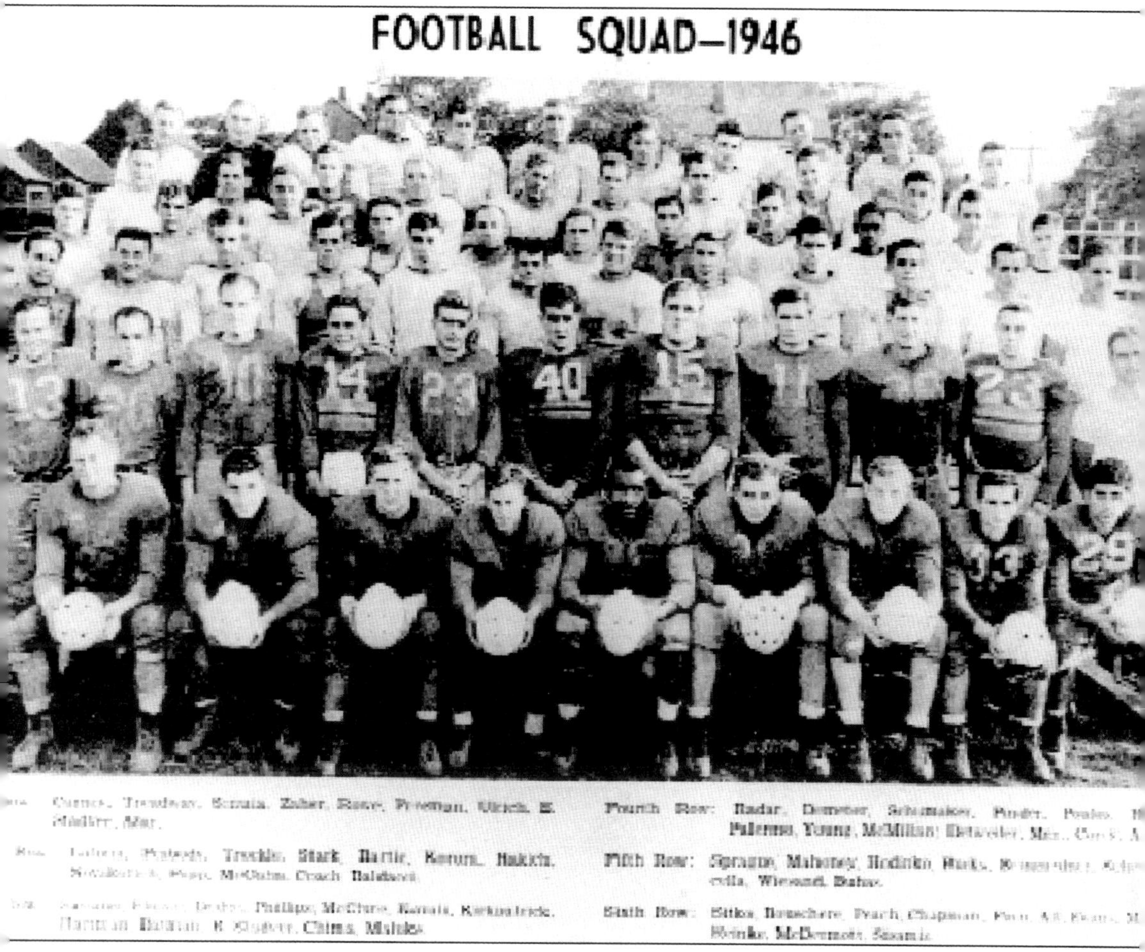

Akron experienced integration very early in its history. Here you see an integrated high school football team as early as 1946. There were at least two African Americans on this team.

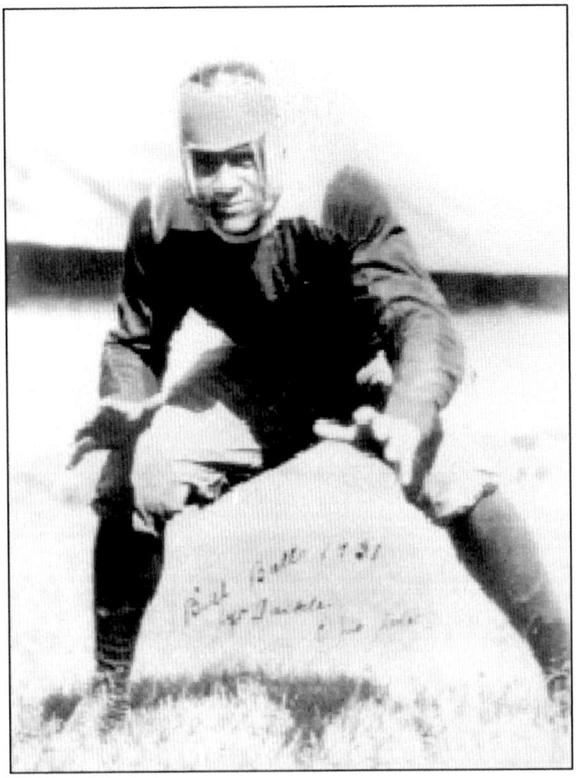

Bill Bell, an Akron native, played left tackle for Ohio State in 1931. Akron's high schools had great success in developing young football talent.

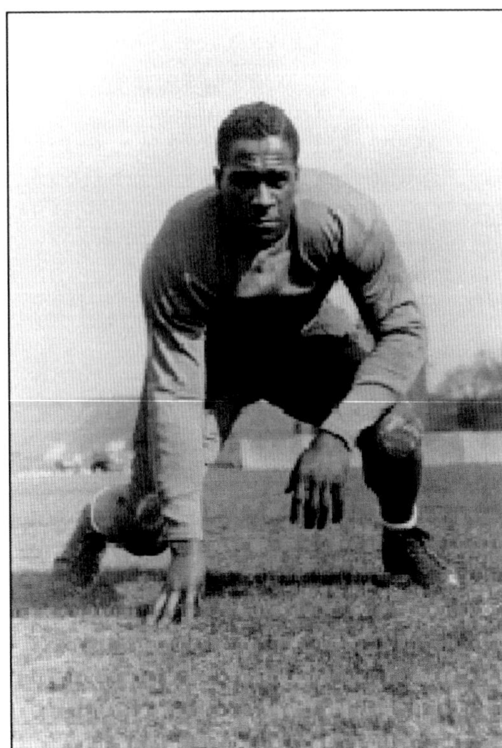

Horace Bell was one of the most feared football players during his time. Here he strikes an imposing pose.

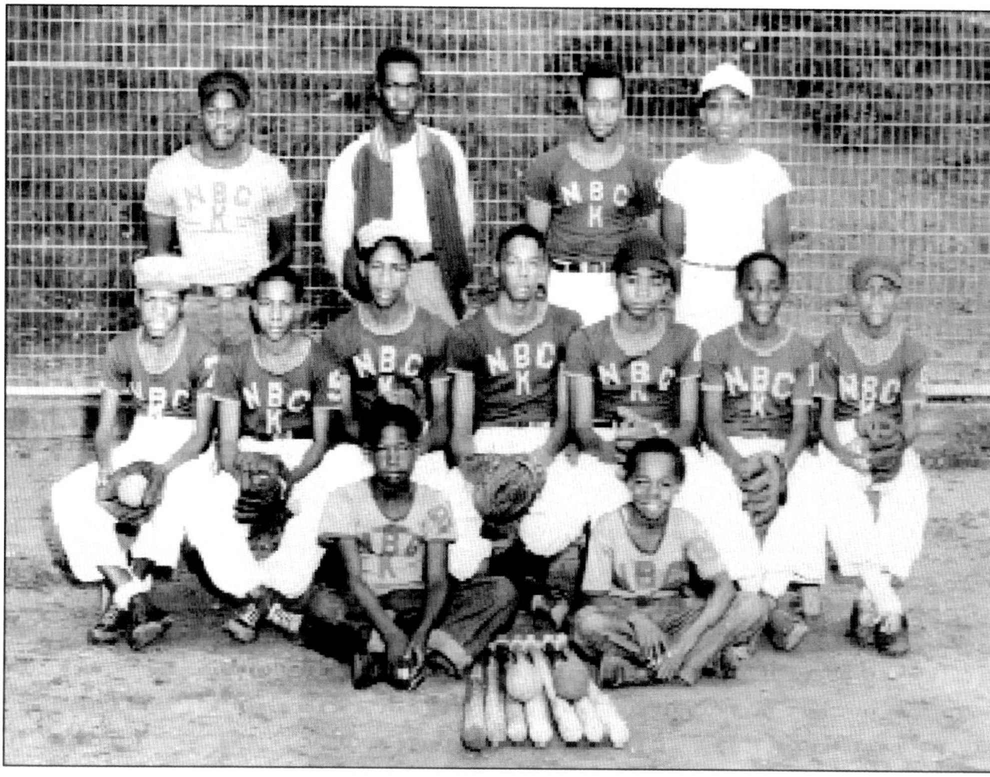

Akron's African-American youths were very active in a number of sports. This photograph shows an all-Black little-league baseball team.

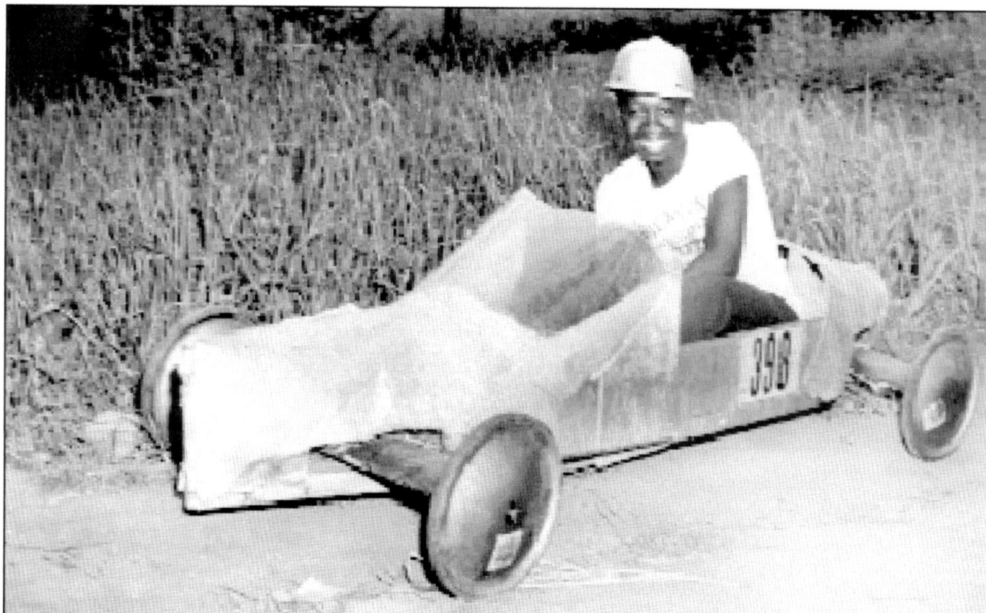

The annual Akron Soapbox Derby is one of the most popular events in Akron. An unidentified African-American youth prepares to participate in the event in this picture.

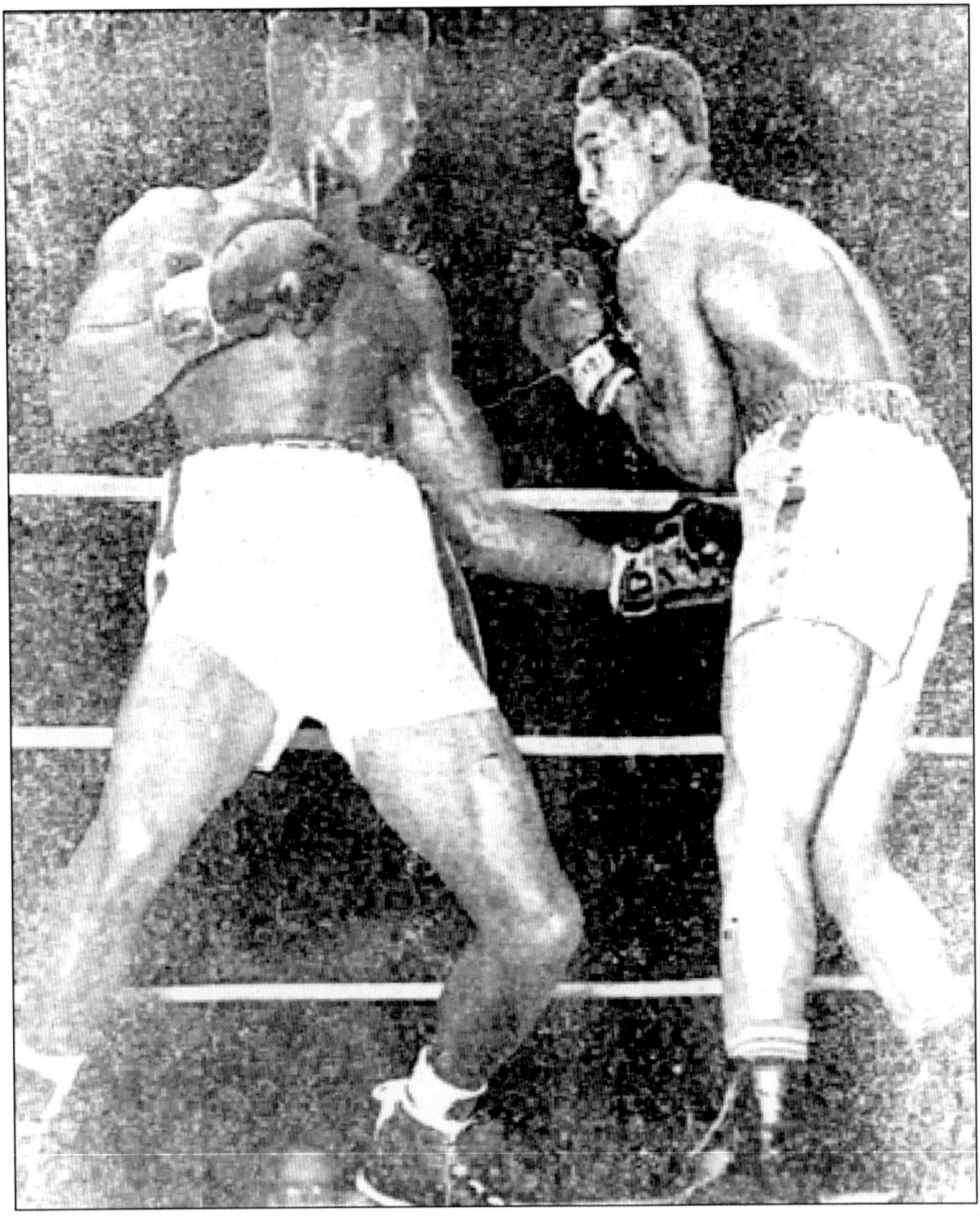

Former boxing champion Sam Baroudi throws one of his signature punches. Baroudi would tragically die in the ring, as a result of a boxing match.

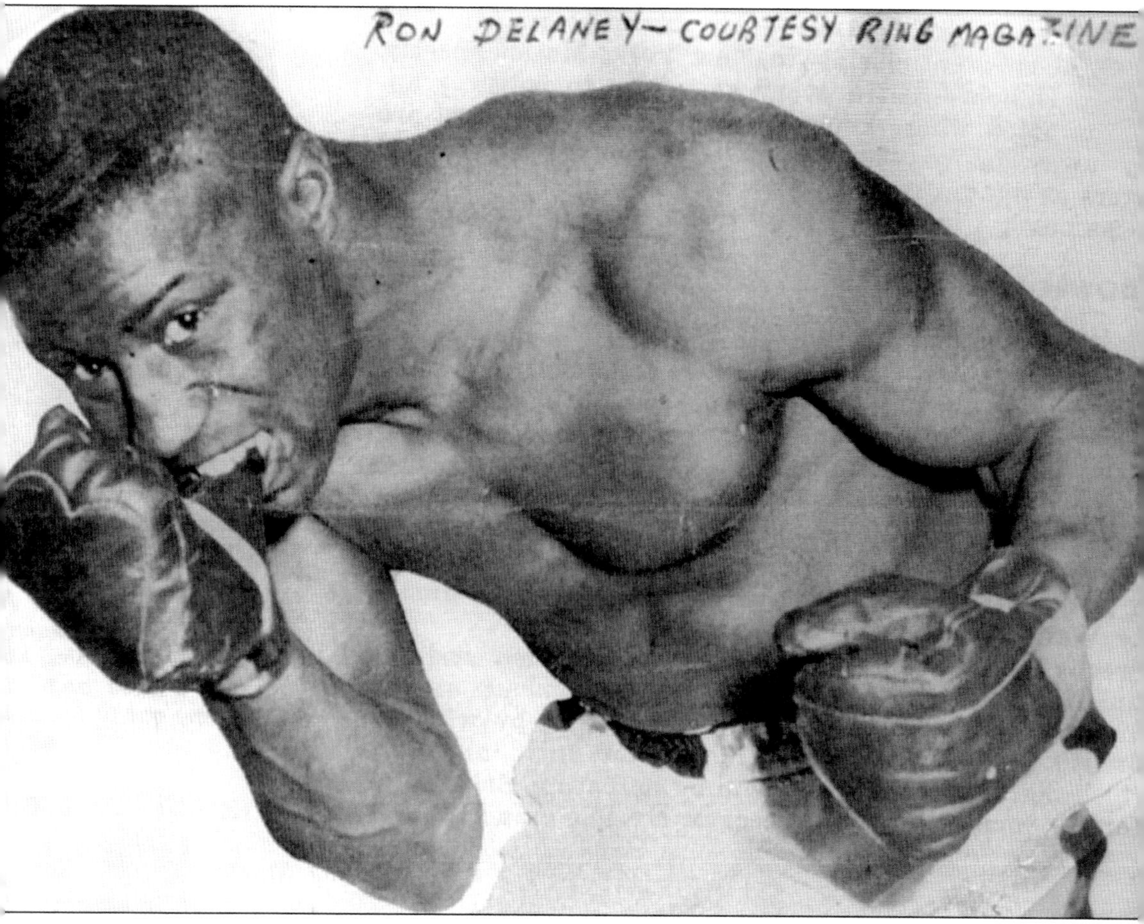

Former lightweight contender Ron Delaney fought out of an Akron gym.

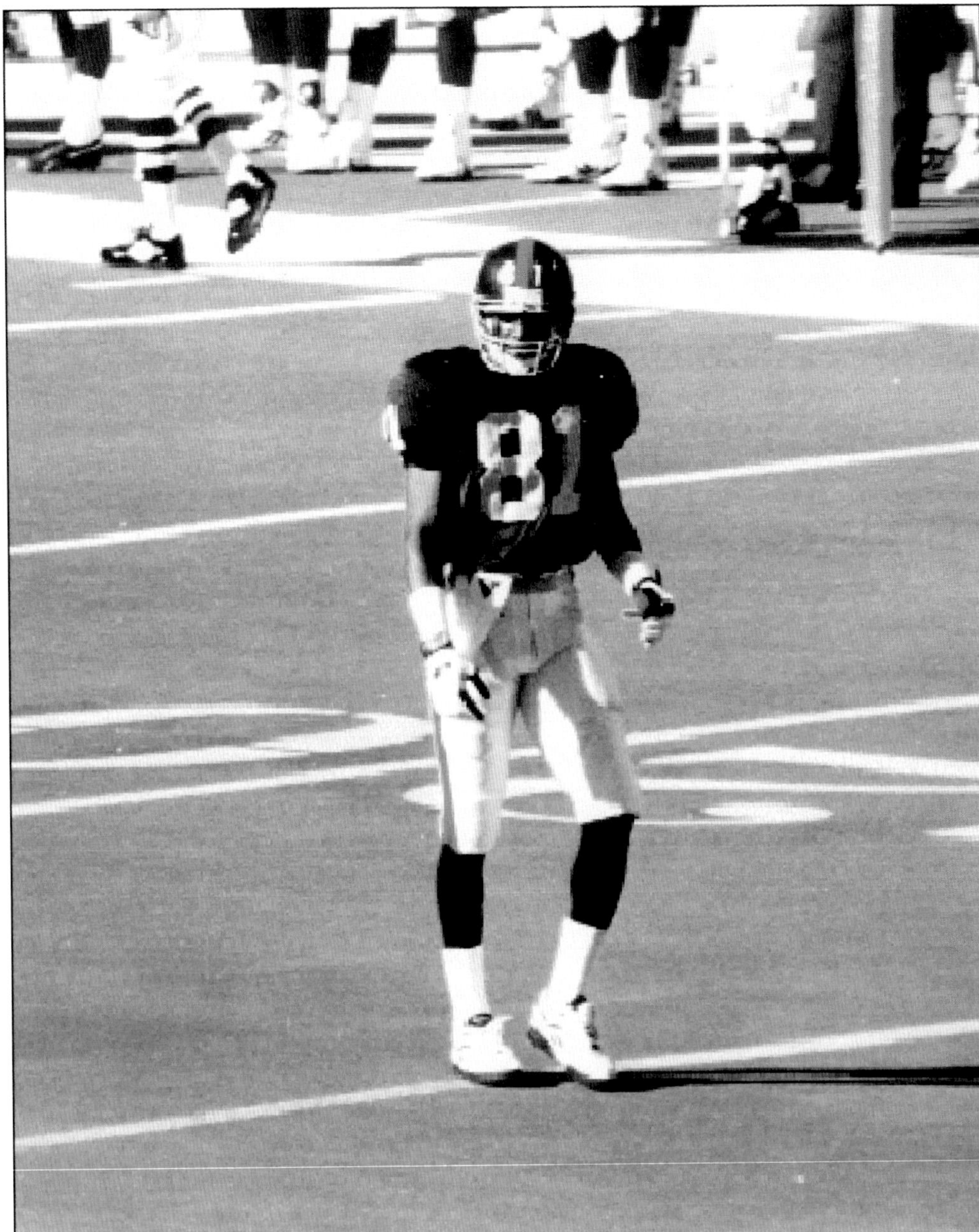

Former NFL wide-receiver Thomas Lewis was a native of Akron who had a standout high school career.

Richard Delaney holds his touchdown trophy, awarded to one of the top football players in Ohio.

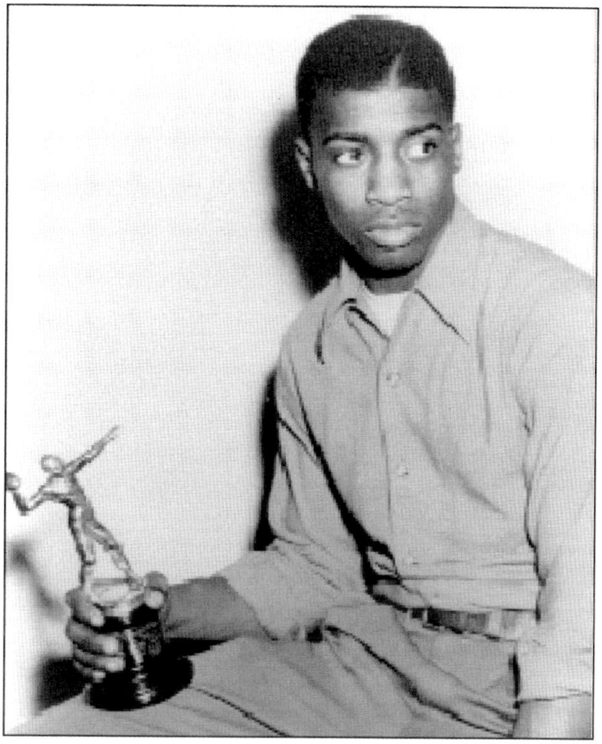

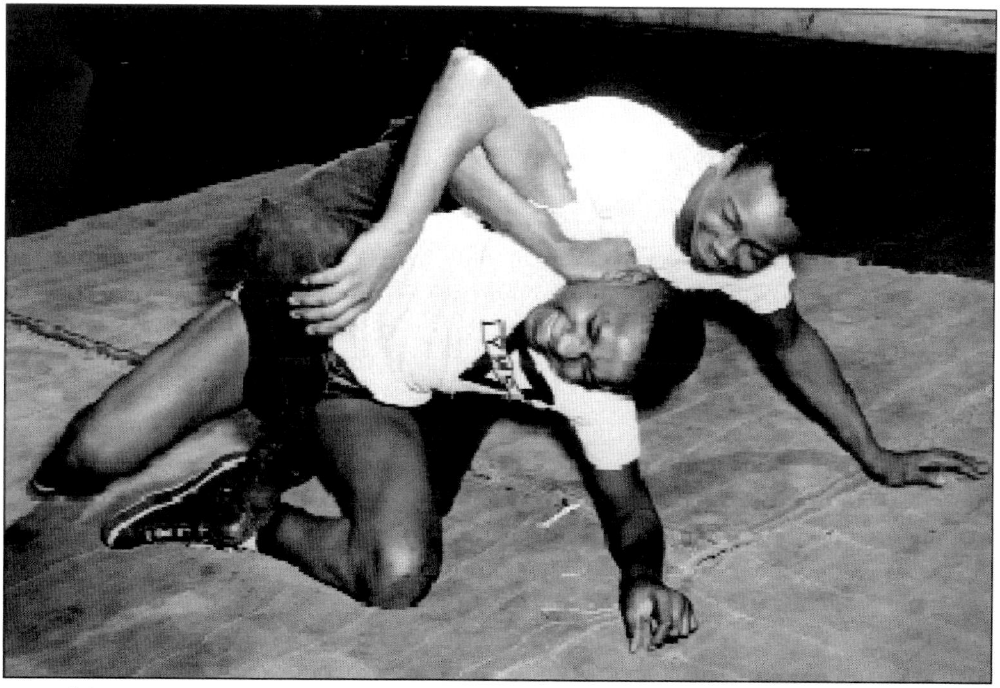

One of the many organizations that helped mold and shape young men in Akron was the YMCA. The YMCA summer programs provided African Americans with an opportunity to work on their skills and to be involved in different activities. Here two young men are wrestling.

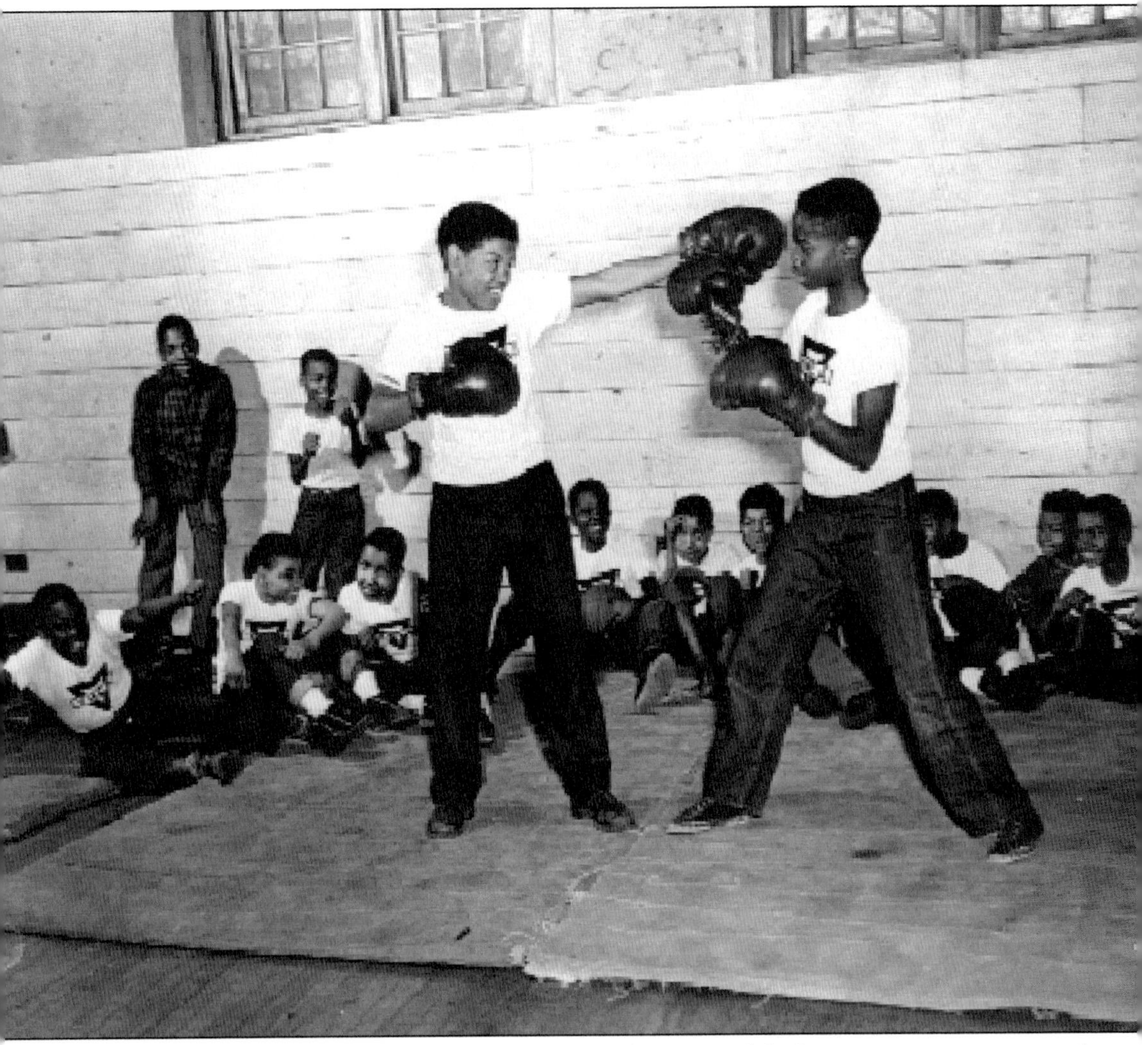

Two youths participate in a youth boxing program. Akron's youth had access to numerous sports' venues, which gave them an opportunity to develop their skills.

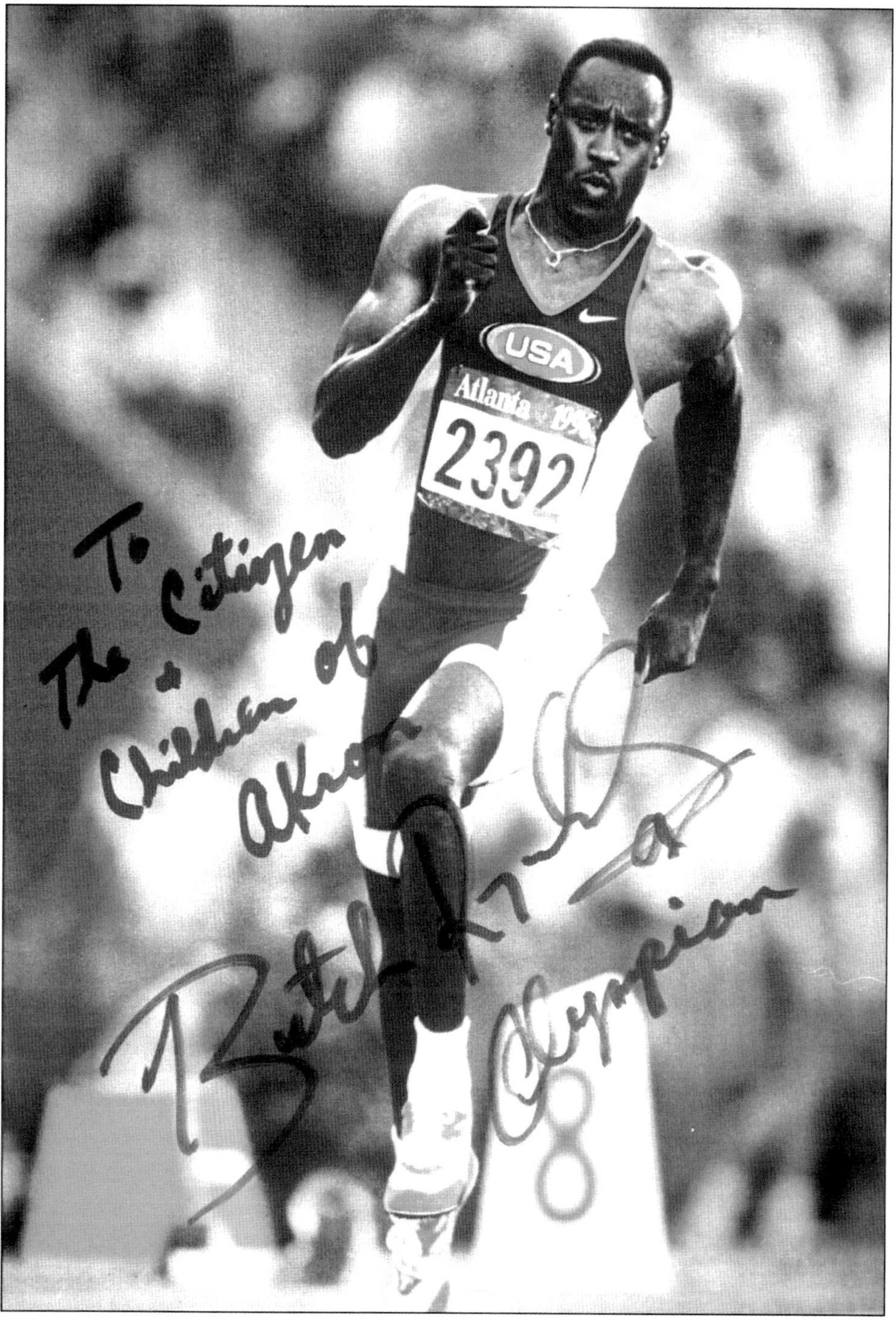

Former Gold and Silver Olympic medalist Butch Reynolds is a native of Akron, Ohio, and a graduate of Hoban High School. Reynolds made the Olympic team three times and in 1988 set two world records in Zurich, Switzerland. He held world records in the 400 meter and was a member of the world-record-setting 4-by-100 meter team. The former Ohio State star continues to reside in Ohio.

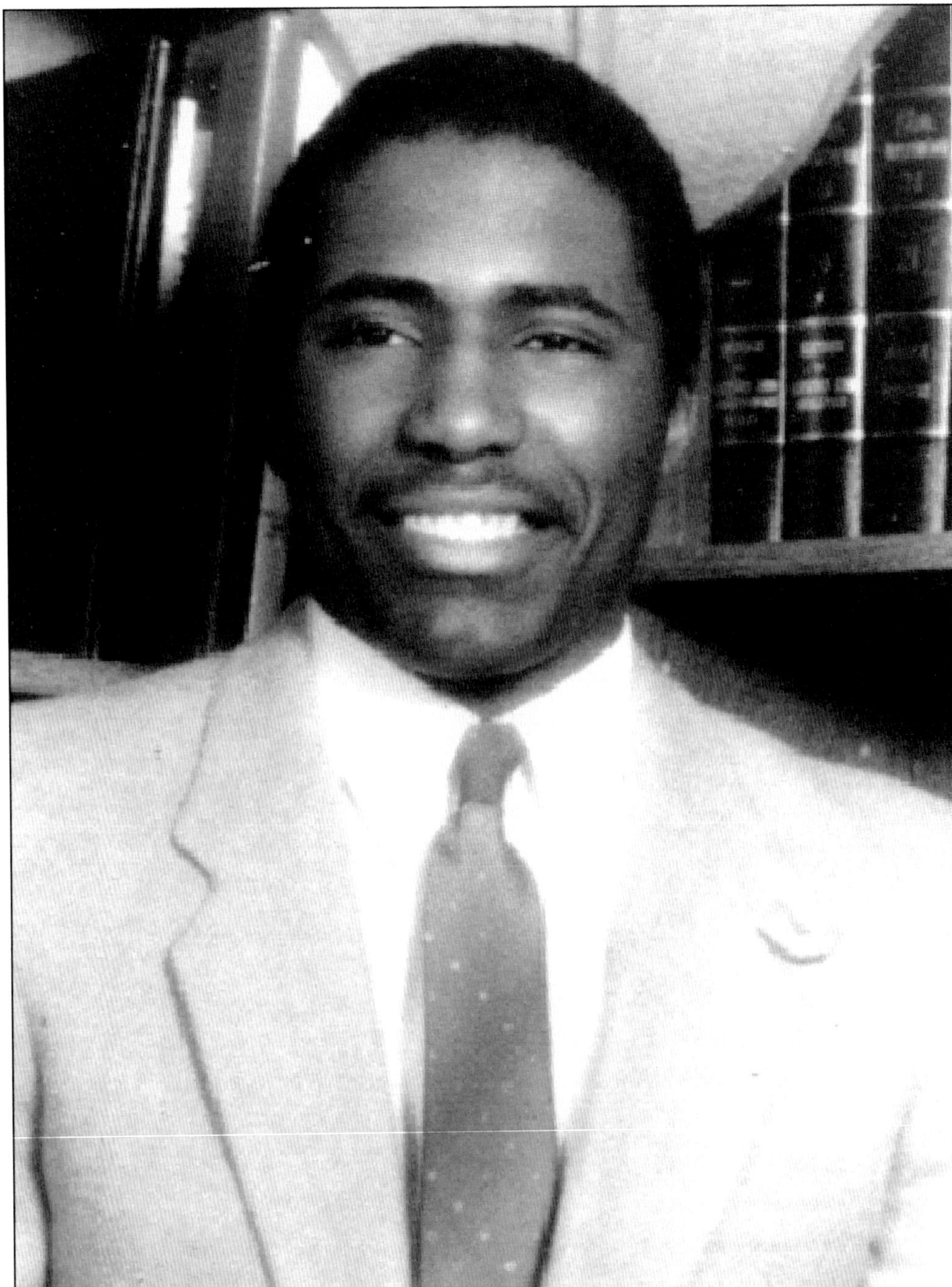

Tony Purnell was an outstanding high school athlete who graduated from Firestone High before receiving a track scholarship to the University of Akron. Purnell was a world-record-holding high jumper who set a world record during a meet in Akron.

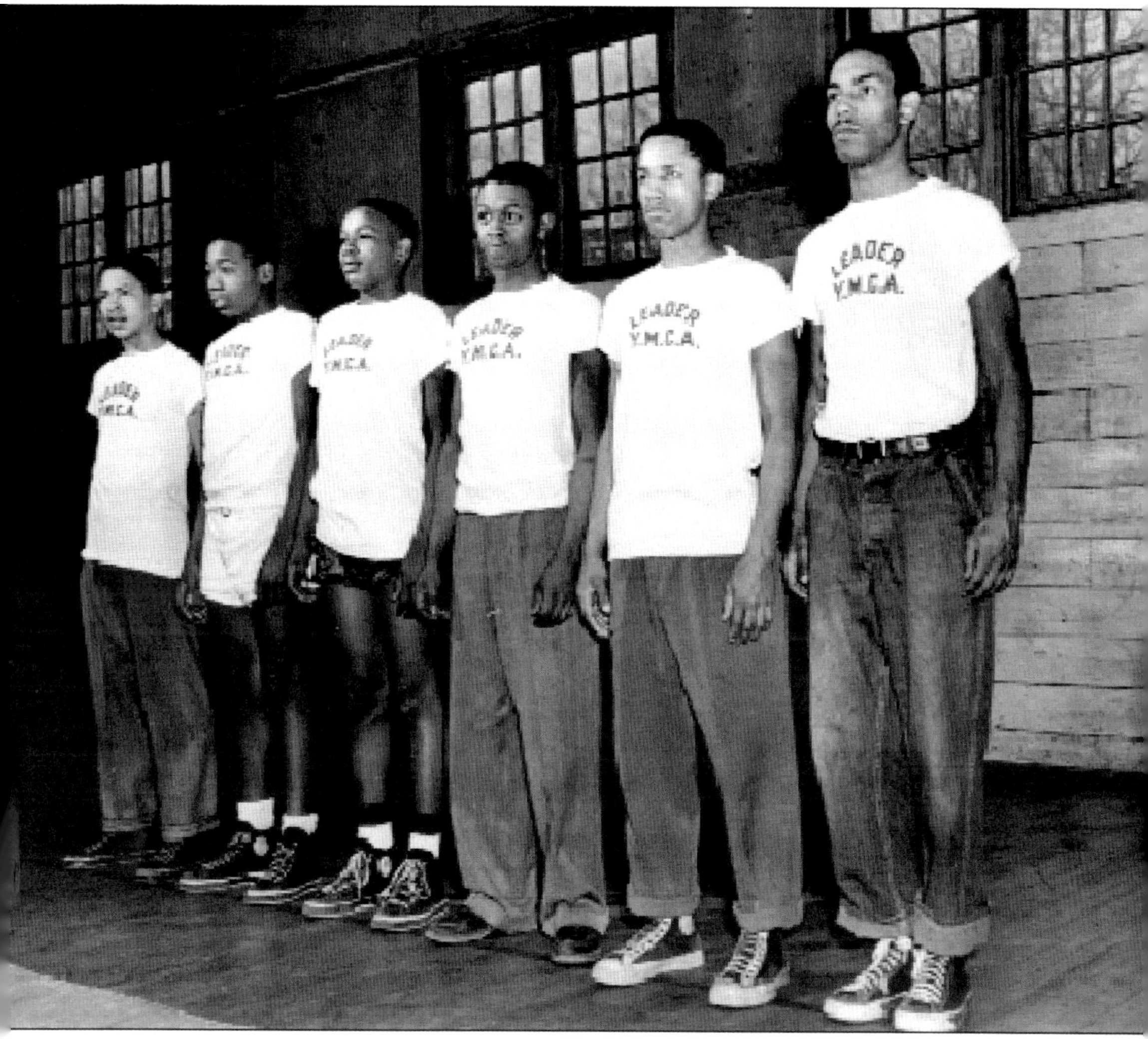

Akron has a number of organizations that are beneficial to African-American youth. This unidentified youth served as a leader in a YMCA-sponsored summer youth program.

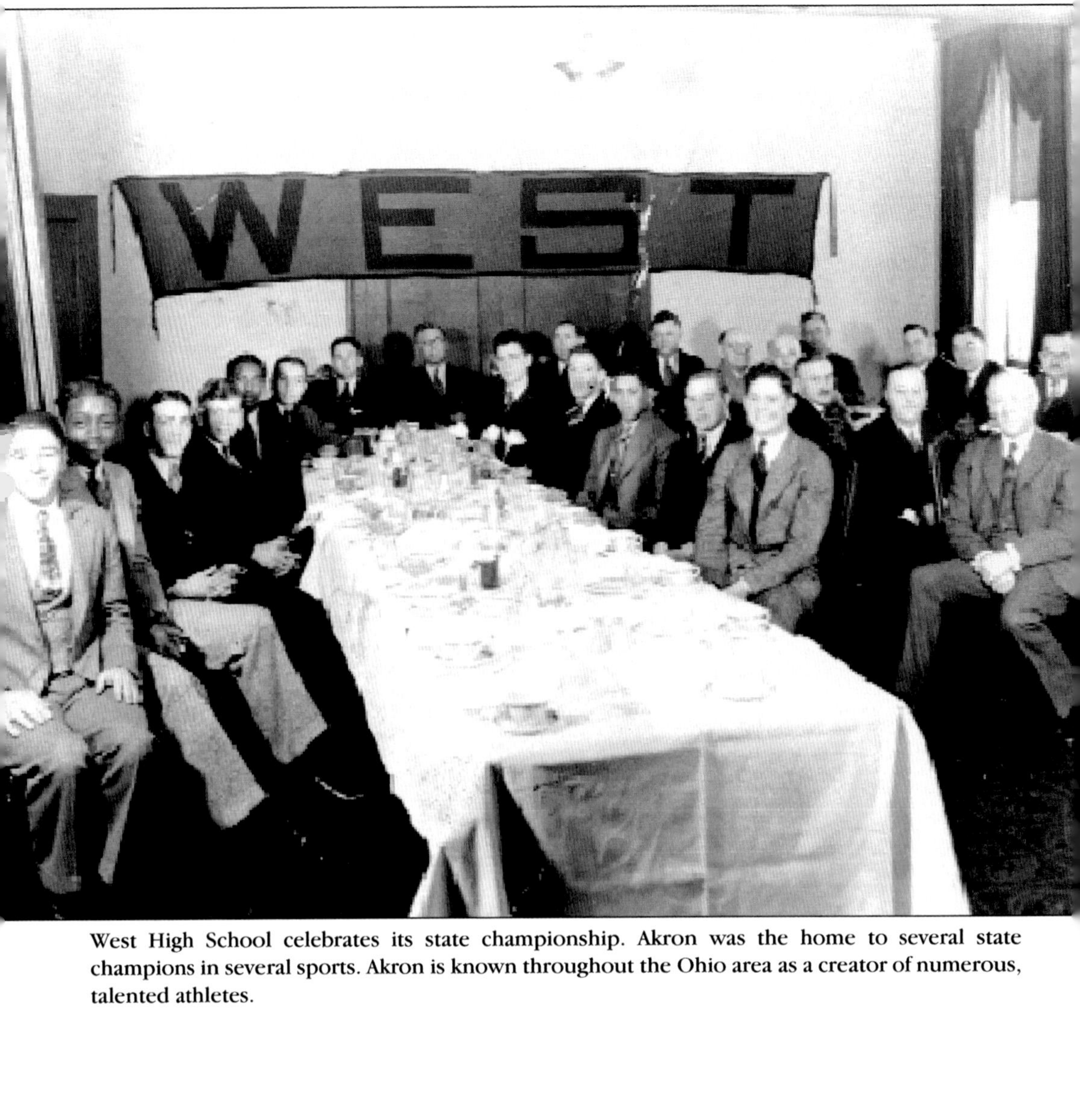

West High School celebrates its state championship. Akron was the home to several state champions in several sports. Akron is known throughout the Ohio area as a creator of numerous, talented athletes.